THE PAPAL PRINCES

THE PAPAL PRINCES

A History of the Sacred College of Cardinals

by Glenn D. Kittler

FUNK & WAGNALLS · NEW YORK

To
LAURIAN CARDINAL RUGAMBWA
Rutoba Diocese, Tanganyika

*—In gratitude for many kindnesses and
in recognition of an outstanding member
of the Sacred College.*

In obedience to the decrees of Urban VIII than March 13, 1625, and June 5, 1631, and to other salutary Pontifical Laws, the author declares that the observations made in this book are his own and do not necessarily reflect those of the Church.

Acknowledgments

The history of the world during the past two thousand years is, to a large extent, the history of the Roman Catholic Church, and the history of the Church involves, indivisibly, the history of the Sacred College of Cardinals, whose members produce the men who become the popes. The relationships between the popes and the cardinals have given the world some of its darkest as well as brightest moments, moments that began the day the Apostles first set out to teach all nations what they had been taught. Pope Leo XIII felt each such moment was important and he urged historians to touch on all of them, good or bad, in their writings. Such detail would be too great for one volume; this book is an attempt to touch on the high points.

For their suggestions for the structure of this book I am grateful to Dr. Christopher Dawson, of Harvard Divinity School; Dr. Thomas Neill, of St. Louis University; Father Harold C. Gardiner, S.J., of *America Magazine;* and Father E. A. Ryan, S.J., of Woodstock College, Maryland. I am especially indebted to Father Florence D. Cohalan, of Cathedral College, New York City, for his enormous help in checking the final manuscript. To Miss Evelyn Singer, my agent, and Mr. and Mrs. Herbert M. Katz, my editors, I extend gratitude for their skills that produced the final draft.

And I should like to give particular thanks to the scholars and archivists who, over the centuries, produced and preserved the research material from which this book was drawn.

G.D.K.

THE PAPAL PRINCES

I

*I*t was a time for leadership. Jesus was dead and buried, and the men who had been closest to Him hid themselves in the upper room of a house in the city, afraid to show themselves in the streets. All the promises He had made now seemed as dead as He. The three years He had spent wandering through the country preaching were finished now. There seemed every likelihood that the men who were His first friends would scatter as soon as it was safe for them to leave their hiding place. Only one of them had displayed the courage to be with Him as He died on the cross. This man was John, the friend whom people said Jesus loved most. The others were nowhere in sight. Simon had even denied that he knew Jesus.

And yet the matter of leadership had already been arranged; Jesus Himself had taken care of that. One day He had asked His close followers, "Who do men say the Son of Man is?"

They told Him that people were saying that John the Baptist might be the Son of Man, that some thought Elijah might have been, or Jeremiah, or one of the other prophets.

Then Jesus asked, "But who do you say I am?"

It was Simon who answered. "You are the Messiah, the Son of the living God."

Jesus said, "You are blessed, Simon Bar-Jona, for flesh and blood has not revealed this to you, but my Father in Heaven. And I say to you that you are the Rock, and upon this rock I will build my Church, and the gates of hell shall not prevail against it. And I will give to you the keys of the Kingdom of Heaven, and whatever you shall bind on earth will be bound in Heaven and whatever you shall loose on earth shall be loosed in Heaven."

Years later, this vital moment of history, preserved in the New Testament, was recorded by Matthew, who had left his job as a tax collector at Capernaum to become a follower of Jesus. Matthew wrote in Aramaic, the language Jesus spoke, and for the word "rock" he wrote *Kepha;* the Greeks pronounced it *Kephas.* Matthew was still alive when his book was translated into Greek. For *Kephas,* the Greeks used *Petros,* a masculine form of the Greek word for rock, *Petra.* The Romans later said *Petrus;* the English, Peter. Thereafter, Simon was called Peter.

2

Peter began his leadership of Christianity on Pentecost, the Jewish Feast of the Harvests, which came fifty days after Passover. On that day, Peter spoke in public for the first time. Jesus had promised to send the Holy Ghost to grant the Apostles the knowledge and powers they would need to carry out His mission, and it was on this day that the visitation was made. So effective was Peter's first preaching that he converted five thousand people in a single day. Later, when the new Christians went back to their homes in the country and in other lands, they were cut off from the Apostles in Jerusalem. It was therefore necessary to send trained men to them to teach them and guide them in their new life. Out of this need arose the first architecture of the Christian Church.

They still looked upon themselves as Jews. They went to the Temple, they offered up sacrifices, they kept the Law. But something had been added. Jesus had said that the people should be baptized; the priests at the Temple would not baptize. Also, Jesus had the Passover meal in Jerusalem with the Apostles just before His arrest. When the meal was over, Jesus took some unleavened bread, breaking it into pieces. He offered it to the Apostles as He said, "Take and eat all of this, for this is my body." They passed the bread around the table and ate it. Then Jesus took up a cup of wine and He said, "Take and drink all of this, for this is the chalice of my blood, of the new and everlasting testament, the mystery of faith, which for you and for many shall be shed unto the remission of sins. As often as you do these things, you will do them in memory of me." The priests of the Temple certainly would not participate at the memorial of such an occasion.

At first, the Apostles baptized the people. When the Apostles were all together and broke the bread and drank the wine it was Peter who stood in the place where Jesus had stood. People were baptized whenever they were ready for it. The commemoration of the Last Supper most likely took place once a week, on Sunday—the day Jesus had arisen from the dead. As time passed, there were too many people asking for baptism for the Apostles to be able to take care of them all. Having been baptized, the people had virtually outlawed themselves and it became impossible for them to meet publicly. Thus they met secretly in each other's homes. In time there were so many such meetings that the Apostles were unable to attend them all to recreate the Last Supper ceremony. It became obvious that more priests were needed.

By His choice of them at the start of His ministry, Jesus made priests of the Apostles. As His last hours neared He repeatedly assured them that all that had been given Him He empowered in them. He even told them, "Whose sins you shall forgive they are forgiven; whose sins you shall retain they are retained." Authorized thereby to act in Jesus' stead, the Apostles were kept very busy. The best trained men available to assist them were among the one hundred and twenty who had been followers of Jesus before His death. From these men the first priests were ordained to act in place of the Apostles.

Jesus had instructed the Apostles to teach all nations, and they took this to mean they were expected to travel to various countries to establish His Church. Matthew went to Ethiopia, Mark went to Egypt, Andrew went to India, Luke went to Macedonia, John to Ephesus. James the Less remained in Jerusalem to supervise the work. Peter, too, was in Jerusalem, from where he directed the entire project. It was Peter who offered Mathias as a replacement for Judas Iscariot in order to keep the Apostles at the twelve Jesus had appointed. In doing so, he granted to Mathias the same spiritual powers Jesus had given to all the Apostles.

A hierarchy began to appear. At its head were the Apostles, led by Peter. As the Apostles died, most of them violently, other men were chosen to replace them, men like Titus and Timothy, thus securing the Apostolic succession of the Church. The Apostles traveled almost constantly, and in each place where they established the Church they appointed advisory councils to supervise local spiritual and material affairs. The councils were known by two interchangeable terms: the *episkopos,* a Greek word meaning "overseer," and the *presbyteros,* a Greek word meaning "old." The word "priest" was derived from *presbyteros;* the word "bishop" was derived from *episkopos.* The councils, therefore, were comprised, for the most part, of older, wiser, experienced men who were qualified to act as overseers after one of the Apostles moved on. The council members also traveled greatly within their own areas, setting up lesser councils, and when the district was sufficiently organized the leader of the major council settled in a principal city to exercise his broad supervisory authority, subject to Peter. This gave rise to bishops and dioceses.

In Jerusalem, criticism reached Peter from the Jews that indigent Christians were being neglected. If indeed Christianity was a religion, then didn't the Church have a responsibility for its poor? After all, the Jews took care of their poor with alms. Didn't Christians have a similar obligation? Peter realized that the criticism was valid and he took immediate steps to correct the situation. He appointed seven deacons (Latin for "servant") to organize and direct the Church's charitable works.

Thus within a few years after the first Christian Pentecost the Church took on its ecclesiastic architecture: Apostles led by Peter, bishops, priests, deacons. The structure would be broadened, it would be more specifically defined, but it would never change.

One of the earliest converts to Christianity was a man named Saul. Although his father had been a Roman and he was therefore a privileged citizen, he had adhered to the Jewish faith and studied the Holy Law under Gamaliel at the Temple. Saul had been vehemently anti-Christian and had led several forays to suppress the new religion. He was commissioned by the high priest to go to Damascus to lead forces there against the Christians. As he approached the city he was blinded by a great light and thrown to the ground. He heard a voice that asked, "Saul, why do you persecute me?"

Passers-by helped him into the city. When his sight was restored he located some Christians and he lived with them for a while, listening as they spoke about their religion. The experience changed him completely. He returned to Jerusalem and made his way to Peter and the Apostles, and when they saw how he had changed they accepted him as one of them. In the next thirty years, he became the greatest Apostolic missionary, traveling to many countries, establishing many churches and winning many converts. The explanatory letters he wrote to the bishops he appointed were to provide vital guidance to the Church as it evolved.

He became known as Paul, and he was in Jerusalem for the conferences called by Peter regarding the abuses that had appeared in the ritual the Christians had adopted. Because of persecutions, the Christians could not meet openly; instead, they met in small groups in private homes. Warily, they adopted a secret sign by which they would know each other: the sign of the fish, which they marked on the side of a building or gate of a house where Christian services were held. The five letters of the Greek word for fish indicated: Jesus Christ, Son of God, Savior. If a Christian traveling among strangers wanted to find out if there were other Christians around, he would make some reference to a fish or perhaps idly sketch one in the loose soil, and if he got no reaction he knew he was not among friends.

In most of the Jerusalem groups, a kind of voluntary community ownership was practiced, and usually a portion of the community income was turned over to the deacons for the poor. The religious ceremony was simple. It was held on Sunday and centered around a meal. The person in charge would read from the Old Testament, which was followed by the collection or allocation of alms. The Apostles and some of the first priests were gifted with a perception into human hearts and were thus able to detect spiritual or moral failings among those present; this was a regular feature of the ceremonies. Then someone would preach a sermon—a talk about Jesus. The ceremony ended with the breaking of the bread, the sharing of the wine, and the recitation of the "Our Father"—the prayer Jesus had spoken.

Abuses occurred simply because there were not enough trained priests to attend all the secret meetings. Often the sessions deteriorated into ordinary meals—a fellowship that had little or nothing to do with Jesus or the Church. Certainly not everybody could read hearts, and so this aspect frequently was based on little more than gossip. And an untrained man who tried to preach ended up talking heresy and plain fiction. Most important, the bread and wine communion fell from its sacramental dignity because people failed to grasp that Jesus' words at the Last Supper were intended literally.

The council called by Peter resolved the problem by defining a Christian service. The ceremony was separated completely from the meal. As for communion, the council clarified the reverence with which it should be approached by instructing: "On the Lord's day assemble together and break bread and give thanks, having confessed your transgressions, in order that your sacrifice be not defiled." The Apostles also composed a credo of their dogma, which specified the divinity of Jesus, His resurrection and ascension, the virginity of Mary, the universality of the Church, and the necessity of baptism and confession. Important though the council was in overcoming the abuses, its vital significance was in the precedent—set by the Apostles themselves—of having matters of dogma defined and enforced by the rulers of the Church, and particularly the head of the Church, Peter.

There were two more specific occasions when Peter was

the deciding factor regarding the character of the new
church. Both pertained to the nature of Christianity itself.
Two questions arose: Were baptized Jews still Jews, or had
baptism turned them into something else? What was to be
the procedure for gentiles who wanted to be baptized?

These were matters of great concern and they were discussed at length and with some heat by the men of authority. The question of gentiles were considered very serious.
A special council was called to resolve it, but there was no
agreement. Since the first Christians were Jews who still
maintained that the Jews were the chosen people, it was
strongly felt that any gentiles desiring to become Christians
must first become Jews, at least to the extent of submitting
themselves to circumcision, a covenant of Jewish identity.
But interested Romans rejected the idea of circumcision. To
them, this was the mark of Judaism, which represented a
foreign nation as well as a religion, and they refused to ad-
join themselves to a people dominated by their own country.

It was Peter who resolved both this problem and the question about the spiritual identity of baptized Jews. He told
the Apostles that while traveling near Joppa he found himself hungry, but because no food was available that con-
formed to Jewish dietary laws he did not eat. At his prayers,
he experienced a vision in which he was shown all the ani-
mals in the world. A voice instructed him: "Arise, Peter,
kill and eat." Peter replied: "Far be it from me, Lord, for
never did I eat anything common or unclean." The voice
said: "What God has cleansed, do not call common." The
dialogue occurred three times, convincing Peter that the
Lord meant him to be released from the dietary laws—and
by extension from certain other practices identified with
Judaism—a verdict he then passed on to all who were
baptized.

At this time there lived in Caesarea a Roman centurion
named Cornelius who had put aside his polytheism and ac-

cepted the monotheism characteristic of Judaism. He practiced Christianity as far as he could in the circumstances, restricted only by his refusal to be circumcised. When Peter
was in Joppa three Romans approached him and said Cornelius wanted to see him. Peter thought he was about to be
arrested again, but Cornelius explained that while he had
been at his prayers an angel had appeared to him with instructions to send for Peter and to do whatever he said.

Peter said, "Now I really understand that God is not a
respecter of persons but in every nation he who fears Him
and does what is right is acceptable to Him." Later in Jerusalem Peter used the incident as the basis for his decision that
all people—any people—could be baptized without first
having been Jewish.

Thus those who were baptized moved apart from those
who were not, into a new spiritual sphere. It was shortly
afterward, while Paul was preaching at Antioch, that the
Greeks first used their name for the baptized people: Christians.

Peter was in Antioch several years later, and it was from
there, in approximately 55 A.D., that he made his way to
Rome. There were already Christians in Rome. On his
previous travels Peter had always appointed others to supervise the Christian works, keeping himself free to go on to
wherever he felt he was needed. But now he made a different decision. He declared himself to be the Bishop of Rome.
The other Apostles, still on their travels, looked to Peter for
instructions and for leadership, and now in doing so they
looked to Rome. With him there, the authority of the
Church was there.

Persecution existed in Rome, as it did wherever the Christians went. In order to carry out the obligations of their
religion, the Christians went underground. But there was
work to be done, work that required some kind of organization to achieve its ends. Because of the dangers in the city,

overt conduct would have been dangerous, even foolhardy, and so the Christian community found itself relying increasingly on a group of men who knew their way around Rome, who knew which Romans would help them and which would not, which could be trusted and which could not. Their ability to open and close influential or threatening doors gave rise to a nickname: they were called hinge-men. The Roman word for "hinge" was *cardo*.

Cardinals.

II

*D*espite the importance of the first cardinals, they were not to assume a specifically defined role in the Church for almost four hundred years. Then another five hundred years were to pass before they were granted their supreme authority: the election of Popes. In essence, however, they were a vital factor in the Church from the earliest days. The very title given them, secretly at first, indicated their influential positions. Because of their quasi-political activities, they were obviously men of experience and wisdom. Upon what they knew and what they advised, the Church took its first steps on a path that was dark with blood and terror.

There were no intentions among the first Christians that their religion should in any way be involved with politics, but there was no escaping the entanglements. Although Jesus had said that the affairs of Caesar should be separated from the affairs of God, the nations of the First Christian Century did not feel that way. Each had what amounted to a state religion. This was true in Palestine, where Judaism reigned; it was true in Rome and in Athens, where polytheism was distinctly entwined with government; it was true in Egypt, with its worship of Ra, the sun god. The Christian Church, therefore, was confronted by politics whether it wanted to be or not.

Most likely the first Christians in Rome were Romans who had been on military duty in Palestine. Soon after his baptism, Cornelius returned to Rome, and in all likelihood he tried to bring some of his friends to his new religion. Jews also traveled back and forth to Rome; among them surely were converts who influenced the Jewish community in the ruling city of the world. Because Palestine was a conquered nation and because of the monotheistic nature of Judaism, there was anti-Semitism in Rome, occasionally to such an extent that at times a kind of ghetto life appeared and at other times Jews were ordered out of the country. Severity depended on the Emperor, and there was a rapid succession of emperors in Rome. Christians were victims of the same uncertainty.

Most upper-class Romans looked upon Christians as being offshoots of Judaism, which in a sense they were. As such they were, like Jews, people who worshipped false gods, a god, at least, not of the Roman pantheon, and for doing this they were considered to be, at worst, bad citizens of the Empire. But the sophisticated Roman didn't waste much time on them. When, as occasionally happened, a noble family turned Christian they could expect to be ostracized by their friends. If at the moment the public feeling was sufficiently severe, they could also expect to lose their wealth and position, possibly their citizenship, perhaps even their lives. The intensity of the public feelings reflected the influence of the upper bourgeoisie, among which there were men who were more Roman than Caesar. These were the men who, out of their own prejudices and ambitions, stirred the constant persecutions.

Persecutions became an affair of the throne during the reign of Emperor Nero. To provide what he felt would be a proper background to his recitation of a poem on the fall of Troy he set fire to part of Rome. The fire got out of hand, and when the rumor spread of how it was caused Nero defended himself by saying that the Christians had started it. A violent anti-Christian rage erupted and hundreds of Christians were killed. Nero encouraged the massacre by inviting its promoters to use his own lawns for burnings and beheadings. Peter and Paul were in Rome at the time, both in a state of semi-arrest. Their deaths climaxed the Neronian violence: Peter was crucified head-down on Vatican Hill; tradition has it that Paul was beheaded at Aquae Salviae, somewhat east of the Via Ostia. Nero used the public furor as a means of getting rid of his own enemies: when anyone appeared to be threatening his throne, he put his name on the list of Christian suspects, the first step to execution. The chaos led inevitably to sedition, and Nero killed himself.

The deaths of Peter and Paul left the Rome episcopate—and thus the Church itself—without a leader. If at any hour it seemed the Church was doomed this certainly was it. But Jesus had promised guidance to Peter—to the Church—to the very end of the world. The task, then, was to choose the successor to Peter. There already existed in the world many bishops, men who had received their authority directly from the Apostles, men thus qualified to pass the authority on to others. For that matter, some of the Apostles were still alive, and if they thought there was anything wrong in the idea of transmitting Church leadership in an unbroken line from one bishop of Rome to the next they obviously would have said so. A close friend of Peter's in Rome was a man named Linus, from Tuscany. There was some opinion in the city at the time that Peter had actually chosen Linus to succeed him, but this could not be established. Nevertheless, the members of the Roman *episkopos* approved Linus as their bishop. It was customary at the time for all bishops to be addressed as *Papas,* a Greek word indicating fatherhood or guardianship. Bishop Linus, therefore, became the *Papas*—Pope—of Rome. The day was still to come when only the Bishop of Rome would be addressed by that title.

2

Thirty popes reigned in Rome during the first three hundred years of Christianity, a fast turnover brought on by the fact that most of them were killed. This was the era of the persecutions, and a significant feature of it was that the Church—young, virile, resilient—flourished in the face of opposition that should have exterminated it. The Neronian edict which outlawed Christianity did nothing to stop it. In the shadow of each martyr stood battalions of converts. By the sheer power of its intimate influence upon the private heart, Christianity quickly evolved into the strongest factor ever to appear outside the specific realms of governments. Its strength made it the enemy of governments. In Rome, the Christians assured the succession of emperors that they obeyed all laws which did not impinge upon their religious obligations, that they would serve in the armies and that they prayed for the rulers, but this was not enough to save them from the bloodiest opposition.

Nero had ordered that Christians were to be killed wherever they were discovered throughout the empire. Their own admission of their faith was enough to condemn them.

Emperors who succeeded Nero followed the same law, at the same time prohibiting Christians from owning property, businesses or burial places. The possessions of any well-to-do Christians were immediately confiscated. Nevertheless, the number of Christians constantly increased. By their numbers alone they befuddled those who persecuted them.

Outside Rome, particularly in the Middle East provinces, anti-Christian sentiments were not always so strong. Pliny, the governor of Bithynia, reported to Emperor Trajan at the end of the First Century that even the non-Christians in his province were growing highly critical of the brutality, especially of the law which, *ipso facto,* sentenced a professed Christian to death. Pliny also wondered what to do with Christians who were willing to recant in order to stay alive.

Trajan replied with a remarkable rescript that managed both to satisfy the virulently anti-Christian Romans and to mollify the critical provincials. He ordered that Christianity must remain proscribed as a religion. However, Christians need not be hunted down, like criminals; the death sentence was to be carried out only when circumstances caused a Christian to admit his faith in a proper tribunal. Since Christians had shown themselves to be neither revolutionaries against the government nor common criminals, recantation was enough to warrant a pardon. Finally, in view of this moderate attitude, Trajan instructed that no further attention was to be paid to anonymous denunciations of suspected Christians.

The rescript was clever, shrewd and vicious. Tertullian, the Carthaginian theologian, said of it: "The Christian is punishable not because he is guilty but because he is discovered, although he is not to be sought out." It was more than that. For many years it was a weapon for future rulers at any level to use as they saw fit. They could execute whom they wished, they could encourage apostasy, they could listen only to the anti-Christian complaints that served their

own ends, they could stir or quell anti-Christian riots depending on which seemed best at the moment. The only
comfort a Christian found in the rescript was that if he
stayed out of trouble, avoided enemies and practiced his
religion secretly he might be able to escape a martyr's
death.

Roman emperors who followed Trajan to the throne in
the next century all applied his rescript strictly. Throughout
the empire, anti-Christian fevers rose and fell, depending
on how other affairs were going. Sudden epidemics, a re-
pression or a lost battle were enough to ignite uprisings, on
grounds that the gods were angry with the people for being
temperate toward the Christians. As it had been from the
first Christian days of Rome, the emperors, the politically
mighty, and the rich actually fretted little about the Christians. But the middle class, the ambitious, the superstitious,
and the ignorant needed outlets for their frustrations, and
the Christians were a convenient channel. Thus it was usually because of pressures from the lower levels that the rulers
condoned and abetted the persecutions, a situation that was
true in all corners of the empire. A contradiction arose that
seemed puzzling for a long time. How could admirable
emperors like Hadrian, Antoninus and Marcus Aurelius,
who did so much good for their country, associate themselves
with the barbaric and ruthless slaughter of thousands of
Christians? Actually, they didn't. They supported the Trajan rescript because it looked like an easy way to resolve a
knotty problem; otherwise Christians were to them a matter
of little concern. Once, as a matter of fact, Marcus Aurelius
took steps to assure that the deceptive loophole of the rescript was upheld.

The incident occurred at Lyons in Gaul in 177. In the
excitement of preparing for a pagan festival, the people
turned on the Christians, arresting many, attacking the
homes of others, killing some before they could be tried. In

the tribunal, the Christians were charged not only with
their faith, but with incest, infanticide, and cannibalism.
Learning of the uprising, Marcus Aurelius sent the local
governor instructions that the common crime charges were
to be dropped and that the Christians were to be tried according to the rescript. He ordered: "Let those who profess
to be Christians be condemned to death, but let those who
deny the faith be released."

In the first rush of panic, several of the Christians, hoping
to be tried for crimes less than their religion, quickly recanted. The orders from Rome, however, which put the
emphasis exclusively on their faith, made them change their
minds. Those who had apostatized courageously affirmed
their faith to the court. Scores of Christians, from the bishop
down to slaves, were killed. In Rome, Marcus Aurelius was
content with the knowledge that at least the Christians
had been given a chance.

3

The blood of martyrs, Tertullian said, was the seed of the
Church. The deaths gave strength to others who were not
so sure of themselves or the Church. Strengthened, they were
often daring in their conduct and thereby attracted converts
among people who wondered what the new religion offered
that could make people so willing to die for what they believed.

And yet there were many Christians who did not really
know what they believed. From the very beginning there
were Christians who misunderstood what the Apostles
preached or could not bring themselves to accept all of it. As
a result, there were heresies and schisms—internal threats
that plagued the Church through the centuries. During their

lifetime, the Apostles occupied themselves energetically in fighting error. While in Rome, Paul wrote to Phrygian communities reprimanding a group that questioned the authority of Jesus. John attacked Cerinthus, an Egyptian Jew who asserted that Jesus was not divine, that God had not created the world nor had He given the Law to the Jews. Cerinthus claimed that angels had created the world and that it was an angel that the Jews called God. John also worked to overcome the heresy of Simon Magus, a Samarian, who, failing to bribe the Apostles into empowering him to perform miracles, announced that he was God and that his concubine, Helen, was his goddess of Thought. In response, John wrote the fourteen-verse preface to his Gospel, in which he clearly defined the link between God and man.

The destruction of Jerusalem by Romans in 70 A.D. and the subsequent dispersion of the Jews gave rise to further religious confusion. A Christian group that called itself the Nazarenes settled in Palestinian villages and attracted many followers by intermingling Christianity and Judaism and practicing the basic precepts of both. The Ebionites, on the other hand, said that Jesus was merely the last of the prophets and that somewhere in the country was a man named Ebion who would be their true savior. They never found him.

Gnosticism held appeal for the intellectuals who couldn't bring themselves to accept the new religion of slaves and fishermen. It held that God indeed was the Father of all things, but He had isolated Himself from the world. Between Him and humanity were beings called eons. Jesus, the Gnostics believed, was an eon—an instrument of God that had existed for all eternity, and His redemptive influence evolved not from His crucifixion but His knowledge (*gnosis*) of the mind of God. Personal redemption, then, depended not on how you behaved but on how much you knew; knowledge became more important than morality.

Gnosticism continued to be an important heresy for almost two hundred years. It was especially strong in Syria and Egypt, where it developed its own highly ceremonious ritual. The Church fought it by showing historically that she, upholding the teachings of the Apostles, had the sole right to define doctrine and morals.

There were other heresies. Millenarianism maintained that the end of the world would occur when Jesus returned to earth one thousand years after His death. Marcionism upheld a similar doctrine, adding that the pleasure-seekers would be condemned and thereby ordering its followers not to marry, not to eat or drink more than enough to stay alive and not to seek personal comforts. Montanism, which became a very strong heresy, claimed that the sins of apostasy, adultery and murder could not be forgiven. Tertullian himself fell victim to Montanism, particularly regarding apostates. Failing to recognize himself as a heretic, Tertullian argued that the baptisms of apostates and heretics were invalid, and so were the baptisms performed by a priest who either became an apostate or heretic. In this he sided with Hippolytus, a Roman priest, who was so convinced he was right that he actually set up his own papacy, which lasted several years.

A doctrinal matter which confused even some of the best minds of the era was that of the Trinity of God, defined by the Apostles as the Father, the Son, and the Holy Ghost. The heresy of Monarchianism explained that Jesus was the incarnation of God the Father. Adoptionism maintained that Jesus was an ordinary human, born of a virgin, who was endowed with such virtues that He was adopted by God and commissioned to perform the Messianic mission.

Heresies were, in a way, one aspect of the growing-pains of the Church. Because of them, it became increasingly necessary for Church leaders at Rome to take stronger stands on doctrinal matters, to define doctrine clearly. In view of

all else that was going on, the popes found themselves leaning more and more on the men near them who acted as
their advisors: the members of the Rome presbytery—the
cardinals. When instructions were sent from Rome to Carthage regarding the validity of the baptisms of heretics and
by heretical priests, the document was signed by cardinals.
It specified that the baptisms were indeed valid. The question, the cardinals pointed out, was not the validity of the
baptism but the responsibility of the heretic—layman or
priest—to adhere to the obligations of it. The document
also set forth an important foundation of the priesthood. It
said that, once ordained, a man was a priest for the rest of
his life. He might apostatize, he might turn heretic, he
might just pick up and walk out, but nothing he nor anyone else could do relieved him of his responsibilities. Like
any other apostate or heretic, the fallen priest had only to
go to confession and reaffirm his faith to his bishop to be
reinstated.

Cardinals further increased in stature when popes assigned them to attend councils held to counteract heresies.
Most often the councils took place in the Middle East provinces of the Roman Empire, where the majority of them
sprouted. In such cases, a prominent bishop of the area
would be appointed by the Pope to argue for the Church at
the meetings. As such, the bishop became, in fact if not in
name, a cardinal. Some of the heretical leaders audaciously
went to Rome in hopes of undermining the Church on its
own grounds. When this happened, cardinal members of
the Roman presbytery confronted them, privately or publicly, to refute them.

Even in its infancy, the Church was a big and broad institution. Despite heresies, schisms, and persecutions, its
growth was phenomenal. In Carthage, which stretched
along the Southern Mediterranean from modern Algeria to
Libya, there were eighty bishops. There were over a hun-

dred in Egypt. Hundreds more worked in the Middle East, in Greece, the Balkans, Italy, Spain, and France. Quite naturally, the poor communications and slow transportation presented serious problems in maintaining a unity, and it was understandable that remote men who were ill-advised or not advised at all should be weak against heresies or even succumb to them themselves. After all, the Church was advancing new ideas that were not always easily accepted even by the sympathetic. Even when the Church unexpectedly won governmental approval—even governmental support—the basic problems of doctrine were not easily resolved.

4

In the year 312, Flavius Valerius Constantinus, Roman general and self-proclaimed emperor, made his way from Gaul into Italy to fight off competitors for the throne. His father had been Caesar Constantinius I, subemperor of the West, and upon his death in Britain, soldiers recognized Flavius as rightful heir. There were people in Rome who had other ideas, and Galerius, the subemperor of the East, had picked his own partner in running the empire. Undaunted, Flavius made his way slowly to Rome, building up his army and claiming western provinces as he moved along. At last he approached the city. Just before the final battle for power, he beheld in the sky a cross arched by the words: "In this sign, conquer." He knew the cross was a Christian emblem and he interpreted the apparition to mean that from Christianity he would derive special strength. He ordered his blacksmiths to make hundreds of crosses and he gave them to his men as the fight began. He conquered overwhelmingly, and when his troops marched in Rome bearing crosses the Christians wondered what in the world was going on.

Taking the name of Constantine I, Flavius sent word to the new subemperor of the East, Licinius, for a conference in Milan. The two men met in 313, and the result of their talks was an edict granting freedom of religion to everybody in the empire. Christians couldn't believe it. As proof of his sincerity, Constantine ordered that all property and money confiscated from Christians was to be returned, that the rights of Christians were to be protected and that public worship was to be permitted. Most of the popes had been buried on Vatican Hill, near Peter, and Constantine not only allowed a church to be built there but contributed heavily to it himself.

If Constantine had stopped there, the course of Christianity might have progressed far differently. But he was a Roman at heart, raised to believe that the gods especially graced Roman rulers, and now that he was head of the state he considered himself also to be head of all religions in the state. He never hesitated to exercise his self-claimed prerogatives and the Church was in no position to hold him off. Because of this precedent, other rulers of other lands in other times took the same prerogatives upon themselves, much to the Church's deep regret.

With Constantine, the intrusion of the state into Church affairs was particularly disquieting because he was not a Christian himself. Without being asked, he handled Church affairs in the same way he handled state affairs: quell the opposition. When he learned of the dissensions caused by heresies, he summoned a council of foreign bishops and told them they must obey the bishop of Rome. His reasoning was not based, as the Church's was, on the authority of Apostolic succession, but rather on the simple fact that Rome was the capital, the seat of western power. Fortunately, while he obtained obedience with threats the Church went ahead and overcame heresies through discussions based on the Scriptures.

Then a heresy arose which neither the Church nor Constantine could handle from Rome. It was called Arianism, named after Arius, a priest of Egypt, who originated it. Like previous heresies, it concerned the nature of the Trinity. A complex idea, Arianism suggested that the Trinity was not a single substance but a trio of natures that were similar but separate. Jesus and the Holy Ghost, therefore, were apart and lower than the Father, distinct and divided from the Godhead of the Father. This directly conflicted with long-proclaimed Christian doctrine that Jesus and the Holy Ghost were consubstantial with the Father in a single God-head. Any other identity of the Trinity would not have been Christianity. Athanasius, who was Arius' bishop, denounced him, but the priest found support from another bishop, Eusebius of Nicomedia, who had been a student with him.

At first the controversy was confined to the Middle East dioceses, and it was a hot battle. Undoubtedly the argument extended beyond purely doctrinal borders: several times earlier the Eastern bishops had the occasion to resent the Rome authority of the Church. Years earlier there had been a difference of opinion between the Oriental bishops and Rome regarding the day on which to celebrate Easter. The Oriental bishops reckoned the feast by the Jewish calendar and wanted to commemorate the Resurrection on the fourteenth day of the first Jewish month, Nisan, regardless of what day of the week it fell on. Rome preferred to celebrate the day on the Christian Sabbath—Sunday—and directed that the feast would take place on the first Sunday after the fourteenth of Nisan. The issue was really not so important as the Eastern bishops made it seem, but when they finally submitted to Rome authority they did so with the utmost reluctance. Now that the Arian idea had once again separated the Church, the Eastern bishops did not intend to give in as easily as they had done in the past. Politics, too, most likely played a part. To Constantine, a divided empire was worse than a divided Church, and as long as Licinius occupied the subthrone at Byzantium Constantine could not look upon himself as the true emperor of the vast Roman domains. Licinius was aware of this and did what he could to keep the West and East divided. One way he did this was to disregard any complaints that came from Rome regarding Arianism.

For ten years the Arian argument raged, with Athanasius authorized and equipped to argue for Rome. The subject became a world issue when Arian "missionaries" began to penetrate the West. To the people, the disagreement was extremely serious. Riots broke out. Arians set Christian churches on fire; Christians set Arian churches on fire.

Then, in 325, Constantine took over. He called a council of three hundred bishops in Nicaea, in Asia Minor—Licinius' territory—which he himself attended as president. Most of the bishops were Arians; Athanasius spoke for the Pope, and two members of the Rome presbytery were present as the Pope's personal delegates. Long debates ended in defeat for the Arians. Out of the council came the Nicene Creed, a definition of faith which eventually became part of the Mass. The victory for Rome, growing out of doctrinal debate, was in itself a triumph, and yet it had its drawbacks. It was Constantine who proclaimed that the Arians were in error and he who banned Arianism from the empire. Thus the Church found itself even more entangled with the government.

Inevitably, the differences between Constantine and Licinius led to war. Constantine won, and then he moved his capital to Byzantium, which he renamed Constantinople. He expected the Pope to move east with him, but the Pope refused and Constantine went eastward with ill feelings. Despite the imperial ban, Arianism died a slow death. Living in the midst of it, Constantine softened toward it. When, on his deathbed in 337, he asked for baptism, it was an Arian priest who baptized him.

5

So the stage was set for the next thousand years. Church supremacy had been established for the bishops of Rome, the heirs of Peter, Prince of the Apostles. Established, too, was the intervention by the heirs of Constantine, the princes and kings of lands around the world. Inescapably established also was the threat of heresies and schisms still to come, among the heirs of confusion, doubt, and ambition. In each vital realm there would be a unique common influence—sometimes good, sometimes bad: the cardinals.

III

$\mathcal{T}$he title of cardinal was one of special authority. The Latin derivation of the word caused its use to be restricted at first to men in the Rome diocese, men whose work brought them into contact with the popes. Since the popes were the bishops of Rome, their assistants had more authority than those who held similar positions in other dioceses. From the beginning, the Bishop of Rome had his deacons and priests. The city was large: there were therefore more such men than in cities elsewhere. Also, there was the business of directing the entire Church from Rome, and this accounted further for the size of the Roman staff.

It should be remembered that the Church was not always free to function as an organization in Rome. Persecutions frequently sent Church leaders scurrying into the country-side for safety. For many years Church affairs had to be carried on in secret. Several of the early popes were exiled, forcing them to administer their business from other cities and other countries. Of the first thirty popes—from Peter to the time of Constantine—twenty-five were martyrs. Conse-quently the papal reigns often came to sudden ends, and it was mainly through the compact unity of the Church, and its well-defined methods of transmitting authority through bishops, that its entity was preserved.

In other dioceses, a new bishop was usually elected by the presbytery from among its own membership. The impor-tance of the bishopric of Rome, however, necessitated broader considerations. Encompassed in the diocese of Rome was the Campania—the suburbicarian sees: six to eight communities with their own bishops who were in frequent touch with the popes. As bishops they were sub-ject to the Bishop of Rome; living so near, they were more directly under his supervision to an extent which made him their archbishop. He frequently called on them to assist him in his work and he took a definite part in their administra-tions. It was therefore reasonable that these men should participate in the election of each new Bishop of Rome.

Within the city, other divisions of authority arose. It was Pope Evaristus (100-105), the fifth pope, who divided Rome into parishes, called *tituli*. The number varied between twenty-five and twenty-eight and the head of each, because of his influence, was known as a cardinal.

The Roman diaconate took on its own character. Peter had appointed seven deacons in Jerusalem. In Rome, be-cause of the population and the constantly increasing num-ber of Christians, the diaconate rose to eighteen. Each dea-con had his own building (dispensary) where he performed his duties, and attached to it was a chapel. For safety's sake, the dispensaries were usually on the outskirts of the city so that the deacons could be warned whenever Roman soldiers located them and went out to close them down. Because of the important work these men did—raising funds for the poor, building churches when possible, offering medical aid, organizing schools, arranging burial grounds, maintaining contact with distant clergy—they, too, became known as cardinals. Later on, when persecutions diminished to the point where the Church could function openly and with the convenience of working under one roof, the dispensaries were closed. However, the chapels remained in use, and the deacon who directed the work formerly done at the outlying dispensary was put in charge of the chapel.

Thus there evolved three types of cardinals: cardinal bishops, who ruled the suburbicarian sees; cardinal priests, who administered the urban parishes; cardinal deacons, who took care of the material work of the Church and supervised the outlying chapels. For the first few centuries the cardinals averaged fifty in number. They were important men in themselves; they were important as an institution because from them grew the College of Cardinals—something of a Church Senate—and the Curia—the papal cabinet.

This evolution did not take place overnight. The adage that Rome is slow has deep roots. Early developments were held back by persecutions, government interference, by heresies, schisms, friction and personality conflicts, and by the simple problem of transportation which made travel and exchange of mail extremely difficult. Many years were required for the Church to accumulate the external characteristics which now mark her so distinctively. Each generation contributed some thought, some regulation, some clarification of doctrine that added to the Church's fulfillment. Truly a living organization, capable of adjusting to the times, the Church grew strong through meeting crises and challenges, steadfastly demanding her prerogatives as the bulwark of Christian morality and doctrine. There were dark moments, to be sure, because at times there were weak men, but the Church itself, her laws and precepts, remained untarnished, and she survived the centuries as the guardian of the faith which Jesus Christ established.

The parade of popes imposed the distinguishing traits that identify the Church today. It was Linus, the second pope, who decreed that women should enter church only with their heads covered. Sixtus I (115-125) instructed that sacred vessels used at Mass should be handled only by the clergy and also that bishops returning from Rome were not to be received by their people without a letter of greeting from the Pope. Victor I (189-199) set the date for Easter. It was Calixtus I (217-222) who established that there was no such thing as an unforgivable sin. Dionysius (259-268) divided Rome into parishes. The large diaconate was developed by Caius (283-296), who also decreed that before a man could become a bishop he must first serve as porter, reader, exorcist, acolyte, sub-deacon, deacon, and priest. Pope Mark (336) decreed that popes should be consecrated by the Bishop of Ostia, one of the suburbicarian sees. He also granted to the Ostian bishop the pallium, a white wool vestment symbolizing authority, which until then was worn only by the pope and now is worn by all archbishops. As the cardinalate became more crystallized, the Bishop of Ostia assumed the role of head of the Curia.

Under Julius I (337-352) monasticism developed into an important force in Europe. It had been introduced by Athanasius, the Bishop of Alexandria, who had led the fight against Arianism. At that time, monks and hermits were already settled in the Egyptian desert. During the so-called Dark Ages, monasteries were to become the vital seats of education in Europe. Until the reign of Damasus I (366-384), the Scriptures existed only in Greek and Aramaic. This pope assigned Jerome, the papal secretary, to translate them into Latin. Jerome had been a desert monk, a priest at

Antioch, and a student of the great Church scholars before working at Rome. His translations occupied him for the rest of his life.

By tradition, most priests were celibate, a custom that grew out of a desire among the clergy to emulate Jesus and several of the Apostles. Also, Paul had once written that, although married life could be a holy state, the person who put aside marriage in order to serve God exclusively would, by the nature of his choice, achieve a higher spiritual level. In the first years of the Church, many of the clergy were married. It soon became accepted practice, however, that men could marry before priesthood ordination but not after it. In many circles, celibacy was looked upon as the ascetic ideal. Women entering the conventual life were already taking vows of virginity. During the reign of Pope Siricius (383-399), a monk named Jovinian, apparently weary of the strict life, appeared in Rome and began to preach that vows, celibacy, fasting, and good works were worthless insofar as spiritual perfection and salvation were concerned. In the process of winning a few followers among the clergy and nuns, he managed to scandalize the populace and to infuriate the Church. Siricius called a synod to discuss the problem, with the result that Jovinian and his followers were ex-communicated (deprived of the sacraments until they repented) and it was established that henceforth all priests would be celibates. This did not preclude previously married men from becoming priests: Pope Felix II (483-492), a widower upon his ordination, was the great-grandfather of Pope Gregory I (590-604); Pope Hormisdas (514-523) was the father of Pope Silverius (536-537.) All four popes were canonized. In later years there were to be similarly close relations between several popes, but not in such happy circumstances.

Celestine I (422-432) permitted the display of paintings and statues in churches as tributes to saints. Miltiades (311-

314) was the first pope to have a palace in which to live—the Lateran Palace, which Nero had confiscated from the Christian Laterani family, was presented by Constantine's wife to the Church. The first pope to change his name was Mercurius who, upon election on January 2, 533, took the name of John II. Foreshadows of the troubles popes would have with kings appeared as early as 355, when Emperor Constantinus, who favored Arianism, ordered the bishops to condemn Bishop Athanasius. When the bishops explained that such action would be against the canons of the Church, the Emperor said: "My will is the canon." By the reign of John III (561-574), Roman political authority in the west was almost completely destroyed by the Goths. The Roman senate disappeared. More and more the people found themselves looking to the papacy for political leadership—a burden the popes did not want but could not escape. The dangers in it became evident during the reign of Benedict I (575-579), when the remnants of Roman authority in Constantinople demanded the right to approve (or disapprove) papal elections. The next step was inevitable: the right of kings—any kings—to choose the pope.

2

Because of the growing link between the Church and the state, whatever happened in the world politically affected the Church. Beginning with Constantine, the friendly emperors who ruled during the next century displayed their sentiments toward the Church by granting her certain lands, the income from which was to be used for the poor. Thus the Church early became a land-holder, with its properties steadily increasing. Threats to Rome thereby became threats to the Church as well.

There were many threats. Each one showed the Church to be a world influence, a factor that was to become increasingly evident as Europe matured. The Church influence had several roots, not all of them good. It so happened that the Christian expansion into Europe took place at approximately the same time as the northern tribes were unifying into strong forces. The impact of Christianity upon the people was tremendous. Northern rulers recognized that they would have to deal with it somehow, and out of this grew the need for communication between the men at the top. There were too many such occasions for the popes alone to handle, so they appointed as their representatives other men whose positions in Rome were of such authority that they could conduct Church affairs at the highest level. In the Roman sense, these men were cardinals. Their added responsibility gave them even greater stature than they previously had. They became, in a sense, princes of the Church. As such, they ranked in power with princes everywhere.

In the year 600 religion and politics played almost equal roles, a situation natural in a world in which the head of the state was also head of the religion. Christianity was the exception: the head of the religion was the pope of Rome. His realm was, in effect, strictly spiritual but, with increasing gifts of land, it began to have another aspect as well. As rulers awarded more and more lands to the Church, the Papal States extended up and down the western coast of Italy, including Sardinia and Sicily. There were even papal properties in other countries, granted by rulers who were converted to Christianity during their reigns.

One danger of this practice was obvious from the start: rulers change—not only in fact but in heart. Harmony with one ruler was no guarantee of harmony with his successor. As a land-holder the Church was forced out of its exclusively spiritual realm into negotiations with rulers whose domains touched those of the Church or who found the Church lands attractive enough to fight for. The Church had no armies; to protect itself it had to rely on the aid of friendly rulers or on mercenaries. The risk of mercenaries was that they would readily sell themselves to a higher bidder. And the friendly rulers were not always so friendly.

It was a complex situation, arising to a great extent from the surge of power in the north. The transfer of the Roman throne to Constantinople had weakened the western provinces. There were, to be sure, occasional men as co-emperors in the west who possessed personal strength, and some of them, like Julian the Apostate—Constantine's nephew— showed their strength by a revival of persecution of Christians. Despite Constantine's edict which supposedly put an end to Arianism, this heresy was still strong in the Middle East. To distinguish themselves from Arians, the Christians of Roman allegiance were already being called Catholics, a term taken from the Nicene creed which identified the Church as being "one, holy, catholic and apostolic." Just as Catholics were sending missionaries to the north, so were Arians.

The Arians were the first to reach the Goths, the Germanic tribes that lived in the vast wilderness of Eastern Europe, and they won many converts. In the middle of the Fourth Century, the Huns from Northern Asia began to move into this area, pushing the Goths out. So powerful were the Huns that some of their generals were put on the payroll of the Roman Empire rulers at Constantinople in order to achieve some hint of peace. The first Germanic tribe to make itself felt in Western Europe was the Vandals. Retreating from the Huns, they fought, robbed and ransacked as they moved westward, settling at last in Spain. Then the Visigoths (West Goths) and Ostrogoths (East Goths) began to move. The Visigoths ousted the Vandals from Spain, occupying that country and the southern part of France. The Vandals went into North Africa, conquering the south shores of the Mediterranean. The Ostrogoths, subjected by the Huns, became uneasy allies of the Constantinople government. Zeno was the emperor at Constantinople, and he had already lost control of Italy to a man named Odoacer, head of an army of mercenaries Zeno had hired to serve as his western troops. Odoacer carried his job further than Zeno expected when he headed a revolt by which he made himself the king of Italy. In an effort to get Italy back and also to get the Ostrogoths out of Constantinople, Zeno instructed Theodoric the Great, king of the Ostrogoths, to fight Odoacer. Theodoric won, but instead of turning the country back to Zeno he made himself king. The Ostrogoths thus ruled the western provinces from Switzerland to Sicily, and the Roman Empire was restricted to the eastern provinces. The Ostrogoth rule came to an end after seventy years when, in 568, another Germanic tribe, the Lombards, moved south and conquered Italy. At first, the Lombards divided Italy into some thirty duchies, but after a few years they reverted to an Italian kingdom in order to unify their strength against outside threats. During this same period, the Germanic tribe of Franks had gone westward to occupy Central and Northern France. Further north, the Angles and the Saxons expanded their Germanic influence across Northern Europe and into Britain.

The Church had been involved in all of it. The Goths who weren't pagans were Arians. As Arians, they were sworn enemies of the Roman Catholic Church. In Africa, the Arian Vandals killed thousands of Catholics and destroyed the churches built by Cyprian at Carthage and Augustine at Hippo. Rome itself suffered. In 410, the Visigoth Alaric burned and plundered the city for five days. In 455, the Vandal Gaiseric came up from Africa for an attack.

Pope Innocent I (401-417) tried to hold off Alaric by going to Ravenna (where Honorius, puppet ruler of the western provinces, had moved the capital), and begging for troops to defend Rome, but Honorius was afraid to move. Innocent returned to a ruined city. In 452, Pope Leo I (440-461) managed to check the attacks of Attila the Hun by meeting with him on the banks of the Mincio River and, with persuasive eloquence, talking him into sparing Rome. When, three years later, Gaiseric arrived from Africa, Leo met him outside the city for a similar conference. As a result, Gaiseric agreed not to kill Romans or damage the city, settling for the prerogative of fourteen days in which to help himself to any riches of Rome he wanted.

And yet the relations between the Church and the Goths took some strange turns. Theodoric, an ardent Arian, was worried that Emperor Justin would send fresh armies to recapture Italy. Justin, a Catholic, had at that time moved against Arianism by closing Arian churches in Constantinople. In a show of strength, Theodoric ordered Pope John I (523-526) to go to Constantinople to instruct Justin to reopen the Arian churches. The Pope couldn't escape being shipped out of the country, but he had no intention of following Theodoric's orders. At Constantinople, Justin welcomed the Pope with great honors, asking John to coronate him to make his emperorship official. Uncertain Eastern bishops who weren't sure whether they were Catholic or Arian came forward and pledged friendship and support to the Pope. John headed back to Rome on clouds of glory, but the minute he set foot in the city Theodoric threw him into jail. When John died in prison, Theodoric arranged that the next pope would be on his side by personally pushing for the election of Felix III. Fortunately, Theodoric then died, freeing Felix III to fill his position in a manner that subsequently won sainthood for him.

Before his own death, Felix III did an unusual thing. Distressed by the open conflict in the city between the pro-Goths and the pro-Byzantines, he sought to avoid a definite rupture by appointing his own successor—the cardinal arch-deacon Boniface. Tradition already established that the bishop of Rome should be elected, so Felix's gesture did not go well at all. While Boniface was being consecrated at the Julian Basilica, the people and clergy had their own choice —the diplomat Dioscorus—consecrated at the Lateran Basilica. For a month, then, the Church had two popes. Then Dioscorus died. The populace decided to turn to Boniface. A little perturbed over his earlier rejection, Boniface at first tried to assert himself by naming as his own successor the deacon Virgilius, but when he thought it over he recognized that this was wrong and retracted the appointment. Virgilius nevertheless made it on his own, but in circumstances that were rather unpleasant.

There existed at the time two heresies, both the result of Arianism. Again the nature of the Trinity was involved. Arians had claimed that Jesus, although a member of the Trinity, was apart and below in substance from God the Father. The Church maintained that the Trinity was of a single substance. Then an idea began to grow in the Middle East that there was a distinction between Jesus, Son of God, and Jesus, son of Mary. Early in the Fifth Century, Nestorius, Patriarch (archbishop) of Constantinople, championed this idea. He said: "Mary merely engendered the man in which the Word became incarnate. Jesus is God, however, because He contains God. I worship the vase because of its contents, the vestment because of him it clothes." A tremendous controversy sprang from what became known as the Nestorian heresy, heretical because it denied the divine maternity of Mary and the indivisibility of the natures of Jesus.

The companion heresy to Nestorianism was Monophysitism, which went to the opposite extreme. Monophysitism was a little fuzzy around the edges, but basically it suggested that the combination of the two natures of Jesus had produced a third, just as hydrogen and oxygen when combined produce a third substance, water.

In a short time the Church found itself being pulled in two directions, by Nestorianism at Constantinople and Monophysitism at Alexandria. In the midst of the fray was Cyril, the great bishop of Alexandria, who held the orthodox view. A council at Rome condemned Nestorius, but that didn't quiet him. Cyril continued to attack him skillfully, unaware that he was inadvertently encouraging Monophysitism. Despite the Church condemnation, Nestorius still hoped to win out, with the aid of Emperor Theodosius II at Constantinople. The Emperor thus convoked a council at Ephesus on June 7, 431, and there was nothing the Church could do but send two delegates to discuss a subject that had already been resolved. Nestorius' lone argument was one that revealed the narrow horizons of his own faith. He said: "Never will I recognize as God a child who was two months old, three months old, four months . . ." Cyril himself debated privately with Nestorius before the council began, and when the first session was called Nestorius refused to appear. Cyril presented his arguments to the forty-three bishops present and won them entirely.

The Emperor, reluctant to contradict a decision favoring the patriarch of his own capital city and forced to act against the loser, decided to imprison both Cyril and Nestorius. Delegates from both men visited the Emperor to discuss the issue again. In the end, Cyril was released and allowed to return home and Nestorius was deposed. The heresy died, except in a small area of Persia, from where it made no attempt to expand. The dismal aspect of the controversy was, in the long view, the Emperor's participation in it, and the worst of it was that the Church had accepted the position of simultaneously trying to keep the government out of religion and yet leaning upon the throne for support of its own actions.

The Monophysitic reaction to Nestorianism was, in a way, quite natural. Throughout history, public sentiment has swung from one extreme to another. Abetting this particular situation was an Alexandrian named Diocorsus (not the one-month pope) who had never liked Nestorius and wasn't especially fond of Cyril. Monophysitic ideas were already spreading throughout the Middle East. It was Dioscorus, who succeeded Cyril as bishop of Alexandria in 444, who organized Monophysitism and began to encourage it. Soon Monophysitism was stronger in the Middle East than Nestorianism had ever been. It took firm root and thrived and found favor in high places. It had been a Constantinople emperor who banned the Nestorian heresy in the fifth century; in the sixth century another Constantinople emperor supported the Monophysitic heresy.

Actually it was the emperor's wife. Theodora had been an actress when she married Emperor Justinian. Her fame and the high position she acquired upon marriage deluded her into fancying that she was also a theologian. Monophysitism attracted her, and she made up her mind that somehow she was going to get at least part of its concept approved by the Church at Rome. She came astonishingly close to success.

The Gothic invasion of Italy had weakened the Ravenna exarch to the point where he could scarcely defend his castle, let alone push the Goths out of the country. The Church suffered greatly. Hoping for relief, successive popes pleaded with the Constantinople rulers for armies to restore peace and order to the land. Meanwhile, Virgilius, the appointed and then rejected successor of Pope Boniface II, made his way to Constantinople and won favor with Empress Theodora. He wanted to be pope very badly, and out of this he made a deal with Theodora: for a sum of money and his promise to give Church approval to Monophysitism she would urge Justinian to send troops to Rome, recapture the country and make Virgilius pope.

Pope Boniface died in 532 and was succeeded by Pope John II, who reigned for two years. There was some shady politics involved in the election that moved Gothic King Athalaric to enforce an earlier Roman Senate decree against bribery in papal elections. Athalaric had the decree carved in marble and placed in St. Peter's Basilica, and he warned that in the event of future disputes in papal elections the Church would be fined. The next pope was Agapetus I, who had the unusual experience of being shipped to Constantinople by the Gothic King Theodahad, with orders to talk Emperor Justinian out of attacking Italy. Once in Constantinople, Agapetus was too busy fighting Monophysitism to carry out his errand. The Monophysites had managed to get one of their men appointed patriarch of the city. After many arguments with Justinian and Theodora, Agapetus succeeded in having the man replaced with an orthodox patriarch. But the battle was too much for the aged Pope and he died before he could return to Rome.

The next man to become pope was Silverius, a sub-deacon and son of Pope Hormisdas. He was, of all things, the personal choice of Gothic King Theodahad, but because of his good reputation in Rome he was approved by the clergy and people. Afraid of attacks by Justinian, the King wanted a friend in the papacy who might win public support for him. But it was a futile hope. Near the end of 536, Roman General Balisarius swept up from Sicily, defeating the Goths, and, on December 6, he led his forces into Rome without opposition. He went for Silverius and accused him of helping the Goths, ordering him to recall the ousted Constantinople patriarch and approve the Monophysite idea. When the Pope refused, the General announced that Silverius had been deposed and that a new pope should be elected. In view of the circumstances and the pressures from Constantinople there was little doubt who the next pope would be: Virgilius.

3

Now the Church was on the threshold of the Middle Ages, the period of its great expansion, its most thorough penetrations. To some, these were the Dark Ages—but they were far from dark. This was the era of the printing press, of great universities and cathedrals, of new powers rising in the north. For the Church, the centuries ahead were to bring both triumphs and fresh wounds.

Pope Virgilius alarmed Empress Theodora when he turned out to be an orthodox pontiff. Undoubtedly, in putting on the pallium he had undergone a change of heart. Instead of embracing Monophysitism, he fought it as had his predecessors. Egged on by his wife, the Emperor was furious with Virgilius and ordered him to come to Constantinople to resolve the matter at a council. In the fifth century there had been three ecclesiastics who had written against Monophysitism and in doing so almost tumbled backward into Nestorianism. They had corrected their error, however, and died within orthodoxy. Their writings were known as the Three Chapters, and it now became Justinian's intention to have the writings condemned officially in order to placate the Monophysite population that was growing so strong in the Middle East. Involved in the matter was the 451 Council of Chalcedon at which the Church had irretractably defined Jesus, second member of the Trinity, to be co-equal God-Man, separate but inseparable. To condemn the Three Chapters inferred condemnation of the Chalcedon council as well as implied approval of Monophysitism. On arriving at Constantinople, Pope Virgilius at first refused to discuss the situation, but the pressure on him was so heavy that in the end he yielded. However, he still would not join in the condemnation of the Three Chapters. He saw the personal danger in this and tried to save his life by sliding down a rope to escape from the palace. Justinian coaxed him back, while at the same time sending into exile those bishops at the council who had sided with the Pope. Thinking it over, Virgilius decided that in protecting the reputations of the Three Chapters authors he was risking the lives of his bishops, so he took another stand. He condoned the condemnation of the Three Chapters with the clear understanding that this in no way changed the definition of the Chalcedon council, a specification that still kept the Monophysites on the outside. Bishops in the West thought Virgilius had gone out of his mind and there was some talk of deposing him. Virgilius hoped to explain his position to them effectively when he returned to Rome, but he died before he got there. His successor, Pelagius I, managed to support him and yet win back all but two or three Western bishops, who held their dioceses out of Papal jurisdiction for several years.

Although the Monophysites had won a victory, they still were not satisfied. They continued to bombard Justinian with demands for sterner action until he could bear no more of the confusion and began to send leading Monophysites into exile. Indignant, the Monophysites cut themselves off from Rome. Those in Egypt called themselves Coptic Christians—Christians of ancient Egypt; those along the Eastern Mediterranean called themselves Melchite Catholics—from Melech, meaning king, i.e., the royal party; an ex-monk named James Jacob Baradai was a pet of Theodora, and she set him up in Syria as head of the Monophysitic Jacobite Church.

As the Church suffered schisms in the East, she gained strength in the north. An important contributing factor was the conversion of Clovis, King of the Franks from 481 to 511. He was married to Clotilda, a Catholic Burgundian princess, and he permitted his children to be baptized. In 496, while fighting the pagan Germanic Alemmani tribe he vowed to become Catholic if he won. He did both, bringing into the Church with him three thousand of his men. His subsequent victories in France and Germany opened the door for Catholic missionaries.

The event that brought the early era to a close and served as the beginning of the Middle Ages was the unification of the Lombard duchies into the Kingdom of Italy. Although the Church had suffered severely during the Lombard invasion, during the decade of the duchies many bishops moved into positions of unusual authority. The Lombards had been Arians, but with time they converted to Catholicity. Despite their common background, the dukes fought among themselves almost constantly and had little time for affairs in their own duchies. Thus bishops gradually became magistrates and, in effect if not in fact, ran the duchies. Even after the unification of the country they retained much of their influence. Without realizing it, they were setting a pattern that was to spread throughout the continent, preparing for the vital roles that were to be played by cardinals.

IV

𝐼t is remarkable that, during the first thousand years of the papacy, despite the questionable methods by which various men worked their way to the papal throne, none of them in any way contributed to heresies. The Church expanded theologically as well as geographically in this period, and yet it remained consistent in tenets and precepts. In view of the turmoil that frequently rocked the papal throne, this was indeed extraordinary. By ordinary measures, the Rock of the Church should have been reduced to gravel in its early years, so severe was the intrigue that surrounded her. But the Church proved to be greater than the men who ruled her. God-founded, she was God-protected. She strengthened the weak and survived the wicked. Some popes who seemed unlikely choices at the time of their election became men of mountains once the new responsibility settled upon their shoulders. Other popes who never measured up to the job nevertheless failed to shake the Church despite their own weaknesses as rulers and as men.

As there were good and bad popes, so were there good and bad cardinals. A major cause of difficulty was the Church's land holdings, and the relationships with foreign governments necessary as a consequence. Affairs would have been much simpler had governments restricted themselves to temporal concerns and had the Church restricted herself to spiritual concerns. This did not happen, nor was it always possible. The Patrimony of Peter—the lands owned by the Church—was at one time so vast that the popes held domain over areas as great as any ruled by contemporary kings. In itself, there was nothing particularly wrong with the idea that the Church should own land. For more than five hundred years after Constantine all Christian rulers awarded the Church certain properties, and they were put to good use. Governments did not build schools, hospitals, orphanages, nor did they take care of the poor; the Church did, with earnings from her properties.

So widespread were the properties that they could not possibly be supervised solely by the popes, most of whom had much more demanding issues to handle. The patrimony, therefore, was usually under the direction of cardinal-deacons who lived at Rome. Locally, the land was managed by bishops. As important as the property was to provide support for Church work, it frequently proved to be a great problem. Sometimes the heirs of rulers who had granted the land wanted it back for themselves; sometimes churchmen in charge of the land got the idea it was actually their own; sometimes regional rulers—dukes, princes, barons—wanted more control over these lands and often contrived to have their relatives chosen as local bishops. And the time was to come when Church lands in Italy were to be such important obstacles in the unification of the country that the Church and Italy were to be quiet enemies for years.

In one sense, it was extremely important that the popes should have temporal realms of their own, no matter how small. Had this been the case from the beginning—or at least from the end of the Roman persecutions—there might never have been any Church-State controversies to disturb the world, even in our time. But for nineteen hundred years, the popes were considered citizens—often captive citizens— of whatever political power ruled the Rome area. If the popes were friends of the ruling power, they were then ene- mies of all opposing powers. The reverse was equally true. It was also true—and this cannot be overemphasized—that political rulers would not leave the Church alone. The Church possessed spiritual power to which Catholics freely submitted, and the political rulers wanted, if not always to control that power, at least to influence it for their own ends.

Also, the Church was rich. Land, art objects, precious jewels, and even commercial projects found their way into Church possession from people who sincerely wanted to help the Church and from others who hoped to win favor. This wealth was attractive; men both in and out of the Church went after it. It was possible for the Church to deal with am- bitious men within her own ranks, but when the avarice came from outside there was nothing for it but to look outside for protection. Had the Church from the start possessed her own property, respected by all as a separate realm from which financial support and consequently spiritual treasures could emanate to everyone equally, then surely there would have been fewer moments in the Church's life to embarrass those who now cherish her. However, our present concern must be not with history as it could have been, but as it was.

2

As the Church grew older it became increasingly obvious that more centralized authority was necessary if there was to be any freedom of action. The imperial demand for the right to approve papal elections was a serious problem. Often weeks—sometimes even months—passed between the election of a pope and his consecration, and there was always the chance that the emperor at Constantinople might not approve the choice. To avoid this, an interesting pattern arose. For years, the second most important post in the Church was that of legate to the imperial court. Men who held this position usually got to know the emperors well and to win their confidence. The election of such men as popes practically assured imperial approval, and so there were periods during the fourth and fifth centuries when five or six popes in succession were men who had worked at Constantinople. The city came to be known as the cradle of popes; actually the men at Rome who made the choice were taking the path of least resistance. In most cases the choices were good.

Each generation brought special difficulties to the papacy. The decay of western imperial power in the sixth century brought on the dismissal of the Senate. Thus Pope John III (561-574), the leading figure west of Constantinople, found himself with more temporal responsibilities than any previous pope. The decay of the secular power opened the door to internal politics in the religious organization. Men vied for the papal throne; some even tried to buy it. In 687, the cardinal-archdeacon Paschal bribed John, the exarch at Ravenna, for support in winning the papacy, and he almost got the prize. However, the contest reached a stalemate between Paschal and the cardinal-archpriest Theodore, and in the end the papacy went to Sergius, a Syrian priest living in Rome.

The rise of Islam, the religion of Mohammed, proved to be a long-lasting problem for the Church. Mohammed was born in Arabia in 571. Orphaned young, he earned his living driving camels and shepherding. At twenty-five, he caught the eye of a rich widow who hired him and then married him. His new wealth enabled him to spend long hours in the religious meditations he enjoyed, and he subsequently claimed that an angel had appeared to him with instructions from God to rid the land of paganism by destroying the idols in the Kaaba, a sanctuary at Mecca. In a short time, he attracted many followers and carried out his plan. Mohammed considered himself to be the last and the greatest of the prophets, greater even than Jesus, whom Mohammed classified merely as his predecessor. Islam's immediate appeal was its promise of riches and power to its heroes—heroes that were to wage a Holy War against infidels, i.e., Christians and Jews. The Islamic conquests in the Middle East, Africa and Eastern Europe were part of that war. In an effort to complete their victories, Islamic generals invaded Spain and held it for centuries.

The Islamic push northward from Spain was stopped by Charles Martel, king of the Franks. He also subdued Germanic tribes in Central Europe and helped the popes against the Lombards. His son, Pippin the Short, was an even more vigorous defender of the popes, and it was he who restored lost properties to the Church, awarding additional ones. As a result of Pippin's battles with the Lombards, Pope Stephen III (752-757) was put in control of the exarchate of Ravenna and thus became the first pope-king.

Control of the papacy was now a double temptation, a fact that quickly became evident. Even before Pope Stephen took his last breath opposing factions were at work to push through their own successors. One group supported the cardinal-archdeacon Theophylact, another was behind Stephen's brother Paul, and Desiderius, the duke of Istria, wanted the duo-throne for himself. Desiderius went so far as to make an alliance with the remnants of the Eastern Empire, promising restoration in the west in return for personal backing. The only thing that stopped him was the decision of Ratchis, the ex-king of Lombard-unified Italy, who had abdicated to become a monk and then, during the tussle for the papacy, left the monastery determined to challenge the ambitions of Desiderius. Paul won the election. Worried, Desiderius pledged support of Paul if Ratchis would go back to the monastery. Pope Paul I convinced Ratchis to return, then had to call on Pippin the Short to help keep Desiderius in his place.

The next pope, Stephen IV, had similar troubles before his election. This time it was Toto, duke of Nepi, who tried to capture the papacy. He entered Rome with his own army and threatened to set it on fire unless his brother Constantine was made pope. Constantine was not even a member of the clergy. Papal officials got a Lombard army to evict Toto from Rome, and before the air cleared a Lombard priest staged his own election and proclaimed that Philip, a monk, was pope. Once again fighting broke out in the streets, and it came to an end only when high-ranking Church leaders were able to arrange an honest election. Stephen, a Sicilian cardinal-priest with excellent experience in Rome, was chosen.

Stephen recognized that the haggling over papal elections could not go on. Regulations had to be enforced by which the elections were taken out of competition and removed from the influence of self-aggrandizing noblemen. With this in mind, he called a synod in 769 which decreed that henceforth the popes should be chosen from among the cardinals. The clergy would elect the man; after the election the public would have the right of acclamation; the nobility would have nothing to do with it.

The decree had several important effects. It raised the cardinalate to new heights. Previously the cardinals obtained their titles because they were pastors of Rome, deacon-assistants of Church affairs, or bishops of the surrounding sees, all under the direction of the Pope. Aside from their individual responsibilities, they were called to the Lateran Palace for conferences with popes and to take part in various religious ceremonies, and the bishop of Ostia consecrated new popes. But now their positions took on an added significance: one of them would become pope when the vacancy occurred. The distinct advantage in the arrangement was that the popes appointed the pastors and deacons of Rome and had a say in the election of suburbicarian bishops, all of which provided a certain control over candidates for the papacy. The control, as has been seen and will be seen again, was not always effective, but at least it was a step in the right direction.

It turned out to be a step that the nobility was ready to take as well. Cardinals who had ordinarily gone their way undisturbed by top-level controversies now found themselves in the thick of things. Whereas in the past they had performed papal missions with capability and thoroughness, then returned to obscurity in Rome, now they were received everywhere as crown princes, heirs to the papal tiara. They were pursued, feasted and favored. Among cunning noblemen, the friendship of a cardinal was an investment in the future. It was understandable that there should be a few cardinals who lacked the equilibrium to live with their new dignities without being swept away by them.

The dozen popes who reigned in the century following the 769 decree had all been cardinals—deacon, priest or bishop —and they were able men. In view of the times, they were surprisingly free from political pressure. Only once did the nobility manage to get its own candidate elected—Eugene II (824-827)—but he worked out well. This was the era of Charlemagne, of Louis the Pious, and Lothair, the Frankish kings who brought most of Europe under their control and laid the foundation for the Holy Roman Empire. In their own ways, they were all friends of the Church. Charlemagne came to the rescue of Pope Leo III (755-816) when an opposition factor tried to depose him. The Pope subsequently crowned Charlemagne officially in St. Peter's. His grandson, King Lothair, son of Louis the Pious, was also crowned in Rome, as his father's coemperor, by Pope Paschal I in 823. Some years later Lothair tried to use his papal friendships to get a divorce and marry his mistress, but reigning then was the strong-minded Pope Nicholas I (858-867), who not only refused the divorce but also ousted the Frankish bishops who favored the divorce in order to keep Lothair friendly. Contrary to popular fears, Lothair submitted to the Pope and kept his wife.

Quite plainly, the papal freedom could endure only as long as mighty kings, or at least the mightiest, respected it. Charlemagne respected it for a long time, but then he got the idea that he was more pope than king, just as some popes considered themselves more king than pope, and as a result Charlemagne encroached more and more upon the strictly spiritual domain of the Church. He frequently summoned synods and preached to bishops about the Church. He considered all Church property to be his and administered it with more attention than he paid to his own. He issued regulations regarding chant and liturgy. He gave orders to bishops and priests in his kingdom as to where and how they should live. Because the popes were indebted to Charlemagne they had to be cautious in pointing out to him that he was becoming too presumptuous and something of a nuisance.

His son, Louis the Pious, set the Church back a hundred years. It came about in this way: As the cardinals grew in stature the popes detected increasing efforts by the local aristocracy to work their way to papal influence via side doors. To put an end to this, Pope Paschal I exiled several blue-blooded families from the city, an act that stirred much resentment among other aristocrats. The Pope appealed to Louis the Pious for help, but before the help arrived Paschal died and was succeeded by the nobility-backed Eugene II.

The help was in the form of a new agreement between the papacy and Louis. Louis offered to continue the protection given the Church by previous Frankish emperors, but with stiff provisos. He specified that although the Papal States would remain under Church jurisdiction Louis would be their overlord. He also ordered that Frankish law as well as papal law would be in effect, and that people should have the choice of which they wanted to follow. He announced that he was sending two men to Rome to see that this was done and to pass on all ecclesiastic and administrative appointments made in the Papal States. Finally, he insisted that the decree limiting papal elections to the clergy should be revoked, and that the people should make the choice—subject to his approval.

Pope Eugene was in a quandary. If he refused Louis' offer he risked the Emperor's wrath; if he accepted he was putting the Church back in chains. Without Louis' protection, the Church was defenseless, for even the aristocracy that supported Eugene lacked the money and the forces to stave off outside threats. Eugene signed.

In a way, it was good that he did. A few years later, the Islamic armies came up from Africa and attacked Rome. A local contingent under the Duke of Spoleto was defeated. Holding to their agreement, the Franks sent troops to Rome and saved the city.

3

The Frankish Empire fell apart from within. Louis the Pious was unable to control his own sons, and as a result brother fought brother and sons fought their father. The chaos led directly to a decentralization of power in Europe, and this in turn gave rise to the feudalism that gripped the continent for the next six centuries. The effect of it all upon the Church was far from good. No longer was there one strong ruler on whom the Church could depend for protection against ambitious lower-level leaders. The Church was up for grabs—and there were many takers. For the Church, survival was of necessity an internal matter, but unfortunately during the tenth century the Church contained little to work with. It was a time when the Church was called upon to produce her own heroes, but one cannot summon heroes the way one summons servants; they must, like stars, arise on their own, within the plan of God.

One such man did appear in Rome. He was Cardinal Hildebrand. To evaluate him requires us to have a certain perspective.

At the beginning of the tenth century there lived in Rome a powerful nobleman: Theophylactus, Duke, Commander of the Army, Master of the Wardrobe. His wife was Theodora, an ambitious, strong-willed, domineering woman, and those leading men of Rome she could not dominate in the royal court she dominated in the royal boudoir. From numerous influential men she acquired, in addition to their political cooperation, a fortune of her own in villas and castles. Her daughter Marozzia maneuvered in much the same way. At one time Marozzia moved into the Castel Sant' Angelo, a fortress on the Tiber that was the refuge of popes during times of strife.

Undoubtedly, Sergius became pope through the influence of Theodora. He was an unusual man. Previously he had openly campaigned for the papacy but lost out to Pope John IX (898-900). As punishment for conduct that violated both tradition and law, he had been excommunicated. It was Theodora who brought him back and put him on the papal throne. Sensitive to the ways of sovereigns, Sergius solved a delicate problem at Constantinople, where the people were severely critical of the fourth marriage of Emperor Leo. The people were willing to accept two marriages for a man, but they thought four was a bit too much. By the time the matter was placed before Sergius, Leo's first three wives had all died. The Pope pointed this out, explaining that Leo was thereby a free man. This was a fact, and the people reluctantly faced it.

For fifty years the Theophylacts ruled Rome and the papacy, thereby establishing a dangerous precedent. Most of the popes they appointed were weak. Overshadowed by the royal family, they left little impression upon their era. Some of them came to inglorious ends. John X (914-928) was a sad example of such a man. His election had been arranged by Theodora, but halfway through his reign Rome came under the spell of Marozzia, who didn't like John at all. The high point of his reign occurred in 916, when he personally led an attack against an Islamic stronghold at Garigliano and won a decisive, although astonishingly brutal, victory. At the other extreme, in a conciliatory gesture toward Heribert, the Count of Vermandois, John appointed the Count's son to be the archbishop of Rheims—an alarming appointment in view of the fact that the son was only five years old.

When John discovered how much Marozzia disliked him he tried to protect himself by attempting to appoint to the vacant Lombard throne a complete foreigner—Hugh, Duke of Provence. His success would have threatened Marozzia's influence in Rome. In defense, she ignited an insurrection during which John was thrown into prison and smothered to death with a pillow.

These were shocking events, to be sure, but we must view them in terms of the times. The important fact was this: despite the unsavory qualities of several men who held the papacy, not one of them was able in any way to detour the Church from its original theological path.

With John out of the way, Marozzia successively put three of her puppets on the papal throne—Leo VI (928-929), Stephen VII (929-931), and her own son, John XI (931-936). She then reconsidered the murdered Pope John's idea of inviting the Duke of Provence to become king of Italy. She married the man, expecting her son, John XI, to crown both her and his new stepfather. In this, she overlooked her second son, Alberic, who had no use for his stepfather. He raised an army, sent the Duke running home, put his mother in jail where she mysteriously died, and then limited his brother only to spiritual rule of the Church, taking over the temporal authority for himself.

Between 946 and 955, Alberic put four popes into office, and then named his own sixteen-year-old son to the papacy before his predecessor had time to die. The son, Octavian, took the name of John XII, the second pope to change his name. When Alberic died, John took over his temporal authorities as well, thus becoming the most powerful person in Rome before he was old enough to shave. He reigned for eight turbulent years, with most of the havoc resulting from his own conduct. He was definitely a bad pope. Some historians claim he died suddenly while in the act of adultery, which, whether true or false, was certainly in character. At his death the Church was left in complete confusion.

But before his remarkable death, John had gotten into trouble with Berenger, the king of Italy. For help, John appealed to King Otto I, head of the German House of Saxony. Otto went to Rome where he was crowned king of Italy by the young pope; then he set out to prove it to Berenger through battle. John became afraid that Otto intended to rule Rome itself, so he turned around and plotted with Berenger against Otto. Otto returned to Rome and deposed John, replacing him with Leo, a lay official of the papal council. Leo was a layman one day, a deacon and priest the next, a bishop and cardinal the next, then pope the next—a speedy rise for any man in any era. The people of Rome refused to accept Leo and, regardless of his character, they tried to restore John. When John died suddenly, the people still rejected Leo, electing instead the cardinal-deacon Benedict. Otto wouldn't hear of this. He hauled Benedict to Hamburg, leaving Leo to rule. Leo rewarded Otto by granting him the right of approving future popes; he also decreed that henceforth the people would be excluded from papal elections.

But still there was no peace. Leo died in 965, and the people asked Otto to send back Benedict. But Benedict died before Otto made up his mind. Otto then thought it would be clever to appoint another Theophylact to the papacy, hoping in this way to calm the Romans. He chose John, cousin of the playboy Pope John XII. The new pope called himself John XIII; he was a good man and he tried hard, but there was little he could do with Otto constantly looking over his shoulder. Since Otto had to be in Germany, he arranged for closer surveillance by appointing his thirteen-year-old son as his co-emperor and sending him to Rome. John XIII crowned young Otto II, then negotiated his marriage to the daughter of the Eastern Emperor Romanus II. By this marriage Otto hoped to acquire what he had failed to win in battle—control of Southern Italy, if not specifically for himself at least for his heirs. And in doing so he inaugurated the Holy Roman Empire, an ambiguous realm that lasted almost a thousand years. Its emperors were supposed to be God's vicars on earth regarding temporal matters while the popes were to be God's vicars in spiritual matters. The partnership seldom functioned successfully. If anything, it provided the Church with a painful crown of thorns.

The temporal vicariate of the Empire remained principally in Germanic families, a situation which understandably displeased the various other nationals who, from time to time, had to live with it. In Rome, the resentment was savage, particularly in the early years of the Empire. There were bloody battles in the streets. Because of the importance of the papacy, both in the city and the world, there was frantic traffic around the papal throne. Popes were killed and mutilated and deposed.

Opposition leadership came from two branches of the Theophylactus family—the house of Crescentius and, at the turn of the century, the house of Tusculum. In 998, the Patrician Crescentius II created an antipope who took the name of John XVI, to which he had no right either by fact or circumstances because he never got to the throne. And yet he had a certain effect. In 1003, John Sicco, a cardinal-priest, was duly elected pope and chose to keep his own name upon consecration. By rights, he should have been Pope John XVI, but the political ruler of Rome was Crescentius III, son of the antipope promoter. For Cardinal Sicco to insist on keeping the record clear by taking the name John XVI for himself would have proved embarrassing in that it would have pointed up the fact that the father of the man then ruling the city had acted against the Church, so the Cardinal settled on being called John XVII. Ever since then, all popes named John have had the wrong numbers.

Undeniably, reforms were needed in the Church. They had been necessary in the past and they were made; they would prove necessary again and they would be made. At each vital hour, the right man appeared. At this particular time, the man was Cardinal Hildebrand.

Hildebrand was born in 1020 in the hamlet of Rovaco in

the Duchy of Tuscany, north of Rome. He came from a poor family; his father was a shoemaker. Quite likely the family had entered Italy years before in the Lombard invasion. Hildebrand's parents wanted him to be educated—a rare ambition and rarer achievement among the poor. When he was ten, he was sent to Rome and entered into the Benedictine monastery on the Aventine Hill, where an uncle was a monk. At that time the Benedictines were the guardians of European education. Their mother house was at Cluny, in France, and from there they spread throughout the continent. Many modern cities of Europe grew up around a monastery. Often a monastery was started in a particular area at the invitation of noblemen who wanted education for their children. The land was granted by the noblemen; farmhands hired to work the fields built homes outside the monastic walls: the beginning of a town. The children of the poor had to work and did not go to school. Occasionally families like Hildebrand's released one son from his chores and allowed him to enter a monastery. It was an economic sacrifice. Many such sons became monks in later years.

Hildebrand's parents hoped he would become a monk. There was every likelihood of it. He did well at the Aventine school, and he adapted so quickly to the monastic regulations that there seemed small doubt about his destiny. In a move to prepare him even better, the monks arranged to enter him into the Schola Cantorum, the pontifical school in the Lateran Palace, where he came in contact with the sons of Roman nobility. Professors of the school were leading churchmen, among them the archpriest John Gratian. Cardinal Gratian was a man both of means and position.

When Hildebrand was born, the papal throne was occupied by Benedict VIII (1012-1024), a member of the House of Tusculum which replaced the powerful Crescentii. Benedict's brother, Romanus, was the senator of all Rome. Despite his political ties, Benedict was a fairly effective pope.

Upon his death, Romanus decided he might as well be pope, and thereby assume full authority in the city. Romanus was a layman, but this didn't stop him: his influence was sufficient to get him elected. He was a weaker spiritual leader than his brother. During his reign, simony became widespread in the city. When he died, the family held on to the papacy by maneuvering the election of Romanus' twenty-year-old nephew, who became Benedict IX. The young man was poorly equipped for the job. Although he was a cleric, he had no serious intentions toward the Church. He was a wild youngster, openly immoral, flagrantly simonious, utterly indifferent to his responsibilities. He took the throne in 1032; four years later the people threw him off. As justified as the eviction might have been, it was uncanonical: a man remained pope as long as he breathed. True, there had been some overlapping in the past—an embarrassing predicament eventually solved by death. In this case, Benedict was still alive and, despite his conduct, he still wanted to be pope.

During his absence from the city, the people put the bishop of Sabina into the papacy; he called himself Sylvester III. Within two months, however, the Tusculum family, through edicts and force, ousted Sylvester and returned Benedict. There were, then, two popes—one of them, Sylvester, the antipope, due to the circumstances of his papacy. Benedict managed to remain pope until the end of 1044, when he decided he had enough and wanted to get out. He went to his godfather, John Gratian, and asked if it was possible for a pope to abdicate.

Throughout Benedict's papacy, Cardinal Gratian had struggled to straighten him out, but to no avail. The Church was in sad shape. Many important appointments had been fixed by simony, bringing into vital positions men who had no right to their offices. Benefices of all kinds could be obtained for the right amount of money. With such a pope in control, it was not surprising that laxity permeated the entire clergy. Peculiar heresies were cropping up and chastity was disappearing among priests and bishops. There was another problem, a particularly serious one. Feudal noblemen throughout the Holy Roman Empire were taking upon themselves the prerogatives of both choosing and consecrating their own bishops and ordaining their own priests. The grave dangers of such lay investitures was obvious. Men who obtained ecclesiastic positions in this way were seldom qualified. If not members of the ruling family, they were at best pawns. Wherever the situation existed, simony was prevalent, the Church and State were entwined in corruption, and immorality was deep-rooted and widespread.

Aware of all this, Gratian welcomed the opportunity to get rid of Benedict, hoping to replace him with a strong pope who would work for reforms. But it was difficult to locate a man who would remain untainted in the midst of such stormy temptations, so Gratian concluded that the best man to trust was himself. He was, however, in a delicate position. No previous pope had abdicated; a lifelong papacy was a matter of tradition rather than written law. By stretching the point, Gratian assured Benedict that there was no reason not to abdicate if he wanted to. He went a step further: he indicated that he would like to be the next pope. On hearing this, Benedict demanded a large payment for his abdication, and there was nothing for Cardinal Gratian to do but pay it. Benedict abdicated, a hasty election was arranged, and Gratian was elected pope before Benedict was out of the city.

Now there were three popes.

Actually, the people were happy with Gratian, who took the name Gregory VI. He had an excellent reputation in Rome, and was known to be a good and honest man. Approval of him came from stern Cardinal Peter Damian, the Archbishop of Ostia, consecrator of popes, who wrote him: "May Simon, the false-coiner, no longer strike at his base money in the Church. May the golden age of the Apostles return, and under your prudent guidance may ecclesiastical discipline flourish once more."

While at the Schola Cantorum, Pope Gregory had become friendly with Hildebrand, and upon his election he summoned the young monk to the Lateran Palace to be his chaplain, an advisory position of great authority. Hildebrand was then twenty-five years old. He was truly, as his name indicated, a ball of fire. Lean, august, made immobile by his Benedictine training, he was the perfect man for the clean-up so necessary at the moment, and this was a task he was to perform for half a dozen popes.

On taking office, Gregory discovered that the Church was impoverished. Its properties, its holdings, its treasures had all vanished through mismanagement and misconduct. To get them back, Gregory equipped Hildebrand with troops and authority and sent him out into the streets. Hildebrand did a thorough job. Brushing aside resistance and resentment, he reclaimed land, buildings, art objects and religious antiquities, and when actual money could not be retaken he took what he could of equal value. He met with some opposition, but because of the public dissatisfaction with the existing situation, there was not as much of it as might be expected. Previous popes were not alone responsible for the muddle; clergymen from cardinals to curates had participated in the sad affairs, and guilt was everywhere. So broad had been the transgressions that, even if Hildebrand had enough time, complete restitution could not be made.

There wasn't time. Gregory had been in office just a few months when Benedict tried to put himself back on the papal throne. And, back in Sabina, Sylvester kept insisting that the throne was his. Both men were able to muster some support for their claims: Gregory's tactics had won him enemies as well as friends. The question of who was pope became a matter of public debate, and the arguments reached Holy

Roman Emperor Henry III, heir of the House of Saxony, in Germany. It was impossible to hide the fact that Gregory had given Benedict money for his abdication, and to many people this looked like another case of simony. By the time the details reached Henry, they were jumbled and prejudiced. When Henry heard that the arguments had developed to the point where ducal armies were being lined up, he went himself to Italy and summoned Gregory to meet him at Pavia.

No matter how Gregory explained his conduct to the Emperor he couldn't clear himself of suspicions of simony. Henry decided the problem could be resolved only by the installation of a new pope. He called a council, over which he himself presided, a throw-back to the old Constantinople interference in Church affairs, and the result was that Benedict was denied any claim to the papacy because of his abdication, Sylvester was told once and for all that he had never been pope, and Gregory was deposed for simony. To prevent further confusion, Henry chose a German as the next pope: Suidger, a bishop of Bamberg. Bishop Suidger, who took the name of Clement II, was the first man to become pope without having seen Rome until he arrived to be consecrated. Because of the financial plight of the papacy, Henry allowed Clement to retain his Bamberg see as a source of income.

The Emperor accompanied the Bishop to Rome for his consecration, and then went to Southern Italy in hopes of stemming the slow but steady encroachment of Normans, but the attempt failed. On his way back to Germany, he picked up Gregory in Rome and made him a house prisoner at Cologne. Hildebrand volunteered to go with his former teacher as a companion and attendant. When Gregory died five months later Hildebrand resumed his monastic life at the Cluny monastery, determined that he would never again set foot in Rome. Future events were to change his plans.

A stranger in Rome, Pope Clement II was shocked by the

state of Church affairs. Strongly supported by Henry, he took daring steps to correct simonious abuses among the clergy, threatening offenders with excommunication and imprisonment. He was, however, a bit more lenient regarding lay investitures, which were being performed by many of the Emperor's friends. Because of the turmoil in Italy, Henry returned in a year and the Pope traveled with him on a study of conditions. A northerner, Clement had difficulty adjusting to Italian weather and did not succeed. He died on the trip and, according to his wish, was taken to Bamberg for burial.

Immediately the Roman cry went up for Hildebrand to be the new pope, but Emperor Henry wasn't taking any chances. He consulted with Germanic bishops for a successor and decided on Poppo, the bishop of Brixen, in Bavaria. The Romans, already displeased by the fact that they were ruled by an outlander, cringed at the idea of having another foreign bishop in the city, and for this reason enough of them banded together to return to the throne—of all people —the abdicated Benedict. Henry was furious. He sent word to Benedict to get out or he would come down after him. Roman nobles knew that he would; again Benedict went on his way. Bishop Poppo arrived in Rome in July, 1048. The city was an oven of summer heat, far too much for the new pope to tolerate. In a month he was dead.

Again the people asked for Hildebrand. Instead, the Emperor chose his own cousin, the Bishop of Toul. For a member of the imperial family, the new pope—Leo IX—took an unusual stand: he refused to accept the papacy from the Emperor until the clergy of Rome elected him. This surprised both the Emperor and the Romans. The clergy elected him with a mixture of hope and apprehension.

The new pontiff wasted no time in asserting his independence. Despite his personal connection with the Emperor, Leo declared that his primary concern was the Church, that he

would tolerate no meddling by the imperial throne, and that
he intended to devote his papacy to the chore of cleaning up
the mess into which the Church had deteriorated. One of
his first acts was to ask Hildebrand to leave the Cluny monastery to help in the work ahead. Hildebrand's willingness to
cooperate indicated further the steadily expanding conviction that at last there was a pope who was going to get things
done. Also, the very choice of Hildebrand assured others of
Leo's independence from the Emperor: having ousted
Hildebrand's close friend, Gregory VI, it was obvious that
the Emperor and the Cardinal shared no affections. Evidently Leo didn't care; he wanted the best men available to
help, and Hildebrand clearly met that requirement.

France particularly needed a house-cleaning. Most of the
French bishoprics had been filled through simoniacal arrangements. The clergy engaged in carnality of all kinds.
Heresies similar to Adoptionism cropped up, and there was
a resurgence of the Manichean heresy—a third century
heresy which maintained that good and evil were actually
two forces (God and Satan) which battled for the soul of an
individual; the individual was therefore the victim of which-
ever force conquered and was thus not responsible for his
own conduct. The appeal of Manicheanism, in view of the
moral conduct of France, was obvious.

So grave was the situation that the pope himself left Rome
to conduct corrective synods. He consulted with Hildebrand
and authorized him to officiate at similar synods. The assignment was important. In a way, Hildebrand was to act as another pope, with the power to depose, punish and reform.
That he was qualified for the immense task was evidenced in
a remark made by Pope Leo soon after the two men became
acquainted. Leo said: "If you ever become pope, which God
forbid, you will see the whole world ablaze."

Throughout Leo's five year papacy, Hildebrand kept a

fire going. At Rheims and Le Mans he ordered synods and achieved sweeping reforms. If there were any men present whose laxity had weakened their respect for Rome, Hildebrand restored it. By his own forcefulness, he revived the strength of the Church's seat of authority, an essential if Church discipline was to have any effect. Without men like Hildebrand there might well have been serious schisms in the European branches of the Church, growing out of ambitious desires for local rule if nothing else. To go into a strange and unfriendly city, to summon the bishop (invariably an intimate of the local duke or baron), to point at the man and declare: "Get out!"—this required an individual whose character, personality, and reputation were such that his orders would be obeyed without question. Hildebrand was able to command such obedience. To be sure, he had behind him not only the authority of the Pope but the support which Henry, as Emperor, offered to the Church. But military might would have been useless in imposing moral corrections upon the clergy. When a man, by his priesthood, had pledged to remain chaste, only another man of supreme moral authority could penetrate his conscience deeply enough to convince him to put aside his paramour and return to the life to which he had dedicated himself. This Hildebrand achieved repeatedly at every level of the clergy. With the same vigor, he put canyons between the altar and the castle, severing ties between the Church and State at the local level. In some areas, this was nothing short of miraculous, so entwined were the affairs of the two realms.

A remarkable example of Hildebrand's power of persuasion occurred in the south of Italy where the Normans were digging in to solidify their occupation. The fact that many Normans were Christians made no difference to them: in the process of overthrowing southern duchies they confiscated Church property, killed bishops and priests, massacred the laity and plundered savagely. Popes and emperors had been helpless to stop them, even to agree with them on compromise. Then Pope Leo decided to reach an agreement with the Normans, and on his trip south he took Hildebrand along. In the midst of discussions that Leo hoped would result at least in respect for Church prerogatives the Norman leaders announced that the Pope and his entire party were prisoners. There seemed to be no escape. To send to Emperor Henry for help would have meant a delay of months as well as the chance of war. In the end, it was Hildebrand who went to the Norman leaders. Exactly what he said to them never became known, but when he returned to the Pope he was able to reveal that the papal party was free, that the attacks against Church property would end, and that henceforth the Normans would be allies of the popes.

Hildebrand was again in France when Pope Leo died. Once more the people clamored for him to accept the papacy. But he knew how Emperor Henry felt about him and he assured his ardent supporters that it would be a mistake to make him pope and thereby risk Henry's disapproval. Instead, Hildebrand suggested that he be appointed to a legation to discuss with Henry the various men who seemed best suited for the papacy. The suggestion was bold and clever. It brought the two men together, it showed that Hildebrand had no fears of Henry and it gave Hildebrand the opportunity to display further his genius at diplomacy. During the discussions, it was Hildebrand who proposed that the next pope be Gebhardt, the count of Calvi, Tollenstein and Hirschberg, Bishop of Eichstatt and intimate advisor to the Emperor. Gebhardt had an additional personal attribute: he was a good man. Being friendly with the Emperor, he was able to win imperial cooperation in furthering reforms among the clergy. He gave evidence of his intentions to make broad corrections when he appointed Hildebrand to be treasurer of papal affairs. Thus, however indirectly, Hildebrand maneuvered to return responsibility for Church leadership to Rome, where it belonged.

Hildebrand continued to act as papal representative at synods in France, and he was there in March, 1056, when Emperor Henry died. Shortly before his death, the Emperor appointed his six-year-old son to succeed him, with the Empress Agnes as regent. The Empress had no desire to pursue her husband's strict supervision of the Church, but she felt that the right to approve papal elections should remain with the imperial family. Obviously her son was too young to make such decisions, so she took the prerogative upon herself. She was ready to exercise it the following year when Gebhardt died.

The decline of imperial influence, due to reign by a woman, was all the Tusculum family needed. Gebhardt, knowing that his death was near, had advised the Rome clergy to await the return of Hildebrand from France before holding elections. Taking advantage of the delay, the Tusculum faction, eager to regain control of the papacy, collected its supporters among the clergy, held an illegal election and slipped the bishop of Velletri into the papal office. Many Romans were happy to have the papacy back in Italian hands, but most of the cardinals, including Cardinal-Archbishop Damian of Ostia, knew that the election was illegal and fled northward. They met Hildebrand at Siena, where they elected the bishop of Florence to be their pope —Nicholas II.

The new pope might never have got anywhere near his throne had Hildebrand not taken affairs into his own hands. First he wrote the Normans in the south, telling them what happened and reminding them of their promise to protect the popes. Then he went to see the Empress Agnes and explained the situation to her, convincing her that the cardinals had acted properly and that Nicholas was indeed the true pope. With the Normans ready to move up from the south and the Empress prepared to send her troops from the north, the Tusculum faction in Rome faced slim chances for success and retreated.

Pope Nicholas had been in office just a few weeks when he issued a decree which clearly showed the hand of Hildebrand behind it. Nicholas decreed that henceforth the popes would be elected by the six cardinal-bishops of suburbicarian Rome. The clergy and the people of Rome would have the right to acclaim the choice, but they could not reject it. Imperial control would be restricted merely to a confirmation of the election.

The decree set off violent repercussions everywhere. In Rome, the cardinal-priests and cardinal-deacons complained that they were being denied a privilege they had enjoyed since the Church's first days. Up north, the Germanic hierarchy pointed out that Emperor Henry III had consulted with them in the choice of popes and they resented the end of this opportunity to influence Rome. Empress Agnes was not clear on where she stood in the matter, but Hildebrand calmed her and she agreed to wait and see how things worked out.

She had to wait two years. On the death of Nicholas II in July, 1061, the German bishops rushed to Agnes and asked her to appoint the next bishop of Rome—the new pope. Before she could act, Hildebrand summoned the suburbicarian bishops to the Lateran Palace, and there they elected Anselm, the bishop of Lucca. Roman nobles saw in the speedy election their own downfall as a papal influence, and in an effort to hold on to the slipping reins they did a complete about-face and threw their strength in with the Empress. Flattered by all the attention she was getting, Empress Agnes allowed a council to be called at Basel, at which the anti-reform bishop of Pavia was declared pope. Hildebrand was about to lose out, when suddenly the powerful Duke of

Tuscany came to his defense, threatening war against any unauthorized person who took so much as one step toward Rome. The quick retreat by the Empress' forces encouraged the Duke to go further: he had her removed as regent and put Archbishop Anno of Cologne in her place.

Hildebrand had won.

4

It was a victory that almost made Hildebrand the next pope. However, he still maintained that he was far too controversial a man to hold the high office, and he insisted that Anselm, the bishop of Lucca, had been duly elected to the papacy, and Anselm became Alexander II. To assure himself of Hildebrand's close counsel, the new pope appointed him cardinal-archdeacon of Rome. Alexander reigned for twelve years, to 1073, a period of continued reform. To declare reforms and to enforce them were, however, two different things. Lay investitures, simony, and unlawful marriages continued among the hierarchy in the north. Alexander deposed many unworthy bishops, only to find a short time later that their replacements weren't much better.

Hildebrand, meanwhile, was busy at Milan, where a group of laymen who called themselves the Pataria were struggling to rid the city of immoral clergymen. As justified as the effort was, care had to be taken against further lay intrusion into ecclesiastic spheres. Through pressures from the nobility, the rightful bishop of Milan had been ousted. All that was necessary was to have him restored. Cooperating with the Pataria, Hildebrand worked toward that end, and achieved it. He then clearly defined the role of the Pataria in future Church affairs, emphasizing that they were to assist the bishop in cleansing the city but that they were not to

take matters into their own hands. Hildebrand's management of the situation precluded any danger of a relapse into
the lay control that wracked the Church in Germany. That
he was able to do this and still hold the affection of the laity
was another mark of his diplomacy and perception.

He had another assignment that required the utmost perceptive diplomacy: Empress Agnes. Although she was no
longer regent, she remained an important person. She had
indicated, despite the split with the Church, that she still
practiced the faith, and that she wanted to re-establish
friendly relations with Rome, but that in the circumstances
she felt she was due an apology. Hildebrand offered it
through cordial visits to her, assuring her gently that she had
been removed as regent not because she was a bad influence
but because her good influence had failed to penetrate the
hard core of evil that had settled around her son.

Young Emperor Henry IV was certainly in need of a good
influence. In his teens he had been introduced to every
known vice, and he wallowed in them. By the time he became of age he was a complete debauchee. As Emperor he
appointed to his cabinet young men he evaluated not by
their administrative abilities but by their good looks. Life
at the castle was one big party. Hildebrand wrote young
Henry, urging him to mend his ways. Resentfully, Henry
replied with a sweet pen held in a bitter hand. Nobody was
going to tell him what to do, but he would wait for the
right time to say so.

Alexander died in 1073. During the funeral march, a cry
went up from the people: "Hildebrand, our Bishop!" This
time there was no chance for a refusal. That afternoon, Hildebrand, an archdeacon, was ordained priest. An election
was held and he was chosen pope. He took the name Gregory VII. Before going ahead with his consecration, he wrote
young Henry of his election, thereby extending to the new
emperor the right of approval. Henry ignored the friendly

gesture and did not attend the consecration. However, his mother was present.

Hildebrand—now Gregory—had behind him twenty years of service in the Church. He knew the problems and the weaknesses; he knew what had to be done. Early in his pontificate he issued two decrees, the enforcement of which was to occupy him for the rest of his twelve-year reign. He decreed, first, that any bishop or abbot or priest who had been invested by a layman or received his appointment from one must immediately resign or face excommunication. Next he decreed that any clergyman of any rank against whom simony could be proved would be deposed. Previous popes had given similar orders, but Gregory knew he would not have to wait long to back his up. Coming from him, it was a specific challenge, and the man at whom it was aimed wasted no time in accepting it. Within a few months after the decrees, young Emperor Henry appointed three bishops and an abbot, personally handing them their crosiers and uttering the words that supposedly made lay investitures official: "Receive the Church."

Gregory immediately deposed Henry's appointees. Then he wrote all the Germanic bishops, citing in a long list the many occasions when Henry had violated papal rights. Two reactions were to be expected: bishops indebted to Henry openly criticized the Pope; bishops who knew Gregory was right openly criticized Henry.

Now the two-man war had begun; ahead was a double defeat.

Both men had gone too far to stop, and neither wanted to stop. Gregory was determined to free the Church from Henry and everything he represented; Henry was determined to assert what he considered his divine rights as heir to the Holy Roman Empire, now a cluster of feudal states. If the two men had only each other to contend with, the battle might have been swifter, but each man had problems within his own organization and thus their personal war was lengthened.

Cencius, a Roman nobleman closely associated with certain crafty clergymen, wanted desperately to get rid of Gregory. For weeks he quietly organized his forces, awaiting the chance to get at the Pope. The chance came on a stormy Christmas Eve. A severe rain struck the city and the people who had planned to attend Gregory's Masses at St. Peter's were unable to leave their homes. Only a few were present at the first Mass, and at the second Mass there were just some of the papal staff. At midnight, while Gregory was at the altar, Cencius' men broke into the basilica, rushed down the aisle and seized the Pope at his prayers. One rebel swung his broad sword at Gregory's head but succeeded only in nicking his forehead. Then others grabbed the Pope and stripped him of his papal robes. The fight was short. Gregory and the few men with him were rushed to the Castel Sant' Angelo and locked in the tower. In the past, the fortress had always been impenetrable. Now Cencius intended to hold the Pope prisoner in his own castle until he either abdicated or was killed.

Nobody expected the city to react as it did. News quickly spread that the Pope was Cencius' prisoner. Despite the storm, men left their homes and made their way to the fortress. In an hour, thousands were outside the walls, fully armed. Cencius had hoped that the rain-flooded streets would serve in his favor. But the Romans would not be held off. They attacked the fortress, broke down the doors, and ran through the corridors killing every Cencius man they could find. As soon as Gregory realized he was free, he ordered the Romans to stop fighting. On Christmas Day he excommunicated Cencius and exiled him from the city. Gregory discovered that another man involved in the uprising was Cardinal Hugo Candidus, who had already been found guilty of simony twice and both times had been forgiven. Hugo was also excommunicated.

Henry was having his troubles with the Saxon lords who were supposed to be subject to him. His disregard for imperial affairs and then his conflict with the Pope had encouraged the Saxon noblemen to break from him. They stopped sending him taxes and they refused to receive his delegations. Hoping to win papal support, they announced that they had turned against the Emperor because of his sinful life and his disobedience to Gregory. Gregory responded only to the point of instructing bishops and abbots to have nothing to do with noblemen who remained friendly to Henry. He then announced that a council would be held in 1076 at Tribur, near Mayence, at which a conference of bishops would examine the charges against the Emperor.

Henry didn't wait. He summoned his own council at Worms in January, attended by the simoniacal members of the hierarchy who needed his backing to retain their offices. Henry officiated at the council himself, and the result of it was a decree which was sent to Gregory, saying: "Henry, king, not by usurpation but by the will of God, to Hildebrand, who is no longer Pope but a false monk. Having been condemned by the sentence of our bishops and by our sentence, vacate the place which you have usurped."

Gregory replied by calling another council at the Lateran Palace at which he excommunicated Henry and released all his subjects from allegiance to him. Gregory then attended the Tribur council where he gave all the sordid details for his actions against Henry. The council approved the excommunication and the feast of Candlemas (February 2), 1077, was set as the date to determine what should be done with the Emperor.

Having been excommunicated, Henry was deprived of all his rights as temporal emperor of the Holy Roman Empire.

Thus he was not emperor at all. He was not the kind of man who would accept such condemnation without a fight. He raised an army and went north to fight the Saxon lords who had severed relations with him. He won a series of small battles before he once again turned his attention to the Pope. Henry recognized that despite his battlefield victories his excommunication seriously weakened his position as a ruler, and would most certainly give rise to endless insurrections by men who either sincerely wanted to protect the Pope or would use the excommunication as an excuse for revolution. Confident that he had things under control in the north, he decided to confront Gregory face to face before the Candlemas council.

In January, 1077, Henry made his way south to Italy. Gregory was already on his way north for the council and had stopped in Tuscany to visit the ruling noble family there. One day in a blinding blizzard Henry appeared at the gates of the Tuscan castle and asked to see the Pope. He sent word that he had come to apologize, but Gregory did not believe him.

Gathered outside the castle was a group of people who had made a penitential pilgrimage to see the Pope. It was customary for such pilgrims to spend two or three days at some kind of penance while awaiting the Pope's appearance and blessing. The people remained outdoors, praying in the snow. To give an impression of his sincerity, Henry joined the pilgrims. He knelt barefoot in the snow, put on a hair shirt, and let Gregory know that he was out there praying for forgiveness. After three days, Gregory began to wonder if perhaps Henry was truly sorry, and he allowed the Emperor to come into the castle for a talk. Henry wept when he saw the Pope and he made all sorts of promises to amend his life. Deeply moved, Gregory forgave him and returned him to the Church.

That night they celebrated their friendship with a big

banquet. Next morning, Henry was allowed to attend the Pope's Mass. As Gregory distributed Communion, he said to each person the usual words of blessing: "May the body of our Lord Jesus Christ preserve your soul for everlasting life. Amen." But when he reached Henry he said: "If you are approaching with a good heart and intend to observe what you have promised, may this Sacred Body be to you the salvation it was to most of the Apostles. Otherwise you will receive it unworthily and without doubt will eat judgment to yourself."

Henry accepted the Host.

The Saxon lords and the bishops who had adhered to Rome were annoyed by the reconciliation and did not trust it. Gregory wrote them that although the Emperor was restored to the Church he would still be held responsible for his civil conduct, past and present. The bishops wanted to proceed with the Candlemas conference and they asked both Henry and Gregory to be present. This displeased Henry. He sent word that he would be unable to attend the meeting, adding that he was also unable to guarantee safe passage to the Pope. Furthermore, he was still burning with resentment toward those bishops who had voted against him. Within a few weeks after his penance he deposed three Lombard bishops and replaced them with his own men. The loyal bishops needed no further evidence of the kind of man Henry was. They adjourned their Candlemas meeting until March, when they held another council, this time in the presence of many Saxon princes. Henry was deposed and his brother-in-law, Rudolf of Swabia, was appointed the new ruler of the empire.

Henry retaliated with another council of his own, again deposing Gregory, appointing the bishop of Ravenna to be pope. The first person to sign the decree was Cardinal Hugo Candidus, who declared himself to be "cardinal of all Romans." Knowing that a big war was now inevitable, Can-

didus went south to the Normans and tried to get them to
support Henry, but they refused. Gregory again excommunicated Henry.

The armies of Rudolf and Henry met repeatedly over the
next months. War in the eleventh century was not the steady,
unrelenting battle that wars subsequently became. Time was
needed to prepare for each fight. Often months passed between attacks. The soldiers were mercenaries, hired from
princes who were on one side or the other, and as long as
they got paid they fought to the best of their ability, but
they had little knowledge of or feeling about the issue that
had sent them into combat. The fighting months lengthened
into fighting years. One thing was clear: although Henry
won some of the battles he was definitely suffering the loss
of military might as his sources of supply diminished.

The decisive battle was fought at Merseburg in 1084.
Henry lost the battle but he won the war. Rudolf was killed,
and without him there was no one to carry on the fight. Victorious by accident, Henry led his army south to Rome.
After a siege of three months he captured the city, and then
had his antipope crown him in St. Peter's.

Gregory took refuge in the Castel Sant' Angelo, on the
banks of the Tiber within sight of St. Peter's. Just by being
there he was Henry's prisoner, and he knew the Emperor
would come for him whenever he was ready. The moment
seemed near, and then help came. The Normans remembered their promise to protect the papacy, made to Gregory
when he was cardinal. Strong Norman forces attacked from
the south, battled Henry and brought about his retreat.

But unfortunately the Normans didn't stop there. For
years they had longed for a chance at Rome. Now that they
were there and saw how beautiful the city was, they decided
to take it over. In trying to do so, they instigated a strange
civil war. Romans who had looked to the Normans for aid
against Henry now found themselves fighting the Normans

instead. It was a street-by-street fight, and whenever the Normans were pushed back they set fire to the areas they lost. In a short time, one-fourth of the city had been destroyed by flames. The Romans refused to give up, and as the fighting continued the Normans realized they could not last much longer. The people blamed Gregory for what had happened, for he had been responsible for the arrival of the Normans. Thus the Pope who had tried to save Rome actually lost it. When the Normans finally gave up and withdrew, Gregory was forced to go with them.

He retired to the Benedictine monastery at Monte Cassino, where on May 25, 1085, he died. His last words were, "I have loved justice and hated iniquity; therefore I die in exile."

It was a sad death for a man who had given his life to the Church, who more than any man before him had crystallized the cardinalcy and strengthened the papacy. At the cost of disgrace he had given the Church its first few hours of freedom in centuries. He set the rules by which the Church could remain free as long as it kept itself free from imperial interventions. His decree against lay investitures was in itself a revolution and definitely contributed to the downfall of Henry.

In asserting the Church's prerogative to judge the morals of kings and commoners, Gregory wrote: "When Christ gave to the blessed Peter the power of binding or loosing, He excepted no one and exempted nothing." By this, Gregory gouged a deep line between the Church and the State, clarifying the duties and responsibilities to God and the people of each, explaining that both could exist together harmoniously, but that whenever the State invaded the Church's realm, whether administrative or moral, the Church had the right to denounce the State. The implications were far-reaching: the Church could exist under any form of government as long as the government respected

Church affairs. Respect was not the same as total subservience; it required merely that everybody remember to render unto Caesar the things that were Caesar's and unto God the things that were God's.

Everybody found this very difficult to do.

V

*G*regory VII had been the first pope to be elected by popular acclamation. The great cry that went up during the funeral of his predecessor had been enough to convince the electors that Hildebrand, who had served the Church so well and so long, could no longer elude the papacy. That such a beloved man should eventually be exiled for a predicament of which he was basically innocent was sadly typical of Rome, of Romans, and of the times. The times required a strong man like Gregory. Gregory himself realized that he—and all popes—should be even stronger.

With this in mind, Gregory had issued, shortly before his eviction, a set of principles by which he tried to define a pope's position in matters of Church affairs and faith and morals. An important part of the statement was that, in these realms, the pope was above criticism. In effect, this was a forerunner of the papal infallibility doctrine that was to materialize eight hundred years later, during the reign of Leo XIII. Citing the papal authority which Jesus had granted Peter, Gregory listed precedents supporting his assertion, ranging from Peter's decisions on diet and circumcision to subsequent papal opinions on heresies and schisms. On the surface, Gregory's statement was a move to wrest Church authority from the hands of laymen and disobedient bishops, but it had deeper significance. It reiterated that the Church was divinely established and divinely guided— a reminder that was to prove tremendously important in years ahead. Nevertheless, it was not surprising that there were many people who did not enjoy Gregory's statement. Later some even tried to discredit the statement by claiming that Gregory had never written it.

The objectors were people who stood to lose something. They were noblemen who resented being excluded from Church affairs, they were bishops and abbots who disliked the invasion into their personal prerogatives, they were cardinals who feared the loss of their own influence. In all cases, the opposition was purely selfish. To be sure, it was scandalous that selfish men should be in the Church, and that they should have risen to high positions in it, but it must be remembered that a great number of them had acquired their positions by simony, by lay investiture, and by the practice of noble families which frequently consigned a son to the Church just to keep an eye on it. There simply was too much lay interference with the Church, which Gregory had detected and tried to overcome. To claim that laymen, in the Church for their spiritual salvation, ought to have had a voice in its administration would have been the same as claiming that a patient, in a hospital for physical salvation, should have a voice in its administration. The authority of the Church belonged where it had originally been placed: with the popes.

Had the Church been rich in Gregory's time, the desire of outsiders to intrude would have been understandable. But the Church had become poor, at least in Rome. Popes who followed Gregory in the twelfth century had to borrow money from wealthy bishops in France and Germany to keep things going. The intrusion, then, sprang from a desire for power or the desire to retain existing power.

This unsavory state of affairs could not be blamed entirely on the Church *per se*. Weak and bad popes were certainly responsible for part of it, but more was involved. Christianity, expanding rapidly through pagan Europe, was a vital moral force, and yet Christian morality was so completely opposed to pagan morality that it could not be easily grasped. To be good out of a fear of punishment was one thing; to be good out of a love of God was quite another. The first type of goodness might assure a man a long life; the second made him a saint. Most of Europe in this period had yet to learn the difference. The nature of feudalism was a contributing factor: the materially strong ruled, and might made right. When, as happened in many places, bishops were merely vassals of princes and barons, the people expected from their bishops the same conduct they had come to expect from their noblemen, and unfortunately they got it. As for their own behavior, the people felt it made no difference what they did as long as they didn't get caught at it. Human life was cheap, war provided an income and a reprieve from boredom, and morals were low.

There were, assuredly, some exceptions. The same era that produced evils to plague the Church also produced Francis of Assisi, Clare, Bernard of Clairvaux, Dominic, and Aquinas: spiritual giants who, being removed from the corruption of Rome, were nearer God.

2

The popes who followed Gregory tried to uphold the principles he had put forth, and the most important of these at the moment was the matter of lay investiture. With it out of the way, the Church could take a step toward freedom.

Two opposing groups appeared. The Imperialists believed that the Emperor had the right to make episcopal appointments, just as he approved papal elections, and that he likewise deserved control of income from ecclesiastical properties. The Gregorians maintained that since the consecration of a bishop was a spiritual act it could be performed only by a spiritual superior and that any benefices from ecclesiastical properties, which were directly under the bishop or held in fief by others, belonged to the Church. The two opinions were so strongly maintained that for a time there seemed to be no solution. Under Pope Paschal II (1099-1118), the debate grew so serious that Emperor Henry V took him prisoner. Paschal felt the only way out of the argument was for the Church to give up all its holdings and depend for its future existence upon tithes and donations from the faithful. Henry didn't want this because it would have shattered his strongest tie to the Church: its need for his financial help. Feudal lords didn't want it either; many of them held Church land in fief, and Paschal's solution would force them to return it to the Emperor.

Under pressure from Henry, Paschal changed his mind, put aside his idea, crowned Henry and permitted him to continue lay investiture. On learning this, the Gregorians turned against Paschal with such violence that he was forced to leave Rome. The middle-of-the-roaders saw the error in such extremes and brought the Pope back, where he remained ineffectual for the rest of his reign. His successor,

Gelasius II (1118-1119), was an ardent Gregorian and revoked Henry's right of lay investiture. Gelasius had other
problems in the feud between two Roman families—the
Frangipani and the Pierleoni—who contested for local influence upon the Church. Bewildered, Gelasius left Rome
and went to France. Henry, meanwhile, put up an antipope,
and consequently found himself excommunicated.

Several cardinals had gone to France with Gelasius, and
when he died they elected the archbishop of Vienne to
succeed him as Calixtus II. Because Rome was closed to the
bona fide leaders of the Church, the new pope was enthroned
at Vienne. Henry was soon in trouble in Germany. By his
excommunication, his subjects were automatically released
from allegiance to him, but he hadn't expected many of
them to take advantage of it. However, unrest was widespread. Feudal barons openly told Henry that they would
not listen to him until his differences with the Church were
resolved. Under the circumstances, this was a strange thing
for the barons to say, but they really didn't expect peace
between Henry and the popes, so they felt encouraged to
flaunt their independence of both. Henry knew something
had to be done.

All France ardently supported Calixtus. Influential Gregorian prelates, like the archbishop of Milan, were also behind him. When Calixtus decided he wanted to go to Rome,
where he belonged, he had no worries about protection
along the way. Even the Frangipani and the Pierleoni were
reluctant to start trouble. Thus the new pontiff arrived at
Rome with a great show of strength. The antipope was at
Sutri. Calixtus had a blockade put up around the city. And
after a week the penitent antipope presented himself
dressed in bloody sheepskins and asked to be forgiven.

Henry was not prepared to go that far, but when he saw
how hopeless things looked for him he suggested that a
meeting be held at Worms for a final discussion of the lay

investitures that had put him at odds with the Church.
Calixtus agreed. A date was set for September, 1122. Weeks
before, bishops began to arrive from all over Europe. Calixtus sent three cardinals to represent him. Henry was there
himself.

The meeting produced an unusual compromise. It was
agreed that a bishop actually had jurisdiction in two spheres,
spiritual and temporal. He was responsible, at the same
time, to the popes, the source of spiritual authority, and to
nobles—that is, the Emperor—who both protected him and
gave him his income-providing lands. Among his accoutre-
ments, the crosier and ring signified his spiritual authority,
the scepter his temporal authority. The two spheres were
separate and yet linked. The Worms meeting decided that
henceforth bishops were to be elected by their clergy, with
acclamation by the people and without interference from
the nobility. Popes would then be free to approve or disapprove the choice. If they approved, they would present
the crosier and ring to the new bishop and would then permit his consecration, to be performed either by the pope or
by appointed bishops. Only then would the emperor—or
other appointed nobleman—present the new bishop with his
scepter.

For Henry, this was an enormous compromise to make
because it definitely put an end to lay investiture. He insisted, however, that German bishops receive their scepters
after approval by the popes but before being consecrated.
This, he felt, would at least give the impression that he
had the upper hand with the German bishops. He was particularly concerned about this in order to extend his own
influence upon the lesser nobility and the people. He further
insisted on the right to settle any disputed elections—another
effort to save face. In return for all this, he pledged allegiance, obedience, and protection to the popes and the return of all properties confiscated by him and his father.

Here again was an agreement—a concordat—between the Church and State that looked better on paper than it did in practice. Henry, like his father, had an inconstant heart, and everybody who realized this was aware that sooner or later he would take advantage of his position in the compromise by refusing to grant the scepter to any elected bishops he didn't like. True, the Church was freer from imperial influence than it had been for a long time, and it seemed there would be no interference in papal elections—from Henry at least. But there was still an area of overlapping interest between Church and State, and as long as it existed there could be trouble.

There was plenty of trouble in Rome. Lambert, cardinal-bishop of Ostia, who had worked out the compromise at Worms, was elected to succeed Calixtus. Lambert was the favorite of the Frangipani family and was undoubtedly elected on that basis, but Cardinal Saxo, who had also been at Worms, was the popular choice. Sensing this, and afraid of trouble, Lambert wisely resigned in favor of Saxo. He was walking in the procession to consecrate Saxo when Frangipani claques sent up a cry in the streets: "Lambert, our bishop!" Though there was no greater disturbance in the proceedings than that, Lambert was taken out of line and put on the throne. Saxo was embarrassed and annoyed, with good reason. To avoid a schism, Lambert offered to resign again, but for the sake of peace the cardinals re-elected him, and he became Honorius II.

Honorius was saved from serious conflict with Emperor Henry by a kindly act of God: Henry died. In the competition for a successor, Honorius supported Lothair of Supplinburg against Henry's nephew, Frederick of Hohenstaufen. The House of Hohenstaufen, however, was to be a major influence in Church affairs in the years to come.

In Rome, the Pierleoni were impatient for Honorius' death so that they could get another chance at the papal throne. When, in 1130, Honorius realized his death was near, he removed himself from Pierleoni pressures by going to a monastery on the Celian. One member of the Pierleoni, a cardinal, openly declared that he would be the next pope, and when the family learned how ill Honorius was they stormed the monastery to find out how soon he would go. To discourage them, the Pope got up from his deathbed and showed himself at a window.

The next four popes were victims of the Frangipani-Pierleoni feud. All of them were forced out of Rome to save their lives. Twice the Pierleoni set up antipopes. Additional woes came from the south, where the Normans were again stirring in Sicily, siding with antipopes, and from the north, where Frederick Barbarossa, son of Frederick of Hohenstaufen, had gained control of Germany.

Barbarossa was a perplexing personality, an ardent supporter of the Church on the one hand and an enemy of popes on the other. He was responsible for the Christianization of the Slavs and even went on one of the Crusades, but he didn't like the idea that he was supposed to rate second to the popes, and to prove his superiority he burned Milan to the ground and attacked Rome. He was particularly opposed to Pope Hadrian IV (1154-1159)—the only Englishman to become pope. In trying to ease the estrangement, Hadrian, in exile in France, wrote Barbarossa that they ought to be friends, if only on the basis of the "beneficia" the Pope had given the Emperor. Barbarossa took the word to mean that the Pope felt he had given Barbarossa the empire as a fief, and he replied sternly that he was emperor "through an election of the princes, from God alone." The hint at an election was a great exaggeration of the fact; Barbarossa was emperor by force. Hadrian wrote back, explaining that he had not meant fiefs but benefits, spiritual and temporal. Barbarossa would not be appeased.

Infuriated, Barbarossa hurried to Rome in an effort to en-throne his own antipope. Before he could do so, Hadrian died. The cardinals with him at first considered electing a new pope among themselves, but then they saw this would lead only to further chaos. The wisest course, they decided, would be to return to Rome for a proper election. They took Hadrian's body with them, and after the funeral they prepared for the election conclave.

In Rome was Cardinal Octavian, a nobleman, an Imperialist and a rich man. He was desperate to become pope, and with Barbarossa on the way to the city he felt that the other cardinals would choose him as an insurance for peace. The cardinals, however, were more interested in Cardinal Roland Bandinelli, chancellor of Rome, a brilliant scholar and a strong advocate of education for all people regardless of rank. Bandinelli didn't want to be pope. When he heard he was being discussed for the role, he asked his friends not to vote for him.

On the first day of the election, thirty-one cardinals gathered behind the high altar of St. Peter's Basilica to vote. The results showed that Bandinelli received the most votes; Bernard, bishop of Porto, next; Octavian, least. On the second day, those who had voted for Bernard announced that for the sake of unanimity they would put aside their candidate and choose between Bandinelli and Octavian. Thus Octavian picked up a few more votes. On the third day, the trend changed. Octavian received only three votes—his own and those of two other Imperialists.

The majority felt there was no reason for further ballots and they declared Bandinelli to be the new pope. Stunned, he stepped away, saying, "No, I am not worthy. Please, I cannot accept." The archdeacon ignored the protests and approached carrying the papal mantle. When Octavian saw this, he went out of his mind. He cried out: "Roland, in the name of Emperor Frederick Barbarossa, I forbid you to don that mantle!" He rushed forward, grabbed the mantle and put it on himself. Panic broke out. A senator who was present ripped the mantle off Octavian's shoulders. Octavian turned and called to his aide to bring the mantle he had had made especially for what he thought would be his election. In his excitement, Octavian put the mantle on backwards and the cowl almost hid his face. Then he ran around to the front of the altar, rushed up the steps, turned and faced a few men waiting in a far corner of the church and shouted: "I am Pope—Pope Victor II!"

The waiting men cheered him, then were startled to see the cardinals come running around to pull Octavian off the altar. At that moment, the basilica doors burst open and in dashed armed men, soldiers in the service of Octavian, who rushed to the altar, pushed the cardinals aside and carried Octavian on their shoulders, out to the crowd. On seeing a man with a mantle, the crowd shouted its joy without seeing who it was. Inside, other soldiers made for the cardinals. Side doors and back doors flew open as the cardinals scurried for safety in the Castel Sant' Angelo at the Tiber. Octavian blockaded the fortress for eight days, during which time he summoned all the bishops of the Papal States to witness his consecration. Only one showed up.

Sensing his unpopularity and hoping to ease the situation, Octavian left Rome for a few hours, withdrawing his men from the castle and thus allowing Bandinelli to get away. Amid great cheers, Bandinelli and the cardinals made their way through the city to the Appian Road and south to the small town of Nympha where, in the Church of St. Mary Major, he was duly consecrated Pope Alexander III.

For twenty years there were excommunications and cross-excommunications; depositions and cross-depositions; anti-popes and anti-antipopes; wars, civil wars, and insurrections on both sides of civil warriors. The Lombard duchies fought each other, then united to fight Barbarossa, then went back to fighting each other. Barbarossa won and lost, signed peace treaties and then broke them; he apologized to Alexander, then swore to see him dead. Alexander was out of Rome more than he was in it, moving from one Italian city to another, then to France, then back again, to Rome and out of it, winning the friendship of the Normans, then the Lombards, then losing both.

In the end, the Church was back where it started. Safe in Rome at last in 1178, Alexander faced the same problem which had troubled several of his predecessors: something had to be done so that papal elections could be held without so much fury. Discipline was essential. The voting had to be conducted in such a way that the results were honest and accepted by everybody. The process needed more stature.

It had already undergone many changes. In the beginning, the Christians elected the bishop without any fuss. But when people who were Christians in name only entered the Church, the thing got completely out of hand. When the people lost the vote to the clergy, these latter violated their precious prerogative to elect. The decree by Pope Nicholas II in 1059 that only the half-dozen cardinal-bishops of suburbicarian Rome should elect the popes never actually took effect.

Alexander knew all this. He summoned over three hundred bishops and abbots to Rome for a council to which he submitted twenty-eight decrees, and he let everyone know that he expected everyone to heed them.

The decrees dealt with many subjects. Many of them concerned the poor. An educator himself, Alexander ordered that every cathedral should acquire an instructor to teach the poor reading and writing without charge. He advised that priests ought to study with the instructor as well, to learn more about their own religion. He ordered usurers to cut down their interest rates on loans to the poor, and he told bishops to decrease taxation on churches in their dioceses because it was the poor who, in the end, had to pay. He threatened excommunication to mercenary soldiers who, under orders from petty despots, were forcing poor farmers off their land and then confiscating the property in the name of their employer.

As for the city of Rome, Alexander decreed that gambling must end, and that sports or any other entertainments that might contribute to immorality were outlawed. He pointed out that Rome was a holy city, sanctified by the blood of thousands of martyrs, and he charged that anyone who stirred evil in the city deserved the wrath of God.

With the clergy, Alexander was particularly explicit. He set the age for the ordination of priests at twenty-five, at least. Bishops had to be thirty before their consecration. Bishops were also told to stop traveling around with such large entourages that they were heavy burdens to their hosts. Regarding ecclesiastical courts, the Pope said the number of appeals must be cut. He pointed out that often decisions were being appealed even before they had been reached, with the result that the higher courts at Rome were so swamped with trivial appeals that nothing was getting done at all. Strictly forbidden were simony in the administration of the sacraments or in any other form, the holding of more than one ecclesiastic benefice by the same person, or the promise of one before it was vacant, and laxities which had crept into monasteries regarding discipline, duties, and spiritual exercises.

Especially important were Alexander's opinions on the election of bishops. He said that outside Rome a bishop would be chosen by a two-thirds majority of the eligible electorate—the clergy. In Rome, only cardinals—all the cardinals—could vote, choosing the bishop—pope—among themselves. In case of disputes outside Rome, the matter would be referred to an ecclesiastic superior. In Rome there would be no disputes: the cardinal who received the two-thirds majority automatically became pope and there was no one higher to whom to appeal any disputes.

The council heard the decrees, discussed them, approved them.

Things were beginning to take shape.

3

When Rome was young and strong and the republic was established, the city was divided into thirty political zones, and the free men residing in each zone elected representatives to a governing body called the Curia. In somewhat the same way, the city was zoned again in 115 when Pope Evaristus created the Church's parishes and diaconates. As the years passed and the city came more and more within the Church's realm the Church absorbed the Curia as its own administrative body. Because Rome was the world headquarters of the Church, the administrators—cardinals—of the Rome archdiocese were thereby administrators of the entire Church.

Because they were in or near Rome, the cardinals knew more about the inside workings of the Church, and they were also readily available to the popes for discussions and assignments. Some of them were of the nobility, and although this could be bad as well as good it nevertheless added to their importance. Each successive pope found himself leaning increasingly upon his cardinals: the sheer bulk of Church affairs made this necessary. No one man could run the Church entirely by himself; he needed help, and the cardinals were best qualified to give it.

As the bishops of Rome, the popes appointed their deacons, pastors, and suffragan bishops, and this gave them distinct control over the men who worked with them. It could only be hoped that men who worked well with one pope would work equally well with the next, but this was not always the case. Aware of this, new popes, especially those with experience in Rome, usually made many changes in their staffs. Changes were easiest among the deacons, who could be promoted or demoted at will; they were not so easy among pastors, who usually held their positions for life; they were difficult among bishops, who rarely were moved from their dioceses. Deacons, therefore, sometimes were more important in Church affairs than bishops because of the ease with which they could be promoted to vital missions. While the world capital was at Constantinople, most of the papal legates to the city were cardinal-deacons, and many of them subsequently became popes. Hildebrand, probably the most outstanding cardinal in the Church's first thousand years, was first a deacon and then archdeacon while he effected the reforms in France and later served as treasurer of the Church. He did not become a priest until his ordination was necessary in order for him to be the bishop-pope of Rome as Gregory VII. Thus, although in terms of religious orders he ranked below the French priests and bishops whose conduct he judged, they had to listen to him and obey him as long as he stood before them with the authority of his cardinalate. As cardinal, he was a man from Rome, a man from the front office, a man authorized to act for the pope.

In the early days, the responsibilities of the suburbicarian cardinal-bishops to Rome itself were primarily spiritual. There were six of them. One day a week, each took his turn going into Rome to substitute for the pope at the solemn religious ceremonies held first at St. John Lateran and then at St. Peter's. After a while, the bishops were called in after the ceremonies to assist the pope with his paper work.

It was traditional that a bishop should remain in the diocese to which he was consecrated for his lifetime. By custom, the bishop was chosen from among the people who lived

in the diocese and, in the early days, he could be anything
from a layman to a priest. The decree by Pope Caius (283-
296) that only priests could be made bishops limited the potential field; in Rome, the decree by Pope Stephen IV
(768-772) that the bishop of Rome had to come from the
cardinalate limited the papacy even more. The first bishop
to become pope was Formosus, the cardinal-bishop of suburbicarian Porto, who reigned from 891-896. Because he was a
cardinal, there wasn't much question about his giving up one
diocese to take over another. In effect, he was a suffragan
bishop of Rome who had moved up.

It was Formosus who first gave evidence of a pope's ability
to appoint bishops outside of the usual local-elections
method. In Rome during his pontificate was a man named
Sergius, openly an enemy of the pope and a self-acclaimed
candidate for the papacy. To get rid of him, Formosus consecrated him bishop of Caere, thus making him ineligible for
the papal throne. The incident, hardly a proper one, backfired when Sergius, using his politic influence with Roman
nobility, quit his episcopate, had himself elected pope in
904, denounced the deceased Formosus by invalidating all
his consecrations, thereby reducing himself to deacon and
making himself eligible for the papacy—which he already
held. That Sergius never rated as a particularly good pope
should be no surprise.

Other outside bishops became popes by various means.
Some were Roman priests who had gone to other cities to
work and were later duly elected bishops. To Romans, such
men were still Romans and there were no objections to the
fact that, to become pope, they were actually changing dioceses. Other bishops reached Rome through political pressures, either by Roman nobility or the emperors, and when
their elections were undisputed they were legitimate popes.
The importance of all this was that precedents were being
set. The time came when the Romans tried to reject certain

popes on the basis that they had been bishops elsewhere and bishops could not transfer dioceses, but the objections were put aside when the properly authorized electorate, for reasons of its own, endorsed the men in question.

This led to vital changes in the Church's structure. It was inevitable that the Church rulers, beholding misadventures like lay investiture, should realize that the Church could best be governed from within. The idea of having the laity participate in episcopal elections might have been attractive at first but it was also dangerous, as the early decree by Pope Caius indicated: the laity could be too easily swayed by politics and personality to assure a good choice. The 1059 decree by Pope Nicholas II, limiting the electors of the Rome episcopacy to six cardinal-bishops, showed even further the great care that had to be taken. Imperial interferences weakened Nicholas' decree, so it was understandable that Pope Alexander III, in 1179, decided to emphasize the importance of papal elections by extending the responsibility to all cardinals everywhere.

This was a particularly significant act. As long as the cardinalate remained a Roman domain, there was always the risk of local interference and severe factions. Nicholas had taken the first step against that by appointing the first cardinal outside the Rome area: Desiderius, the abbot of Monte Cassino Monastery. To preserve the original nature and historical importance of the cardinalate, Nicholas gave Desiderius the title of pastor of a Rome church, thus making him a cardinal-priest of Rome while he remained abbot of the monastery. The importance of this became evident years later when, after the death of Hildebrand (Gregory VII) in 1085, the cardinals in Rome were unable to agree on a successor for almost a year. In the end they turned to the only eligible man outside their factious environment—Desiderius.

Further evidence of Alexander's concern about the cardinalate came in 1163, when he appointed the first cardinal outside of Italy. He chose the archbishop of Mainz, making him a member of the Rome clergy by permitting him to remain in Mainz while serving as titular pastor of one of the churches in the city. Thus it was Nicholas who created the Sacred College of Cardinals and Alexander who gave the College its universality. With the precedents now set, subsequent popes had only to carry on the policy.

From the start, the core of the College was the Curia. In modern terms, the College might be described as the congress of the Church, whereas the Curia is the papal cabinet. Since, however, the pope is the supreme authority of the Church, the College and the Curia function more as administrators and advisors rather than as deliberative bodies that can oppose or overrule the popes. But the evolution of this effective arrangement was accompanied by many difficulties.

The Curia was active in the earliest days of the Church. Pope Cornelius (204) appointed men to the Sacred Penitentiaria, the first tribunal of the Church. By the time of Pope Benedict (684), the tribunal was headed by cardinal-priests. Basically, it was a tribunal that dealt with disciplines. Persons who committed crimes against the Church, its clergy or properties were adjudged by the Sacred Penitentiaria. It had the powers both of excommunication and absolution; it could apply fines, imprisonment, interdicts and penances. It could delegate its authority to lower courts in other places, and in this way it also acted as a court of appeals. This was the tribunal to which Alexander III referred when he complained that the Church courts at Rome were swamped with appeals that could have been resolved elsewhere. When St. Bernard of Clairvaux, the great French abbot, visited Rome at this period he criticized the tribunal for bothering itself with trivia that did not merit its time. The court was obviously in need of major reorganization; Alexander contributed some, and the rest was added by later popes. Although all residents of the papal states and

Catholics everywhere were subject to the tribunal, the cases it handled mostly concerned the clergy and its conduct.

In addition to the Sacred Penitentiaria, the Curia handled the administration of the Church's temporal affairs. Legates to royal courts were members of the Curia; so were social reformers like Hildebrand who acted in the pope's name throughout Europe. The papal fleet, of all things, was under Curia direction, as were papal estates, the treasury and library, the chancery, and major churches such as St. Peter's. At times when the Church held unusual temporal powers in Italy the Curia members were men of tremendous authority and influence. More accessible than the popes, they were important social prizes and political contacts.

4

In the Middle Ages the Church structure allowed for fifty-two cardinals, but seldom were all the offices filled. Usually there were about thirty-five; sometimes the number dropped to as low as twenty. Since elevation to the cardinalate was made by the popes, the number depended on the popes themselves. Some popes preferred to have Church authority centralized in themselves and thus did not appoint cardinals who could have eased their work load. Other popes who were better executives welcomed both the advice and help cardinals could give them.

There were other factors as well. At times Rome was so laden with political intrigue instigated by the nobility that it was difficult for a pope, provided he had a free hand, to choose cardinals who would be free as well. Also, the morality of men eligible for the cardinalate was not dependably high, and there were times when a good man was hard to find. The expansion of the cardinalate, therefore, beyond Rome and even beyond Italy, enabled the popes to utilize the abilities of valuable men who would not be so influenced by conditions in Rome.

One very capable man from Rome was Lotario de' Conti. The Conti family was one of the oldest in Rome, one of the most respected and one of the most influential. Between 1198 and 1721, this family produced thirteen popes, forty cardinals, a queen, seven prefects of Rome, five senators and thirteen generals. Lotario was a brilliant young man. After finishing his studies in Rome, he entered the University of Paris and majored in canon law, completing his work at the University of Bologna. While he was still a student, news of him began to seep back to Rome. With the papal courts in the shape they were, the Church needed a legislator of the type he promised to be. He was in his mid-twenties when he was called to Rome by Pope Gregory VIII and made a canon of St. Peter's, which made him a member of the tribunal. At twenty-nine, he was appointed a cardinal-deacon by Pope Clement III, said to be his uncle.

For eight years Lotario served the Church as an outstanding judge. So perceptive was his view of canon law that his court was always filled more with lawyers anxious to hear his opinions than with the clients they affected. It was said that when he summed up a case, his presentations were so thorough and impartial that nobody could tell until the very end what his decision would be. His cases were usually the more delicate matters of jurisdiction and privileges over fiefs and benefices, requiring intimate knowledge not only of the papal decretals but of pertinent regional laws as well. He was able to quote both, evaluate both, and exercise both with such complete justice that many times his verdicts, so astutely reached, brought applause, even from the losers.

Lotario was probably the only honest candidate in Church history who knew he was going to become pope long before the occasion arose. He had enormous popularity in

Rome; people often told him that he ought to be pope and cardinals openly assured that they would vote for him at the first opportunity. The opportunity came in January, 1198. On the very day Celestine III died Lotario was unanimously declared pope—Innocent III—by the cardinals. He was only thirty-seven years old.

For a man who was so loved and respected, Innocent had a stormy reign, a great deal of which was his own doing. But the age he lived in made its contribution: Germanic wars had once again leveled Europe to chaos, Rome was torn apart by competing factions, the Patrimony of Peter (the Church properties) was in the hands of barons who disregarded their obligations to the popes, heresies were appearing in France, anticlericalism was rife in Germany, Jerusalem was back in the control of Saracens, immorality was widespread. Innocent's neat legal mind abhorred such disorders and he determined to clean everything up.

He was a severe centralist, a strong supporter of Church supremacy, an advocate of spiritual authority over the temporal. He said: "Just as the moon receives its light from the sun, so the royal dignity is nothing more than a reflection of the papal dignity." This was an opinion that did not sit well with royalty, but Innocent was the kind of man who knew how to make his opinions stick. By the sheer force of his own personality he made radical changes during his first year as pope, and circumstances conspired to aid him.

The death in 1197 of Henry VI, son of Barbarossa, had left the empire without a ruler. His widow, Queen Constance, was made regent of Sicily and Naples, and she reacted to Innocent's overtures by declaring herself to be his vassal and banishing German margraves from her kingdom. When she died early in 1198, she willed that her four-year-old son should be a ward of the Pope; Innocent assigned two cardinals to take care of the boy and to manage his realm.

With no emperor to challenge him, Innocent had a free

hand in Rome. He appointed a new prefect and a new senator of the principality, both of whom were required to take
oaths of submission to him. By this, Innocent reduced the
importance of factions of the nobility. At Ravenna was
Markwald of Anweiler, the imperial majordomo, and he was
beginning to see the handwriting on the wall. In an effort to
retain his position and some of his authority he tried to
reach an agreement with Innocent whereby he could continue as seneschal but in obedience to the Pope. Determined
to get Germans out of Italy, Innocent wouldn't have any part
of Markwald, and under growing pressure he was forced to
withdraw.

Another powerful German in the country was Conrad of
Urslingen, appointed by Henry VI to be duke of Spoleto, a
large duchy in Central Italy which Charlemagne had given
to the Church but which Germanic rulers had taken away.
Innocent wanted it back. Living there as vassals of the duke
were several Lombard lords, who had no love for Conrad.
Encouraged by Innocent, they began a series of insurrections
that Conrad could not quell. He too then tried to make
terms with the Pope, offering to pay an annual rental to the
Church and to cooperate fully in any plans the Pope might
have for the duchy. The Pope's plan was to get rid of Conrad, and in a short time he did.

Other papal lands were under the control of Lombards
who earlier had vowed allegiance to Henry VI. Innocent was
willing to let the Lombards keep their positions, with the
understanding that they were his vassals and that a percentage of their incomes was to be turned over to the Church.
They quickly agreed. Thus in less than a year Innocent
brought the entire Italian peninsula under the control of the
Church, a phenomenal achievement for a man without an
army and whose coercive power lay only in his assertion of
historical prerogatives.

Innocent's tremendous influence extended far beyond

Italy. In England, John Lackland, youngest son of Henry II, had maneuvered his way to the throne and proceeded to enrich his personal treasury by confiscating Church properties and funds. Ignoring Innocent's complaints, he topped his arrogance by refusing to recognize the election of a new archbishop of Canterbury. Innocent excommunicated him, then urged King Philip Augustus of France to attack England. Worried, John Lackland capitulated, going so far as to announce that Innocent was actually the ruler of England and Lackland was merely his vassal. Innocent held this unique role when, in 1215, the barons of England forced Lackland to sign the Magna Carta, a document which not only defined the individual rights of citizens but also restored the feudal prerogatives of the barons and guaranteed freedom for the Church. Oddly enough, Innocent declared the document null and void because approval of it had been extracted from his vassal under duress. Innocent never did approve the Magna Carta, but his successor, Honorius III, did on the first day of his pontificate.

An important innovation by Innocent was the introduction of consistories. Previously, when popes wanted to discuss current issues with their leading advisors—cardinals, bishops, abbots—they called councils, at which the matters were deliberated and decisions made. If the popes were strong enough, the decisions went their way. Innocent changed this. He limited his advisors to the cardinals, most of whom could be summoned easily, and when he was in Rome he held meetings with them three times a week. The consistories differed from councils in that deliberations and decisions were replaced by discussions. After hearing everyone speak, Innocent then expressed his opinions. When he finished, he asked: "What do you think?" The cardinals knew who was pope, and they knew the particular pope they had was a man who not only did his own thinking but who had clearly defined to them and the world his position as supreme authority in the Church, so they answered: "We agree with you." Also, it was in this way that the cardinals indicated their acceptance of papal supremacy.

Innocent's convictions regarding his authority were far-reaching. When Philip Augustus wearied of his wife Ingeborg he pressured the French hierarchy into granting him an annulment. Ingeborg appealed to Rome, for which Philip Augustus put her away in a convent. Innocent wrote him: "The Holy See cannot leave persecuted women without defence; the dignity of king does not dispense you from your duties as a Christian." He ordered the king to return Ingeborg to her position as his wife, and when the king refused Innocent placed all of France under interdict, depriving the entire country of Mass and the sacraments. Repercussions among the people were so severe that Philip Augustus finally yielded.

In Germany, Innocent again displayed his authority when he made the choice for the successor to Henry VI. Actually he didn't have much to choose between. The pretenders were both Hohenstaufen: Philip of Swabia, Henry's brother, and the Saxon Otto of Brunswick. Already the two men had resorted to battle to win control of Germany, and when Innocent indicated his disapproval both men appealed to him to choose between them. Of Philip, Innocent said: "Born of a race which has always persecuted the Church, Philip would only turn against the Church the weapon we placed in his hand." He picked Otto.

No sooner had he crowned Otto than the new German king seized papal lands he claimed were his by royal inheritance. The Pope tried to reason with him, then finally excommunicated him. Innocent next nudged the Lombard lords into action against Otto by intimating that there was no reason why they should subject themselves to him. He then hinted to Philip Augustus that it looked to him as though Otto and John Lackland were about to join forces against France. The French king took to the battlefields first and crushed Otto's armies. Sitting in Sicily was the Pope's ward, young Frederick, son of Henry VI. Confident that the boy had been raised properly, Innocent proposed him as the new king of the Germans and he was accepted. But being ruler of the Germans invariably stirred dreams of world conquests in men, and Frederick ran true to form. He was to remain a problem to popes as long as he lived.

Despite Innocent's broad activities in temporal affairs, he was an extremely spiritual man. As cardinal, he had written two books—*On The Holy Eucharist* and *On The Contempt Of The World*—that revealed a deep piety and a reverent faith. His concern for temporal things during his papacy was, he indicated, to strengthen the Church, not himself. He was a rich man, and as cardinal had used his own money to rebuild his titular church, Saints Sergius and Bacchus, which stood in the ancient Forum. (The two saints were converted Roman soldiers who were martyred in 303.) During his papacy, Innocent purchased many art objects with his personal funds and gave them to the Church. In order for popes to live nearer St. Peter's Basilica, where all important religious ceremonies were conducted, Innocent ordered the construction of a palace, toward which he contributed heavily himself. St. Peter's was located on Vatican Hill; the palace became known as Vatican Palace; the term Vatican was thereafter applied to the Church's headquarters in Rome.

As guardian of the faith, Innocent was particularly anxious to recover the Holy Land for the Church. From the start of his reign, he wanted to send another crusade against the powerful Islamic rulers of Egypt and Palestine. The first three Crusades hadn't accomplished very much, but in paving the way for Dominican missionaries they did result in the return to Rome of the Maronites, some 300,000 people whose church had earlier fallen into the Monotheletic heresy. Innocent was able to send the Fourth Crusade on its way in 1202. All went well until the Crusaders reached Venice, from where they were to sail to Jerusalem. Venice then figured high in world trade, in competition with the Dalmatian city of Zara. Wealthy Venetian merchants bribed the Crusade leaders into attacking Zara, already a Christian city, and when Innocent heard about it he was furious. But before he could prevent the attack, the Crusaders had taken the city. Then they moved on to Greece where, again at the instigation of the Venetians, they overthrew the Byzantine Empire and settled down to rule for almost fifty years. As a Crusade, the effort was a miserable failure and a great embarrassment to the Church.

In 1212, a French shepherd boy named Stephen attracted hundreds of children to follow him in a pathetic attempt to capture the Holy Land. The Vatican tried to halt the Children's Crusade, but before anything could be done the youngsters, some fifteen hundred of them, boarded ships at Marseilles and were on their way. Those who didn't die at sea were sold into slavery to the Moslems by the ship-owners, so the aims of the Crusades again were frustrated. Innocent tried again. The Fifth Crusade, inaugurated by him in 1215, left for the Middle East after his death in 1217. It was making progress in Egypt when a quarrel broke out between Cardinal Pelagius and King John of Brienne, which delayed an attack on Cairo. The Moslems used the occasion to break the Nile dikes, flooding the Crusade supplies at Damietta and thereby drowning the whole project.

The heresies in Europe were much different from the Middle East dangers.

The heresies prevalent at the turn of the thirteenth century had their roots in the anticlericalism so rampant at the time. Sad but understandable, the people found little to respect in the majority of the clergy. There were plenty of priests—too many, in fact—but few were educated, and their personal conduct rarely reflected much piety. The popular feeling was that men became priests when they didn't know what else to do with themselves. This seemed especially true among the secular clergy—men who worked directly under bishops in towns and on feudal estates. Often there were so many of them clustered around one small impoverished church that they took turns begging in the streets, put price-tags on their prayers, and to brighten their dull lives disregarded their vows. Even at the top of the hierarchy, prayers and politics were so entwined that it was impossible to separate them. Ordinary people were therefore ripe for any movement that allowed them to display their displeasure with the clergy. Royalty, resentful of local ecclesiastical arrogance and squirming under the justified demands by strong popes, welcomed any chance to extricate themselves from Church ties. Heresies, then, lost their doctrinal emphasis and increasingly encouraged their adherents to criticize the Church and to escape personal responsibilities. It was easy for the heretics to convince themselves that they really believed the new ideas. Many did, of course, because priests hadn't taught them better. But for others the heresies were an escape route; the seeds of the Protestant Reformation were being planted.

The Waldenses were started by Peter Waldo, a Lyons merchant, who, mourning the death of a dear friend, decided to give up his wealth and become a mendicant preacher. He translated the Latin Bible into French, which he felt qualified him to interpret it. With a few disciples, he took to the roads preaching. The Archbishop of Lyons, pointing to the heretical dangers in Waldo's preaching due to his lack of theological training, tried to stop him, but Waldo appealed to the Pope for approval. When he didn't get it, his movement took a new twist. He condemned the Church as an unlawful power that had no privileges in either spiritual or temporal domains. He said that Jesus hadn't actually started a church, and he claimed that any man who considered himself qualified had the right to preach and administer the sacraments. In other words, every man a priest. The idea was a definite prelude to Protestantism. The Waldensian heresy was attractive, appealing particularly to the poorer classes through its emphasis on poverty. Small wonder, then, that it caught on quickly, spreading from France into Italy, Germany, Poland and Bohemia. It settled in the Alpine region where it simmered for over two hundred years, awaiting events that made it a sword.

The Amalricians were the followers of Amalric of Bena, a philosophy professor at the University of Paris. In trying to explain the union between Jesus and Christians, Amalric put forth the pantheistic theory that Jesus literally dwelled in Christian souls, thereby making Christians actual parts of the Divinity. Amalric subsequently gave up the idea, but his followers expanded it into a religion. They claimed the Church wasn't necessary any longer because each individual was the Church. Thus baptism was unnecessary, receiving Communion was unreasonable because they were in Communion, confession and penance were unrealistic because they were incapable of sin. The result was a great deal of high living.

The Albigensian heresy was an extension of the old Manichaean heresy, which maintained that God created all goodness and Satan created all evil, that people were just spirits who had been trapped by Satan and placed in human bodies, that salvation was achieved through the denunciation of all worldly things, fasting, mortification, and a baptism conferred by the laying on of hands. Albigensians frowned on desires for fame, money, influence; they considered marriage to be sinful; they urged people to escape from their prisons of flesh by poisoning or starving themselves. Owning property was also wrong, so Albigensians gave up all their possessions—turning them over to Albigensian leaders. They lived in groups throughout Europe, continually sending out their missionaries and winning converts at every social level, even among priests. When a good prospect seemed reluctant the Albigenses didn't hesitate to apply physical torture, believing that in punishing his body they were doing the prospect a favor. Their attitude toward the Church was clear: it was big; it was powerful; it was influential; it was evil.

But they felt the same way about governments and any other authority, and for this reason they were problems to the State as well as the Church. By their nature, all heretics were anarchists, and in this particular era they were double-barreled threats because of the close association between rulers of the State and Church. The Church had survived heresies in the past, but the danger of heresy to established political authorities was something new. It had to be stopped. In the minds of men whose governments were endangered, there was only one way to do it: by physical violence. Significantly, the suggestion for such extremes came not only from rulers who supported the Church but from men like King Henry II of England and King Frederick Barbarossa who had fought the Church. The suggestion was actually carried out in northern France, when an army of 200,000 under Simon de Montfort went south to fight the Albigensians. The war lasted almost twenty years and was shocking in its barbarism. The Church recognized that this was the wrong way to combat heresy and produced its own methods: Inquisitions.

The Inquisition began as a well-organized method of investigation, aimed at preventing wholesale spiritual seductions by heretics. In terms of the times, heretics were rebels, and local rulers were more anxious to punish them than was the Church. In fact, the Dominicans who conducted most of the thirteenth century Inquisitions were severely criticized by the nobility for their leniency. The punishment for penitent heretics was usually an order to attend Mass every day of their lives. Heretics who refused to recant were imprisoned and deprived of their properties by civil authorities.

Interestingly, a heretic was not told who had accused him, but he was allowed to list his enemies in the community and if the accuser was named the suspected heretic was immediately released. Torture and murder of heretics and witnesses were firmly denounced by the popes, and when they occurred it was usually in an area where the investigation was headed by a bishop who owed his position to the local baron. Invariably, the Inquisition became deplorable whenever the civil powers exceeded the ecclesiastic.

This was the case in most of the black moments in Church history. The Spanish Inquisition was controlled entirely by the Spanish kings.

VI

One day in 1244, Margaret, the countess of Flanders and the daughter of Baldwin II, the Latin emperor at Constantinople, was in Rome to visit the new pope, Innocent IV. As she went about the city she found herself facing an unusual problem: she couldn't tell the cardinals from the abbots. They were dressed alike, in long dark robes, low-crowned broad-brimmed hats, and pectoral crosses. Not knowing any of them personally, she extended to abbots the courtesies reserved for cardinals and she treated cardinals as if they were only abbots. When her error was repeatedly pointed out, she was embarrassed. At one of her meetings with the Pope she asked why something wasn't done to enable strangers to distinguish the cardinals and abbots. There ought to be some distinction in their dress, she suggested. Maybe the cardinals could wear red hats.

In June of the next year, Innocent called a council at Lyons for the purpose of deciding what was to be done about Frederick II, the papal ward who had grown up to be a papal problem. He had been excommunicated again, and this time he did nothing to reinstate himself within the required period. The council had been suggested by the French hierarchy. Present were the Pope, kings of France, England and Spain, many princes and barons, the cardinals, patriarch, archbishops, bishops and abbots. It was at this auspicious gathering that the Pope first presented the cardinals with their red hats. Thereafter the presentation of the red hat was the gesture that made a man a cardinal.

The most important duty the cardinals had was to elect the popes from among themselves, and this alone made them worthy of special courtesies. Cardinals living outside of Rome were principally occupied with the jurisdiction over dioceses; those in Rome worked with the popes as counselors and aides.

Pope Innocent II had died in 1216 at Perugia while on a trip to organize another Crusade. There were ten cardinals in his entourage. The day the Pope died, the Perugians took advantage of having some cardinals in their midst. They locked the cardinals in a palace and told them they would stay there until they elected a new pope. With the cardinals removed from politically-confused Rome, the Perugians felt there was more chance of getting a new pope elected without delays and intrigues.

The captive cardinals were uneasy. They tried to elude their responsibility by saying that the election ought to be postponed until other cardinals could be present. The Perugians replied that this was all right, provided the cardinals in the city were willing to remain imprisoned until other cardinals arrived. This would have meant a delay of weeks, perhaps months. The cardinals decided to go ahead with it. But rather than proceed with the normal discussion and numerous ballots, they agreed to appoint two men—the cardinals of Ostia and Preneste—to make the choice. On the second day of deliberations, the two cardinals chose Cencio Savelli, Innocent's cardinal carmelengo, which was an office similar to prime minister. The new pope took the name of Honorius III.

This was a period when the papal states were briefly back again in papal hands. In hopes of keeping them there, Honorius decided against commissioning loyal noblemen to hold the estates in fief because, as he had previously observed, popes could never be sure how long the noblemen would remain loyal. Instead, he appointed cardinals to supervise the lands. In this position, the cardinals were called rectors; some of them had enormous power and handled a great deal of money. With the exception of small areas on the west coast north of Rome, which Honorius permitted a few Lombard lords to rule, all the papal lands were managed by cardinals. The Duchy of Spoleto, a vast area that for a while had been held by papal enemies, was managed by a cardinal-deacon named Rainerius who possessed more authority than most of the princes of Europe.

A cardinal in England had more authority than many kings. When John Lackland bowed to Innocent III and said that the kingdom would be submissive to papal rule, the Pope quickly sent Cardinal-priest Gualo to London to see that Lackland's offer was carried out. Lackland died two months after Honorius became pope, and shortly before his death he asked the Pope (he thought Innocent was still reigning) to accept his young son as a ward and to act as his regent.

The signing of the Magna Carta had not brought peace to England. Prince Louis of France sent over troops to support the barons who opposed Lackland; they held London and almost half the kingdom. Innocent had backed Lackland, even to the extent of refusing to recognize the Magna Carta. Honorius took a different tack. His first papal act was to approve the charter—with amendments that defined the freedom of the Church. Cardinal Gualo expected to be recalled after Lackland's death; Honorius ordered him to stay there, assume responsibility for Lackland's son, and to try to make peace with the barons.

With Gualo in charge, Lackland's son was crowned King Henry III three months after his father died. The crown was placed on his head by the Bishop of Winchester. The barons and some of the English hierarchy declared that the coronation was illegal because it had not been performed by the Archbishop of Canterbury. But the Archbishop—Stephen Langton—whose election Lackland had disapproved, was out of the country. Gualo argued that the Archbishop would only have been acting for the Pope, and since Gualo was already doing that himself the coronation was legitimate. And yet there was something deeper to the hierarchal objections than the coronation itself. During Innocent's reign several bishoprics had become vacant. Instead of permitting local elections or appointing Englishmen, Innocent assigned Italians to the vacancies. He did so primarily to avoid a nationalization of the English Church, which had occurred in other countries due to lay investitures, but the English still didn't like it.

Cardinal Gualo realized this was another situation he would have to clear up if he was to restore order in the country. He informed the Pope of this, and Honorius replied favorably to the idea of appointing Englishmen to future vacancies, but with the understanding that this would not exclude any other nationalities he saw fit to assign.

Gualo was thus equipped to console the unhappy hierarchy with assurances of promotions. Although the promise did not win all of them over, it at least softened their resistance to him. Nevertheless, he was not a man to compromise himself into ineffectuality for the sake of a hint of peace. He was a cardinal, thereby a crown prince of the Church; he was moreover the papal envoy; and he was an Italian: he would tolerate just so much guff and no more. With the Cistercian monks he was severe. A mighty force in the Church because of the importance of their founder, Bernard of Clairvaux, they had sided with the barons. Even after Gualo ordered the clergy to come around to young Henry, the Cistercians refused, feeling furthermore that their position placed them beyond reproach. When Gualo had quite enough of them, he placed an interdict on their institutions, he excommunicated their abbots, and, as one of their own historians reported, "he caused discipline to be publicly inflicted upon their bare flesh before the church-doors."

Gualo handled the barons differently. He pointed out to them that Lackland was dead and there was no reason at all why his son should inherit their grudges. Some saw the logic in this; others still held out. There would always be holdouts as long as Prince Louis remained in the country. Gualo wrote the Pope that Louis must be sent back to France. Honorius wrote Philip Augustus using Gualo's arguments, saying that Lackland's death had removed the cause of strife in England and that Louis' presence there only served to keep old wounds bleeding. He urged Philip to recall his son. However, face-saving was involved. For Louis to leave England without a clearcut victory would give the impression that his efforts for the barons had been stalemated, that he was retreating because he could not conquer. Gualo supplied the way out: he suggested that the English crown pay Louis a large indemnity for his troubles and that since the Crown was in no position to make a peace treaty the treaty be made with the papacy. Louis accepted. Gualo personally escorted him to Dover and waved good-by as he sailed across to France. With Louis gone, the baronial faction weakened and then submitted. Gualo won.

2

European cardinals were most often archbishops and they derived their personal income from earnings of their archdiocesan properties and from taxes, tithes, and donations of the landowners and landholders. Under this group was the bulk of the population: tenant farmers who could not afford to support the Church directly. It was toward these that the Church extended most of its charity, providing doctors and teachers and caring for orphans and the aged. The charity was a personal thing, highly paternal, usually bestowed directly by a priest who knew the needy family. Bishops put aside part of their annual budgets for such purposes.

There were, too, many parts of the world that did not contribute anything to the Church. Africa was impoverished; so was the Middle East. Here the Church had to give without expecting any support in return. In Italy, despite the Church's vast properties there, the Church was frequently bankrupt. This plight grew mostly out of the wars which so often devastated the country. Time and again invaders marched on Rome, and to reach the city they had first to level the surrounding country. When the invasion was over, won or lost, the countryside had to be rebuilt, and always it was the Church that paid for it. And the complicated administration of the Church was in itself a great expense.

The money had to come from somewhere. When pressed, the popes borrowed from other bishops, particularly those in France. At the beginning of the thirteenth century, a voluntary tithe was created called Peter's Pence, by which every household made a contribution to the Church; this annual practice continued through the years. William the Conqueror was the first ruler to offer a yearly donation from the civil treasury, which others took up later. The practice also evolved of donations by bishops. At one time a fifth of the Church revenue in England was sent to Rome.

The Rome cardinals who had no private earnings had to rely entirely on the Vatican for an income, and the higher they rose in influence the more they required. Those who served as rectors of papal estates were responsible for the collection of revenues and, depending on their needs, they were allowed to keep a portion for themselves. Some kept as much as half. In good times, this amounted to a lot of money, adding another realm of influence for the cardinals. Obviously, a few cardinals, because of their positions and influence, ranked above others, and as such they were precursors of the era when cardinals would have more power than popes.

In the election of Pope Gregory IX (1227-1241), the choice again was made by just three cardinals. Among them was Conrad, the cardinal-bishop of Porto, and the story goes that the other two cardinals picked him, to which he said: "Never shall it be said that I had any hand in electing myself." But the cardinal who was chosen—Ugolino De Costi—described the scene differently, reporting that the three electors stepped aside briefly, then, "as though divinely inspired all turned their eyes on our insignificant person. And although we were unwilling to bear the burden which they desired to place upon us, they greatly urged us, and even used violence to place the papal mantle upon our shoulders. Despite, therefore, our reluctance, we at length submitted, fearing to resist the will of Heaven."

It was understandable that no good man in his right mind would want to be pope. The responsibility was tremendous. An unwise move could mean war, persecution, death. There were enemies on all sides, even the inside; there were few impartial counsels, few unselfish friends. The holy and unholy alike were critical and suspicious. But as long as the Church was run by men instead of angels all this was to be expected, and the good men who became popes realized that their only steady source of strength and guidance was God. As great as this was, it was nevertheless lonely.

The ninth Gregory's reign was scarred with further conflict with King Frederick II. Twice again Frederick marched on Rome; both times Gregory excommunicated him. During a brief peace, Gregory gave in to Frederick's suggestion that unrepentant heretics should be burned. As severe as Gregory had been against heretics, this was more than he had in mind. Even so, merely by accepting Frederick's plan Gregory earned himself a reputation in history as a ruthless killer. In the five centuries of Inquisitions, those by the Church and those by the various governments, about a thousand people suffered the death sentence. More in keeping with the Church's purpose in holding Inquisitions was the censorship of heretical books that could endanger the faith of readers who lacked sufficient knowledge. It was Gregory who, in 1231, initiated what became known as the Index when he instructed the University of Paris professors: "Inasmuch as, then, we understand that the books of natural philosophy, which were prohibited by the provincial of Paris, could contain much that is useful and much that is detrimental, we commission your discretion in which we have full confidence, by virtue of this apostolic rescript and in view of the divine judgement, to examine these books with all skill and care in order that what is useful may not suffer from what is hurtful and so that the books may be studied forthwith without danger when all that is erroneous or calculated to scandalize their readers has been removed." The professors offered their cooperation.

Try though he did, Gregory could not sustain cooperation with Frederick. The King invariably took advantage of the Pope's leniency; then when the Pope could stand no more the King attempted to make him out a monster. He accused Gregory of being the Antichrist; he said that in excommuni-

cating him Gregory was only trying to cover up for his own
failure as pope; and he charged that if there was no peace in
Europe Gregory was to blame. In Sicily, Frederick confiscated Church property and forbade the people to go to
Church. He warned that anybody entering Sicily with papal documents—his excommunication papers—would be
hanged. He closed the Monte Cassino monastery because
the monks had dared to proclaim his excommunication.

He worked hard to turn the cardinals against Gregory. In
letters to all of them he said it was sad indeed that the cardinals, "who are the foundation of the Church, its columns, the
assessors of rectitude, the senators of Peter's City and the
hinges of the world," had not taken steps to depose Gregory.
It was their right, he said, and their duty. Two or three cardinals actually went over to Frederick because they thought
he would come out winner in his battle with the Pope.

For two world leaders, the King and Pope behaved like
children at times. Frederick wrote a poem which he had one
of his cardinal friends affix to a lamp in Gregory's bedroom,
saying:

> "The states and fates and flights of birds decree
> Of all the world one hammer there shall be.
> Rome totters, through a mass of error led
> And of the world shall cease to be the head."

Gregory replied with a poem slipped into Frederick's bedroom:

> "Scripture and Fame, your sins, all loudly tell
> Your life but short, and then forever hell."

Holding the territory around Rome, Frederick captured
all papal couriers sent out to get help and he prevented anyone from entering Rome who might work against him. But

there was still the sea. Gregory sent out word by ship that, as far as he was concerned, Frederick's throne was empty and invited other rulers to take over his domains. There were few takers: any such attempt would have meant war. Determined to get rid of Frederick, Gregory sent a small fleet to Genoa, from where couriers hurried throughout Europe summoning the hierarchy to a Rome council at which Gregory planned to declare the temporal throne vacant and use the hierarchal influence to make the declaration stick.

Weeks later the cardinals, archbishops, bishops and abbots gathered at Genoa for the sea voyage to Rome. French ships entering the harbor reported encountering some of Frederick's vessels on the high seas: the King was obviously planning an attack. The news both frightened and angered the prelates. Some wanted to wait for reinforcements before attempting the trip; others said that Frederick, villain though he was, certainly would not have the audacity to attack a fleet of the Church's princes. Anger won out and the journey began. Ninety miles out of Genoa the fleet of twenty-seven ships came upon the vessels commanded by Enzio, Frederick's bastard son. Only five ships escaped; the others were damaged, sunk or captured. Among the prelates taken prisoner were the Cardinals James, Otho and Gregory.

The world turned on Frederick. The King of France threatened to attack if the three cardinals were not released. Stern notes of similar tone came from England and from German princes. But Frederick was not to be stopped. At first the Pope was all for revenge, but then he realized that now the matter was not solely one of power: the lives of three cardinals were in Frederick's hands. One wrong step by the Pope would mean their deaths. Gregory wrote the European rulers and asked them to hold off for a while until he could make a final attempt with Frederick.

But Frederick sent his armies rushing at Rome before Gregory could begin negotiations. Gregory asked the Roman nobility not to fight but they would not listen to him. The battle was on in the fields beyond Rome when, appalled by all that was happening, the Pope died suddenly. Frederick received the news with a cheer.

There were fourteen cardinals. Of the three in prison, one had died, leaving Otho and James in Frederick's hands. Earlier, Cardinal John of Colonna had been assigned by Pope Gregory to be chaplain to King Frederick, and when the final breech occurred between the Pope and the King the Cardinal sided with the King. Upon the Pope's death, Frederick sent Cardinal John into Rome in order to take part in the new election and get himself elected if he could. Two other cardinals were out of Rome at the time and could not get back for the election. That meant that ten cardinals would vote.

As soon as Pope Gregory was buried, Senator Matteo Rosso locked all the cardinals in a jail to keep them away from Frederick and to force them to elect a successor as quickly as possible. But they could not agree on a choice, a division reportedly brought on by conflict over whether or not to select a man acceptable to Frederick. A week passed, and then a second week passed. Frederick got the idea that his presence outside the city walls was causing complications in the election and he moved his armies back some fifty miles. A third week passed. Impatient, Frederick demanded to know which candidates were being favored, but Rosso wouldn't tell him. The favorite was Geoffrey Castiglione, cardinal-bishop of Sabina, but after repeated ballots he could muster only five votes. Seven were necessary for the two-thirds majority. The fourth week passed.

Talk arose in Rome that the stalemated cardinals were about to look outside their own group for a successor. The Romans and Frederick were indignant; the Romans didn't want a foreigner as their bishop; Frederick felt that as long as there was a block he had a chance to get in one of his own men and he didn't want to risk having the compromise choice be a man over whom he had no control at all. In jail, the cardinals were growing weary. It was summer, the Rome heat was intense. Three cardinals fell ill and days slipped by without a vote.

At last the cardinals sent a plea to Frederick: "Free Otho and James and let them help us choose a pope." Cautious against irritating any cardinal whose vote might be swayed in his direction, Frederick permitted the two captive cardinals to go to Rome and took two bishops to hold as hostages.

But the situation didn't change. The fifth and sixth weeks passed. Cardinal Robert Sumercote, of England, died, and it looked as if the favorite, Cardinal Castiglione, was about to go too. When the seventh week went by without a successful vote, Cardinals Otho and James announced that there probably would never be an election and they asked to be returned to prison so that their hostages could be released. Now there were only nine to vote. At last, on October 25, in the middle of the eighth week, somebody changed his vote to Castiglione, giving him six votes—two-thirds of the nine present—and the aging bishop of Sabina was proclaimed pope.

He took the name of Celestine IV. He was very old, and the two months in prison had ruined his health. The significant factor of his election was that he had been a close friend of his predecessor: after his death Pope Gregory had won out over Frederick. But it was a short-lived victory.

Pope Celestine died on his seventeenth day in office. Immediately five of the eight cardinals who had participated in his election fled the city. A sixth—John of Colonna—was arrested by Senator Rosso, deprived of all his personal possessions and put into prison. That left two cardinals in Rome to elect a new pope, which would be difficult since a cardinal was not supposed to vote for himself and the winner was to have a two-thirds majority. Helpless, the two cardinals turned to the canons of St. Peter's for advice. The canons sent messages to the five fleeing cardinals to come back and elect another pope. Remembering the hell they had just gone through to elect the last one, the cardinals' reply was the equivalent of, "No, thanks."

VII

The hinges of Rome, King Frederick accused bitterly, seemed to be getting a little rusty.

Indeed, as the months passed there was every indication that the cardinals, by their refusal to convene, had brought the Church to an end. Celestine IV died on November 10, 1241, and at the turn of the year there was still no sign of a conclave. The two cardinals still in Rome wrote repeatedly to the scattered five, urging them to return; the five cardinals wrote to each other about the sad state of affairs. But nobody made a move. By spring, King Louis of France notified the cardinals that if something weren't done soon he would authorize the French hierarchy to elect a pope on its own. Still no cardinal stirred.

There was great concern everywhere. The entire machinery of the Church had come to a halt. Not only were spiritual events affected, but the many enterprises in which the Church had a primary concern—universities, properties, businesses, negotiations of all kinds—could not move. The Church had involvements, investments, and responsibilities greater than any government, and now nothing could be done.

Afraid to move, the absentee cardinals nevertheless insisted that nothing be done without them. They warned their two confreres in Rome that they were not to proceed with any of the Church's interests on their own and that in no circumstances should they take upon themselves the task of choosing a new pope—even if they could.

But the public demand for an election grew louder. In self-defense, the absentee cardinals agreed among themselves that there could be no election as long as Otho and James were imprisoned. This might have been a legitimate excuse, but to many it looked like a dodge. King Frederick took advantage of this new excuse for delay. He sent delegates to call on the five cardinals, baiting them with all kinds of offers and promises in an effort to secure their allegiance to his own position before an election could take place. Yet at the same time he kept up his threats to the city of Rome, moving in close to plunder and rob whenever he needed supplies for his troops. When he considered it to his benefit, he suggested releasing Otho and James, but he never got around to it.

Further pressures came from France, from England and Spain, from Germany, both upon the cardinals and upon Frederick. Rulers suggested that, if the deferred conclave was a matter of the imprisoned cardinals, Frederick should release them to show his good faith. Everyone knew that he was merely stalling until he could feel confident that the new pope would be favorable toward him. The first indication of his confidence occurred in August, 1242, when he let

Cardinal Otho out of jail. A sigh arose from the rulers on the continent, only to become a gasp when the cardinals said that one man was not enough. The cardinals began to receive queries: Will you not compromise? They would not. To some observers, the stubbornness gave the impression of a certain unanimity and strength of purpose among the cardinals, but others began to suspect that perhaps Frederick was right in his accusation that each cardinal wanted to be pope and that they were all simply stalling until they lined up sufficient votes.

The year ended. Cardinal John Colonna was released from the Rome prison and allowed to join the other two cardinals in the city to do what Church work could be done. Time continued to slip away. The English hierarchy went into mourning for the "widowed" Church, and in France fasts were ordered in the hope that God would soon provide a solution to the crisis.

Then, quite unexpectedly, Frederick released Cardinal James from prison in May. Now all stumbling blocks were out of the way. In June the cardinals met at Anagni, and if anyone wondered what had motivated Frederick to surrender to the cardinals the clue was in the man they finally elected: Cardinal Sinibaldo de Fieschi, an old friend of Frederick's. Evidently Frederick had had his way.

But the new pope, Innocent IV, soon proved he was no puppet. It was he who gave the red hat to the cardinals, enhancing their dignity, and in order to remove the conduct of the College of Cardinals from the hands of so few he quickly appointed twelve new cardinals. He welcomed gestures from Frederick for a peace treaty with the Vatican, but when he discovered that the King was making deals with leading Romans for property in the city and especially to have himself recognized as heir to the papal throne, as his grandfather Barbarossa had done, Innocent annulled the treaty and issued a public statement exposing the King.

This was the act that helped restore much of the respect the Church had lost during its seventeen months without a pope. It made renewed conflict with Frederick inescapable and again risked the peace of the continent, but nevertheless it was worth it. So typical of the times, the political plans of the king backfired when Innocent, having gone this far, decided to go all the way by having Frederick deposed and replaced. Innocent knew Rome was not a safe place for taking action of that sort, what with Frederick's armies sitting just a few miles from the city. Furthermore, he wanted his attack to have as great an effect as possible, which meant inviting the European hierarchy to a council, and this was impossible at Rome with Frederick holding all the roads into the city. It would have to be held elsewhere.

A ruse was necessary. First, Innocent gave a quiet order that Genovese ships should go to Civita Vecchia on June 28. Then he announced that he was leaving Rome to celebrate the Feast of Saints Peter and Paul at the Cathedral of Sutri. He left Rome on June 27, 1244; the feast was June 29. With him was a large entourage, intended for the procession Frederick knew about the ships and he knew about the trip to Sutri, but he didn't associate the two until it was too late. The night of June 28 it occurred to him that something was up and he sent a contingent of his men to Sutri to keep an eye on the Pope.

Only minutes before the troops arrived, Innocent and seven aides, all disguised as monks, had left their quarters at the Sutri cathedral, mounted horses, and ridden slowly away without attracting attention. As soon as they got out of town. they left the road and took to the woods, galloping at top speed through the countryside toward the sea. An hour passed before Frederick's men realized what had happened, and they raced after the Pope. The chase continued all night. Near dawn a storm broke. At the height of the deluge Innocent reached the wharf, where a small boat was waiting to take his group out to the ships. The winds were strong; the seas were running high. The captains warned Innocent that sailing immediately would be dangerous. The Pope replied that it would not be as dangerous as waiting. Frederick's soldiers appeared at the wharf just as the Genovese vessels hoisted anchor.

At Genoa, the Pope sent out announcements of a council to be held at Lyons the following year. The first reaction was world shock: the Pope had left Rome. Evidently he expected to be away a long time. Did this mean he would never go back?

It began to seem so. Illness kept Innocent from going to Lyons for several weeks, and when he finally entered the city he set up his administration there. Taxes from bishops were sent to Lyons. Innocent used some of the money to improve the cathedral and to assist the local poor. The following summer, Church leaders from all over the world met at Lyons, prepared for what they were going to hear: the papal deposition of Frederick.

At the same time, Innocent appealed to the princes of Germany to support him by choosing another emperor. In this he received the support of German bishops and archbishops who, being members of the royal family and also landholders, had the right to vote. As important Churchmen, the prelates also had influence with other German nobility. Innocent suggested Henry Raspe, the landgrave of Thuringia, as the best candidate. So effective were the temporal and spiritual pressures Innocent was able to apply that, in May of 1246, the German noblemen did exactly as the Pope wished. Henry Raspe defeated Conrad, Frederick's son, and Germany was his.

But Innocent was not free to go home. Frederick was still in Italy with a large army and as long as he could afford to pay his soldiers they would remain with him. Furthermore, although Germany was lost, Frederick still claimed Sicily, and that matter had to be taken care of before the Pope could safely return to Rome.

Frederick was at Parma, struggling to put down a Lombard insurrection that had risen against him, when he learned that Henry Raspe had died suddenly in February, 1247. Frederick urged Conrad to form a new army quickly and retake what he had lost to Henry Raspe. Conrad succeeded, but his victory was negated by Frederick's defeat at Parma, the worst defeat of his career. Despite this—with Conrad in command in the north and Frederick's other son Manfred in command in Sicily—Italy was still closed to the Pope. He appealed to King Haakon of Norway to come to his aid, but Haakon replied that although he was ready to defend the Church against its enemies he did not feel obliged to go to war against Innocent's personal enemies, which was all he considered Frederick to be. The Pope then turned to William, the count of Holland, and mustering the cooperation of several bishops and princes he managed to get William named emperor. William went to war against Conrad.

Frederick moved south to Sicily, from where he tried to attract military and financial support from German princes he thought were loyal and from Eastern rulers he suspected would cooperate for the chance of expanding their personal influence. But his defeat at Parma, his deposition and excommunication, and the slow but steady victories of William in the north all worked against him. In December of 1250 he died. His death, in fact, put an end to the Hohenstaufen rule of Europe. His son Conrad called himself emperor and was making a good show of it, and only William's presence and actions kept him from making his claim an actuality. Conrad appointed his brother Manfred to rule Sicily in his name, then devoted himself to William.

For a while, Italy was quiet. Encouraged, Pope Innocent, after seven years away from Rome, began his return in 1251. His trip was slow and triumphal, made greater by Conrad's withdrawal from Germany and escape by sea to Sicily. Northern Italy was in ruins. As Innocent made his way to Rome, he consulted with churchmen and noblemen on the reconstruction of the area. The Pope, said the people, had given them freedom and now he would give them another chance to start life over. With such sentiments widespread, Innocent's return to Italy was glorious. But his troubles were not over.

In Sicily, Conrad and Manfred sought some means to hang on to what they had left of the empire that had dominated Europe for over two hundred years. Cornered, they were still not trapped, and they felt what they needed most was time. Like their ancestors, they tried to gain time through peaceful overtures. They sent representatives to Innocent, asking if he would be willing to end hostilities by letting things stand as they were, with the two brothers in possession of Sicily. The Pope said no. Victories in Europe had led him to believe he could be equally victorious in the Mediterranean. Furthermore, he said, Sicily already belonged to the Church, having been submitted to the Church by Frederick. Even though Innocent knew the word of the Hohenstaufen meant nothing, he was determined to make this one stick. He pointed out that by accepting Conrad's offer he would be indirectly accepting Conrad as a partner in the Holy Roman Empire and that, regardless of the vague entity the empire had become, he refused to do so. The Church, he said, had the right to choose its own throne-mate, and Conrad wasn't it.

This was a strong attitude, effective in some quarters and understandable in terms of the times, but it proved unwise in the long run. To be sure, the world belonged to God and the Church was God's specific agent of communication, but to assert that the world therefore belonged to the Church was unrealistic. Previous popes had struggled to stay out of political government, but now the situation was changed.

The Church was about to enter on the era of its strongest temporal involvement, and it was to be an era in which the Church was itself to bring about the worst problems it would ever face.

While holding Conrad in check in Sicily, Innocent warned the new powers in the north against expanding its horizons south of the Alps. He directly ordered that no attacks were to be made against Sicily without his approval. At the same time, he hunted around for someone he could trust to do the difficult job of getting Sicily back. He offered it to Richard, Earl of Cornwall, but Richard didn't want it. The Pope then turned to Charles of Anjou, the youngest son of King Louis IX of France. Charles, an ambitious young man, was slow to respond, wary of the terms of his rule should he accept. He was willing to accept the kingdom as vassal to the Pope, but he wanted to be sure that vassal did not mean servant. Irked by the procrastination, Innocent offered the Kingdom to Edmund of England. As these negotiations went on, Conrad moved an army across to Naples and damaged the city severely.

Stunned by the surprise attack, Innocent was at a loss. Before he could recover from the blow, news arrived that Conrad had died, reportedly poisoned by Manfred. On top of that came the fantastic news that Conrad, suspicious of Manfred, had previously taken steps to provide that in the event of his death his kingdom should go to his infant son and the boy was to be made a ward of the Church. That the man who had battled the Church throughout his short life should make such a provision showed clearly the amazing confusion of principles that kept medieval Europe in such constant upheaval.

But Manfred was not to be stopped. Typical of his family, he pretended to give serious consideration to Conrad's will and Innocent's efforts to carry it out, but meanwhile he was accumulating all available funds in Sicily and using them to round up the German soldiers who had been left in Italy after the death of Frederick. When he felt strong enough, he began to attack the papal holdings in the south of Italy. Innocent retaliated by getting together an army of his own and sent it against Manfred. The two forces met at Foggia on December 2, 1254. Before the day was over, Manfred roundly defeated the papal army.

Innocent was then at Naples. The rapid turn of events was too much for him. Worn out, he developed pleurisy, and in a week he was dead.

2

Eleven cardinals were with Innocent when he died. A twelfth, William Fieschi, Innocent's nephew, was in the south, in command of the defeated army. The administrator of Naples, appointed by Innocent, was Bertholinus Tavernerius, the husband of Innocent's niece. As soon as Innocent died, Tavernerius locked the door of the house where the cardinals were staying, then sent word to Cardinal Fieschi to come and take part in the election. Innocent died on December 7; Fieschi arrived at Naples on Friday, December 11. He was permitted a few moments to pray at Innocent's grave, then was locked up with the others. By noon of the next day, the cardinals realized that they were getting nowhere. Fearful of another lengthy session, they agreed to pick a committee from among themselves and abide by its choice. The choice was Cardinal-bishop Rinaldo Conti of Ostia, who became Alexander IV.

The circumstances of this election demonstrated some significant facts. More and more, popes were bringing members of their own families into their administrations, probably in the hope of acquiring some trustworthy aides who would be freer from political influence than others might be. Most often the relatives were nephews, which occasioned use of the word "nepotism." In return for loyalty, the nephews often received the best appointments. This custom eventually became so much a part of the papacy that nephews began to look forward to rewards even before they earned them, all of which was to prove to be extremely detrimental to the Church.

The speedy election of Alexander also showed that the people and the cardinals wanted to avoid both the long vacancies and the discomfort and isolation of endless balloting. In a way this was an improvement; but it also led to the hasty election of men who were not fully qualified for the important role thrust upon them.

Alexander's qualifications were unique. When Innocent fled from Rome in 1254 he left four cardinals to direct the routine functions of the Church, and Alexander was one of them. Later he made his way to Lyons for the council, then returned to Rome to continue his work. He knew, then, the basic functions of the Church, and in this he was better equipped for the job than most.

He was, however, chosen by compromise, an indication that once again the cardinals had been unable to elect a man by popular vote. In essence, the choice of the cardinals was supposed to be the choice of God. Often enough in the past there had been occasions when such harmony was scarcely evident, and more were to come. The basic problem was personal ambition. It was said that he who entered the conclave as pope came out as cardinal. Most often this was true. Anyone who actually wanted the position was usually the wrong man for it and the cardinals knew this as well as everybody else. Thus when an ambitious cardinal managed to roll up a few votes others who were aware of his campaign turned against him out of well-founded fear. Resorting to selection by a compromise committee was an easy way out.

Many conclaves ended with reports that the elected man had to be held down while others put the pallium on him: it was understandable that the majority of popes were unwilling to serve. There was no peace in the job. The power and the glory that went with it were certainly no compensation for the constant hounding that came from all sides. The nature of the papacy made it something of a benign dictatorship, and no dictator, even a saintly one, could expect much tranquility. There was always someone who would try to sway him, use him, or get rid of him.

It was therefore evident that although the papacy was 1300 years old it had not as yet developed its character to its full effectiveness. But this was to be expected. In the hands of men, it could not have started out perfect.

3

Pope Alexander did not spend much time in Rome. The city was controlled by Senator Brancaleone, a Bolognese who had been imported by the people and given supreme temporal authority for three years. He began his rule during the absence of Innocent IV. After his first term he was briefly replaced, but his replacement was too gentle for the Romans and Brancaleone was recalled. Again he was supposed to surrender his despotic powers in three years, but when his contract expired he announced that, by the powers granted him, he was extending his rule indefinitely. Nobody seemed concerned enough to challenge him.

Brancaleone had no use for the papacy. He had ruled without a spiritual çollaborator at first and felt he could go on that way. When the popes were ready to resettle in Rome, he restricted their movements, their temporal authority, and their contact with the people. The Church was too weakened by its experiences in the north and the Sicilian matter was still unresolved; rather than become embroiled in the Roman affair, the popes lived mostly at Viterbo, a resort town in the mountains north of the city where there was a papal palace and accommodations for the cardinals.

Alexander IV died at Viterbo in May, 1261. Eight cardinals were there, and after Alexander's burial in the cathedral (it was politically inadvisable to attempt burial at St. Peter's, in Brancaleone's Rome) they convened to elect a successor. Once again there was a delay. Two stories came out of the conclave. According to one, the conclave dragged on for two months because two men who had been elected —Cardinal John Tolet of England and Cardinal Hugh of France—both refused so vehemently that the cardinals decided to seek outside their own circle and finally chose Jacques Pantaleon, the patriarch of Jerusalem who happened to be at Viterbo at the time. The second story relates that after two months of stalemate the cardinals agreed to elect the first cleric to knock on the conclave door. It was the Jerusalem patriarch. The new pope—Urban IV—later said he too refused the election but finally accepted in order to bring the long conclave to a close.

The Sicilian affair was still dragging on when Urban died four years later. Just before his death, however, he managed to convince Charles of Anjou to attack Manfred on the promise that Charles would not only be the ruler of Sicily and southern Italy but Senator of Rome as well. Brancaleone's well-timed death had made the last offer possible, even though Charles realized he might have to pressure the Romans into accepting him.

Urban died in October. By February, four months later, no pope had been elected. This time eighteen cardinals were in conclave, and it was known that a decisive faction of them were sympathetic toward Manfred. For this reason there could be no agreement. Once again the cardinals had to resort to a compromise committee.

The committee chose an unusual man: Guy Fulcodi, the cardinal-bishop of Sabina, who wasn't present at the conclave. Urban had sent Fulcodi to England as his legate in an effort to bring peace between King Henry III, the son of John Lackland, and the barons. The country was in worse condition than Cardinal Gualo had found it years before. By his free-spending, his incurable readiness for war, and his disregard for the rights of the barons, Henry alienated the entire nobility. He was, on the other hand, always friendly toward the Church, and though this saved him from excommunication it didn't help much in his own country.

Urban hoped that Cardinal Fulcodi could restore order. Born in France, Fulcodi had been a successful lawyer, had married and was the father of two girls. When his wife died, he became a priest. His knowledge of law and his connections in the country helped him to rise rapidly. He had been the bishop of Le Puy and the archbishop of Narbonne when he was summoned to Rome to become the cardinal-bishop of Sabina. His mission to England, however, did not add to his list of triumphs.

The English barons were not about to let another papal legate coax them into submission to a king for the second time. When Fulcodi wrote the barons from France to send over a delegation to accompany him to England, they replied that they would not let the cardinal set foot in the country until he realized that he was not arriving to give orders but to participate in discussions by which peace might be achieved. Angered, the Cardinal pointed out that England had been submitted to the Church by John Lackland, that the Pope was King Henry's suzerain, that as legate he was authorized to act in the Pope's name, and if they didn't take care he would excommunicate the whole pack of them. The barons responded with an attitude which indicated that, in view of the Cardinal's feelings, it would be better for all concerned if he headed back to Rome. Henry himself detected the impasse and he wrote Fulcodi that the predicament "could in these days be better conducted by lenity and kindness than by ecclesiastical coercion."

Fulcodi's threat of interdiction was empty talk; he could not very well excommunicate an entire country when the King was supposed to be a friend. Restricting the interdict to the barons was equally futile; many bishops and most of the clergy were on their side. All that was left was force. He wrote the English bishops that if they didn't come for him in a month he would think of some way to punish them. A delegation arrived in seven weeks, bringing along an agreement from the barons defining the methods by which Fulcodi would conduct his mission.

The Cardinal rejected it. Where, he wanted to know, did the bishops get the audacity to hand it to him? Since when was anybody telling a papal legate how to do his job? And how come the English hierarchy had fallen so low as to act as messengers for the illegal baronic holders of the country?

The bishops explained that they were helpless. The barons were in power and nothing could be done about it. No ships were to be made available to bring the Cardinal to England unless he signed the agreement. Fulcodi reacted by having the agreement torn to shreds and thrown into the sea.

Pope Urban died in October. Cardinal Fulcodi felt he could not possibly return to Italy in time to participate in the election of a new pope, so he remained in France, busy at the exchange of nasty letters with everyone in England who would write to him. The year came to an end. There was no pope in Italy and no peace in England. In the middle of January, Fulcodi announced that he ought to return to Italy to see what he could do about the stymied election and to discuss the English problem with the new pope. On February 5, when he had reached the south of France, news arrived that he had been chosen by a compromise committee of two. Aware that no pope was safe without a military escort in a land where Manfred still roamed, Fulcodi disguised himself as an ordinary monk and made his way to Perugia where the cardinals were waiting for him.

As Clement IV, the former legate saw important progress during his three-year reign. Charles of Anjou finally arrived in Italy. He defeated Manfred, then he defeated Conradin, the son of Conrad, who tried to follow in his family's footsteps and actually succeeded in sending troops into Rome before encountering Charles. And events in England took a decided turn for the better. Prince Edward won an important battle at Evesham and the barons were no longer in a position to dictate. Clement immediately sent Cardinal Ottoboni Fieschi to England as legate. The changed atmosphere, the warm welcome provided by the royal family, and the subdued arrogance of the barons enabled Fieschi to achieve what Fulcodi had failed to do. In six months, the Church's affairs in England were much improved, peace of a sort was established, Henry remained king, and the barons had more say about the government. This cooperation accomplished what coercion could not.

4

There was need of the same kind of cooperation at Viterbo. When Clement died there in November of 1268, there were twenty cardinals. Nineteen of them were at Viterbo; the twentieth was in France helping to arrange the Eighth Crusade, headed by King Louis IX. Both the King and the Cardinal died later in Tunisia.

Of the nineteen cardinals at Viterbo, eleven were said to favor the imperial party, which would install an Italian pope who would create an emperor, also Italian, for joint rule over what could at best be considered the potsherds of the old empire. Opposing them was the group, headed by Ottoboni, who favored a foreign pope, with temporal rule to remain with Charles of Anjou. In both groups were men who wanted the papacy for themselves, regardless of who was emperor.

Such was the atmosphere at Viterbo as 1268 came to a close. By this time, a papal vacancy at Rome of a month or two was no novelty. But three months passed, then four, then six. Philip Benizi, superior-general of the Servite Order of priests, went to Viterbo from his Florence headquarters and reproached the cardinals vehemently. He was a man to be listened to. A nobleman, he was additionally powerful through his position as leader of the Servites (Order of the Servants of Mary), a group of monks who had strong support in the north. A stern and voluble man, he lashed the cardinals with each word. When he finished, they suggested that he should be pope. He told them he wasn't a cardinal— a papal requirement the cardinals themselves sometimes overlooked—and before they could say anything more he left Viterbo and hid in the mountains for three months to avoid being forced into the papacy.

Then Vincent, the archbishop of Tours, let the cardinals hear what he had on his mind. They were, he said, the cause of scandal in the world, of infidelity, the loss of souls, and rancor throughout the Church. Heresies were arising, he said, and there was no one to fight them because there was no pope to speak. Their scandal was in the bad example of unity they were showing the world, from the least significant of people to kings, and he warned that if there was in the future any occasion of broad disobedience to the Church the blame would be traceable to the cardinals who could not agree.

Still nothing happened.

The Viterbese grew restless. The conclave was being held at the papal palace instead of the cathedral and each afternoon, when the cardinals finished their deliberations for the day, they returned to their own homes. The Viterbese began to throw rocks at them. When the cardinals went a few days without balloting, the people threw rocks at the palace. The allotment of food to the palace was first cut down, then cut out. At their own houses, the cardinals found the same food shortage. They also found that their servants were quitting.

Chagrined, the English Cardinal John Tolet commented one day that maybe the roof of the palace should be removed to give the Holy Ghost easier access to the minds of the cardinals. Word of his observation reached the people. Next morning when the cardinals arrived at the palace the roof of the conference room was gone. From then on the cardinals dated their pronouncements with: "Given at the uncovered palace."

All of 1269 and 1270 passed without a pope.

Charles of Anjou manipulated the situation in two ways. He knew that men favorable to him were being considered. From time to time he sent some meat to Viterbo, or a little wine. At the same time, he held back the Sicilian tribute payments to the Church, depleting the papal treasury to the point where cardinals had to write to foreign bishops for funds to keep alive. Invariably the bishops replied that they didn't have any money either and didn't expect to see much until the Church became a going organization again.

The bishops of England particularly claimed destitution. Most of what they could raise went to heal wounds left by the Barons' War. On top of that, Clement had been anxious for another Crusade to Palestine. As evidence of royal family loyalty to the wishes of popes, Prince Edward was forming the Ninth Crusade and was taxing the churches for funds.

Edward was in the Holy Land early in 1271, fighting for a Church that had still no leader.

On the death of King Louis in Africa, his son, Philip the Bold, inherited the throne. Like all rulers, Philip was disturbed by the immobile cardinals. In March of 1271 he met Charles of Anjou at Rome and the two of them went to Viterbo to try to pressure the cardinals to reach a decision. A few days later, King Baldin, ex-emperor of Constantinople, and Henry of Almaine, nephew of the King of England, arrived. They, too, begged for action, but to no avail.

By now the number of cardinals was down to sixteen; two died and one became so ill he could no longer take part in the project. The Viterbese began to wonder if the plan was to postpone an election until there was only one man left for the papal throne. Accordingly, they ended their personal attacks on the cardinals to avoid being the cause of diminishing their number even further. Also, with four such important men in the city, the Viterbese were sure the cardinals would do something.

Then, on March 13, the already tense city was shocked by a murder. A leader in the Barons' War had been Simon de Montfort, the earl of Leicester. Two of his sons, Guy and Simon, had taken up residence in Tuscany, where Guy served as vicar for Charles of Anjou. The earl was killed at Evesham, and his sons vowed revenge on the first member of the English royal family to come near them. It turned out to be Henry of Almaine. While Henry was at Mass in a Viterbese church, the two Montforts came up behind him, stabbed him to death, then dragged the body out of the church and threw it into a public square. Before they could be arrested they fled from the town. Viterbo was in an uproar. There were rumors that Charles of Anjou and King Philip had been behind the murder, but it was never proved. The rumor nevertheless incited ill feelings between England and France that lasted for many years.

Naturally the cardinals learned all about the murder. Instead of moving them to bring their conclave to a close it served only to lock them in deeper complications. The summer passed away. By now Church business was in dreadful shape, almost beyond salvage. Even the stubborn cardinals faced the fact that if they didn't agree on a pope soon they eventually could well elect a man who had no Church to rule. It was only then, two years and ten months after Clement's death, that the cardinals decided their only solution was an election by compromise. They drew lots for membership on the six-man committee, and it so happened that most of the six men were foreigners. The choice they made was indeed a masterful compromise.

First, they didn't choose a cardinal. But they chose an Italian. However, he was an Italian who had spent most of his Church career outside of Italy and whose last position was that of archdeacon of Liège, in Belgium. At the moment he was in Palestine with Prince Edward's Crusade. And he was a good man.

When the cardinals finally returned to Rome, jokesters asked why such a noble group of men had to reach below their rank to find someone worthy of being their superior. On the contrary, Archdeacon Tedaldo Visconti was better qualified than most cardinals for his new responsibility. He had served on papal missions to France and Germany; he had been with Ottoboni in England. He had many friends. He and King Louis were close, and he was therefore close to Charles of Anjou and King Philip. The fact that he had gone to Palestine with Prince Edward was evidence of the high regard he earned in England. He was over sixty when he was elected pope. Previously he had turned down a chance to be bishop of Piacenza, his home town in northern Italy, just as he had rejected other important promotions, content to serve rather than lead. His first reaction to news of his election was negative, but then he decided to accept.

He had several vital projects in mind and he could only execute them in the top position of his Church. Having seen Palestine and all the misery there, he was determined to help the country. He arrived at Viterbo on February 10, 1272. After the preliminaries of agreeing to be pope, he spent a week at private conferences with cardinals and kings on the Palestine question, extracting from all of them promises for financial aid for Palestine. He decided to call a council to make the program official.

He also had his own ideas about the future emperor. He felt it should be a Germanic ruler, but no one associated with Saxony. When the time came for him to recommend a man for the northern lords to elect he surprised everyone by naming a nobleman nobody knew much about: Rudolf of Hapsburg. In so doing he raised into prominence the Austrian family that was to dominate Europe for seven hundred years, and have a marked effect even into the twentieth century, when the assassination of one of Rudolf's descendants precipitated World War I.

The archdeacon soon revealed his plans for the Church. When the cardinals asked him about his consecration, they expected him to assume the papal throne at Viterbo, but he told them: "You know, my dearest brethren, that Constantine, the ruler of the world, when in Rome, placed his crown upon the head of Pope Sylvester as a mark of temporal authority. Hence reason, justice and decency demand that in Rome the Church should, in my worthy person, be duly crowned."

Thus he took the Church back to Rome where it belonged. On March 27, he was consecrated Gregory X.

He wasted no time. He initiated his aid to Palestine program; funds poured in from all over Europe. The work won for him the deep affection of Easterners; scores of Churches, schismatic for centuries, returned to Rome allegiance. From a distance, he guided the Germanic princes in the election of

Rudolf; then he got Rudolf to agree that, as emperor, he had no jurisdiction over the papal states or southern Italy, which Gregory left in the hands of Charles of Anjou.

And then he turned his attention to the cardinals.

When he learned about all that had happened at Viterbo for almost three years, Gregory swore that never again would such an occasion arise. In the constitution he wrote for his reign, he gave strict instructions for future elections.

He ordered that when a pope died the cardinals in residence with him—usually the Curia—were to wait ten days to give others a chance to arrive for the election. All present were then to move into the papal palace and set up living facilities in one large room. Each cardinal was to be allowed one servant. No one was to be allowed to leave the room, except in the case of serious illness; no one was to be allowed in, unless all cardinals approved and the newcomer had something to do with the election—in which case everybody in the room was to be told his news. Cardinals arriving late could enter, however, provided their tardiness was caused by travel conditions.

No secret messages could be sent or received. The only item permitted to come from the outside was good food, which was to be passed into the room via the window. If nobody was elected in three days the food allowance was to be cut down to a single dish each morning and evening. After five days, the cardinals were to go on a diet of bread and water.

During the election period, no cardinal at the conclave could accept any revenue from any ecclesiastical source. No cardinal could conduct any business, Church or otherwise. Nothing was to be discussed in the room that wasn't pertinent to the election. Any voting agreements made before the conclave began were void, and if civil authorities exerted any pressure whatsoever upon the cardinals the election was illegal.

Gregory's rules were obviously a reprimand, meant to re-mind the cardinals that the election of a pope was a serious duty as well as a privilege. The cardinals did not like it at all.

VIII

$\mathcal{T}$he next pope was elected on the first ballot. This speed was undoubtedly due to the firm grip with which Gregory had ruled, a grip that held even after his death. Gregory showed his character clearly in yet another way. Soon after his consecration his relatives began writing him for favors, for appointments, for influence. Apparently they knew how generous previous popes had been to their families, and they thought it was now their turn. Gregory denied them all. At death, then, he left the papacy with a clean slate.

His successor, Innocent V, died a few months after taking office. It was just enough time for Gregory's impact to have faded, and when the cardinals met to elect the next pope they reverted to their old intrigues. They were in Rome, where Charles of Anjou was senator, and they began their conclave, as Gregory had prescribed, ten days after Innocent's death. Two weeks later they still had not chosen their new leader. Following Gregory's orders, Charles put the Cardinals on bread and water. They had not actually expected anybody to enforce Gregory's decrees; when Charles did, they were furious. Hunger soon overcame anger. In a few days they agreed on Cardinal Ottoboni Fieschi, the man who had successfully compromised to achieve the English peace. A brilliant diplomat, he was a worldly pope. As Hadrian V, he reigned only a matter of months, but in that time he surrounded himself with luxuries and enriched his relatives with countless benefices. Significantly, he also suspended Gregory's election laws.

Hadrian died at Viterbo, so it was there that the cardinals convened for the next election. Having gone through one long siege with the cardinals, the Viterbese wanted no nonsense this time. Although Gregory's rules had been suspended, the people applied them. Two weeks after starting the conclave the cardinals found themselves back on bread and water. They protested, but the Viterbese ignored the protests. There was nothing to do but elect someone. They elected Peter Juliani, a member of the Curia and the only Portuguese ever to be pope.

As John XXI, the new pope's first act was to repeal the Gregorian election rules. The people were scandalized; now it was obvious that neither the pope nor the cardinals were concerned with what the world thought of them. This was shown clearly the following year. John died on May 20, 1277. The new conclave began on schedule, but it was November before a successor was chosen. The Viterbese constrained themselves until the end of September, letting the cardinals move freely around the town, returning to their homes at night. Then the people cracked down. A day's session closed, the cardinals headed for the doors. The doors were locked. Outside, Viterbese surrounded the palace. The next day the cardinals elected Cardinal Giovanni Gaetani Orsini. It should now have been plain to the cardinals that some kind of control was necessary if they were to carry out their responsibilities with any efficiency, and yet nothing was done to achieve order.

The Orsinis were an old and powerful Roman family, with many of their members in high places in the Church. When the new pope (Nicholas III) died after a two-year reign, the Orsini cardinals tried to keep the papacy in the family. There were not enough of them to swing the election, but enough of them to block the election of anybody else. Again came the great delay. Six months passed with no progress. At last the Viterbese, correctly guessing what was going on, stormed the papal palace and carried off the two leading Orsini cardinals bodily. On the next ballot—or scrutiny, as it was called—the cardinals elected Cardinal Simon de Brion, a Frenchman more concerned with France than the Church.

Charles of Anjou was turning out to be a despot with peculiarly Gallic ferocity. The state of the Church in Rome depended entirely on how Charles got along with the pope. If there was friction, the Church felt it worse than Charles did. In his Sicilian kingdom, the predicament reached the extremes of revolution. He taxed excessively, he confiscated properties, he ignored complaints whether they came from the Church, the nobles, or the people. In time the situation was intolerable—and unfortunately it was a time when the French Martin IV was on the papal throne and practically in Charles's lap. Sicilian pleas for justice fell upon deaf papal ears. The people had no recourse except violence and revolution erupted in Sicily. Even in victory the rebels tried to remain loyal to the Church: they offered Martin the usual papal prerogatives in Sicily if only he would recognize the republic they established. He refused, and he threatened an interdict unless Charles was allowed to resume control of the country.

The Sicilians had to look elsewhere for help. Peter of Aragon had married Constance, the daughter of Manfred, and the Sicilians invited him to be their king if he would permit their republic to remain. He accepted. Indignant, Martin excommunicated Sicily and Aragon. Then he took the money which bishops were submitting to Rome for Gregory's Palestinian works and gave it to Charles to build up a new army to attack Sicily. Again the world was scandalized by papal misconduct. The feelings at Viterbo ran so high that Martin moved his headquarters to Perugia, and it was there he died suddenly in 1285.

Although they were in another city, the Cardinals didn't want to risk the uprisings that had made elections at Viterbo so troubled. On the second day of the conclave they elected as Honorius IV the old and crippled legate Cardinal Giacomo Savelli. Honorius followed in Martin's footsteps in backing Charles against the Sicilians. He supported a French army that tried to invade Sicily but failed. At approximately the same time Peter of Aragon and Charles of Anjou died. Peter's son claimed that Sicily was his; Charles's son was willing to concede the country and settle for his father's lands at Naples, but the Pope wouldn't hear of it. He continued to pour papal funds into French battalions. When Prince Edward of England pointed out that the money could better be used to support a crusade to save Palestinians the Pope said he was the one best qualified to decide that. His qualifications enabled him to leave the Church in astounding debt.

Sixteen cardinals convened in Rome upon his death in April, 1287. With Charles of Anjou dead and his son miles away at Naples, there was no one to lock the cardinals up. There seemed to be no reason to rush. Weeks passed. The city grew hot. From the suburban marshes came millions of mosquitoes, many of them malarial. Bubonic plague, which soon was to kill half the population of Europe, was beginning to appear. By mid-summer three of the cardinals were dead; before the next pope was elected seven cardinals had died.

Of the nine surviving cardinals, only one remained in Rome throughout the vacancy. He was Jerome Masci, cardinal-priest of Palestrina. His method of protecting his health was to have fires burning in his house in every room every day, no matter how hot the weather. Unaware that the dense smoke kept mosquitoes and rats out of the house, he thought the secret was in the fires themselves. Throughout the summer, he wrote the cardinals who had gone to the mountains, suggesting that if they did not want to hold the conclave in Rome they could meet in some cooler place. The summer passed with letters circulating among the cardinals on the subject. It was November before they could agree that since the summer heat was over they might as well meet in Rome. Since Masci was the only cardinal who had done any work all year, he was unanimously elected on the first scrutiny.

Clever though Nicholas IV had been against mosquitoes and rats, he failed to display equal intelligence in papal affairs. He was interested in art and spent most of his time collecting it for the Vatican galleries, and this was something to his credit. He had been a Franciscan monk at one time and now encouraged Franciscans to go to the mission field of the Far East, which was another credit. But he adhered to his predecessor's policy of opposing the Sicilians, and this proved to be a serious mistake. Despite the satisfaction of Sicilians under the Aragon crown, Nicholas tried to get the French to attack Aragon in hopes of breaking up the royal family, but the French couldn't because they were on the verge of their Hundred Years War with the British. When the English made a peace pact with the Aragonese head of Sicily, Nicholas annulled it, and this annoyed the

English. And with the College of Cardinals he straddled a wobbly fence. Instead of breaking up the factions that kept the College at odds, he appointed six cardinals, one to each faction, by which he achieved nothing.

It was no wonder, then, that after his death the Church should go two years, three months and two days without a pope. There were then twelve cardinals, six of them Romans, two French, four from various parts of Italy. They were hopelessly divided on every problem that faced the Church. Some of them wanted to see the son of Charles of Anjou—King Charles of Naples—regain the Sicilian throne. Others favored the Aragonese, and it was said they were even in the pay of the Aragonese. Some wanted to break with France. Adolf of Nassau had succeeded Rudolf of Hapsburg as emperor, and a few cardinals wanted to see some action from him. The Orsini faction planned to put one of its own on the throne; the Colonna faction had similar plans for its clique. And there were others who had designs of their own. Thus there were factions within factions and factions within those.

The interregnum had its usual effect. With no ruler, Rome and the patrimony became lawless. Vice of all kinds broke out; robbery and murder were frequent. With no one to enforce order there was no one to apply law, so nobody feared punishment for his crimes. Cardinal Latinus of Ostia urged promptness in the election so that the streets would be safe again. The other cardinals agreed the matter was urgent, then proceeded to stall as they made bargains, deals and compromises among themselves.

There lived at that time in the Neapolitan mountains a monk named Peter, who for most of his life had been a hermit. His privacy was often disturbed, however, by people who sought his advice. An uneducated man, he nevertheless possessed a certain wisdom in moral and spiritual matters. Every day he left his mountain retreat for a few hours to consult with the troubled persons who climbed the hills to see him. Men who wished to emulate him had also moved into the mountains. With time, he acquired a large number of disciples who looked to him as their leader. He was well known in the surrounding villages, and there were stories that he had performed miracles. King Charles of Naples occasionally sent him money and asked for prayers in return and came to look upon himself as Peter's protector. A humble and saintly priest, Peter wanted only to be left alone; he saw people simply because he felt he ought to, particularly since they seemed to feel he did them some good.

After the papal throne had been vacant for over two years, the cardinals agreed to meet at Perugia for some serious efforts to fill it, but immediately they were at their wrangling and there was slim hope of success. One afternoon several of the cardinals were sitting together chatting when Cardinal Latinus commented that he had received a letter from a holy monk saying that God had revealed to him that the cardinals would be punished if they did not elect a pope soon. Amused, Cardinal Gaetani asked if the monk was Peter del Murrone. Latinus said it was indeed. The cardinals began to talk about Peter, about his miracles, and of the peaceful life he must be enjoying up there in the mountains.

Then quite suddenly Latinus stood up and shouted, "In the name of the Father and the Son and the Holy Ghost, I elect Brother Peter del Murrone!"

There was a stunned silence for a moment, then five other cardinals cried out that they elected Peter too. Another cardinal entered the room at this moment and heard the shouts and added his own; Peter had seven votes. The Cardinal of Milan was ill in his room, being visited by two others. One of the men who had already voted for Peter hurried across to them and gave the news. Struck by the excitement, all three voted for Peter. Now he had ten votes; he was in. The remaining two votes for unanimity came as fast as the absent cardinals heard the news.

When Peter heard the news three days later he said, "Me?" And he fled up the mountain and hid in his cave.

He refused to come out. Even when a committee of bishops came to give him the news officially he withdrew deeper in his cave and told them to go away. The cardinals themselves had to go to the mountain, huffing and puffing their way up, and order Peter to come out.

He was terrified of them. Never in his life had he been in such elite company. He knelt in their midst and begged them to elect somebody else, repeatedly assuring them that he was incapable of so important a position, that he had no training in such complex administration, that he would certainly make a mess of things. The cardinals told him not to worry. The had been inspired by God to choose him. They would guide him through the troubles ahead. Some of them were planning exactly that: the frightened, trembling, meek, befuddled Peter looked like a bit of a boob.

King Charles himself showed up. With him, Peter felt safer. He confided his reluctance to the King, revealing that he knew what kind of men the cardinals were and that he would never be able to stand up against them. Charles comforted him, promising his personal protection, suggesting that if Peter didn't want to go to Rome he could transfer the Vatican to Naples where the King could keep an eye on things.

His mind eased, Peter accepted the decision of the cardinals. He told them, however, that he was too old for anything hasty; he wanted to spend a few days meditating at a valley monastery he had built with his own hands. When he was ready to be consecrated he would let them know. Satisfied, the cardinals returned to Rome.

Meditation convinced Peter that Rome was no place for

him. Leaving the monastery, he went to the Neapolitan city of Aquila and he wrote the cardinals that if they still wanted to consecrate him they could come there and do it. King Charles was ecstatic. The cardinals were appalled. Aquila was not within the papal patrimony; to consecrate a pope in what amounted to a foreign land was extremely ticklish, especially when that land was the kingdom of Naples which was, to many cardinals, enemy land. To the world, a consecration at Aquila would give the impression that the Church was favoring the Naples kingdom—an unwelcome impression in many places. The cardinals wrote Peter that if he didn't want to come to Rome why not choose Perugia as the site of his consecration. He replied that if they wanted to get done with this business they'd better come down to Aquila or they could just forget the whole thing. Peter was consecrated Pope Celestine V in the Aquila cathedral in August, 1294.

The Cardinals waited impatiently for Celestine to make the trip to Rome. After his consecration he said he wanted a little more time alone in a monastery. When he returned to the cardinals he had an announcement that shook them severely: he wasn't ready to go to Rome just yet, but he would set up Church headquarters at Naples for a while. They were to bring to him whatever business they wanted him to conduct.

Petulant though Celestine might have appeared, he was actually afraid. He had no experience in world affairs, no vital preliminary training in the cardinalate at Rome. The mere idea that he was on the same level with kings—perhaps a little above them—terrified him. He did not know Latin; he was unable to converse with cardinals who did not speak his Neapolitan dialect; how in the world could he be expected to govern Rome, the Church, the universe of Catholics? His limitations embarrassed him. He was a most unhappy man. Though pope, he continued to live like a monk. In Naples, the King gave him a beautiful palace overlooking the bay, but he was so uncomfortable in it that he ordered an ordinary wood hut to be built for him in a corner of the garden and he lived there. He ate once a day: dry bread and a cup of wine. And he paced the room as he ate so that he would be merely partaking of necessary nourishment and not enjoying a meal. Many times important cardinals cooled their heels outside while Celestine and two of his monks recited their prayers.

He did not trust himself to make decisions. He suggested to Cardinal Matteo Orsini that he appoint three cardinals to run the Church for him, but the Cardinal said this was impossible because the world would think "the Holy Spouse (Church) had three husbands instead of one." Celestine knew he had few friends among the cardinals, so when he needed advice he turned to the man of Naples he had known longest: the King. Charles was far from an impartial adviser. For a long time Charles had been trying to work out a peace treaty with James of Aragon, ruler of Sicily, and the one he submitted to Celestine for approval was greatly to Charles's benefit. The Aragonese-backed cardinals were outraged when Celestine signed it. James accepted it because, although he was obliged to make a large payment to Charles, at least Sicily was his and the fighting would stop.

At Charles's advice, Celestine wrote to foreign bishops for money for the Crusade Pope Nicholas IV had ordered, and when the money arrived most of it was earmarked to remain in Naples to supply the Crusade.

Charles's influence was most surprising when Celestine appointed twelve cardinals all at once. Seven of them were French—Charles was French—and of the five Italians two worked for Charles as his counselor and chancellor. Of the remaining three, two were members of Celestine's monastic

Order and the third was a native of Naples. With these plus the few cardinals who already favored Charles, the College was stacked.

Then Celestine did the most amazing thing of his short career. He decreed that the papal-election regulations established by Gregory X and revoked by John XXI were again enforced. The astonished cardinals turned as red as their hats. King Charles reminded Celestine that Gregory's regulations had been repealed. Celestine added a postscript to his decree: now reinforced, the regulations would remain applicable forever.

Celestine's problem with the cardinals was that they awed him. Whether they came to see him alone or in groups he lost his voice in their presence. He knew perfectly well most of them were crooked, but he could not bring himself to say so. The old guard, which had so strangely elected him, was the worst of the lot. Papal bulls were—and are—the personal edicts of popes; they might pertain to excommunications, absolutions, privileges to certain countries and hierarchies, statements on particular matters, transfer of properties, taxes, payments of funds, gifts, awards, etc. While Celestine brooded in his hut, lonely for his mountain cave, the Curia cardinals were selling blank bulls, forged and seal-stamped, and the buyers could write in anything they wanted. Celestine was aware of these machinations, but he had no idea how to stop them. The thought of punishing the cardinals could never enter his mind. He could not punish anyone. Persons or places punished by previous popes were forgiven by him. He wanted peace and harmony for everyone, which was fine in a saint but weak in a thirteenth century pope.

He had to get out. After three months in office he was looking for ways to do it. The only book he owned outside of his prayer volumes was a thin collection on canon law. Studying it, he found that bishops and abbots could resign—

because they had a superior to accept their resignations: the popes. Who could accept a pope's resignation? He asked the monks with him. They didn't know, but they felt there ought to be some way to work it.

He talked to Cardinal Gaetani. Gaetani was later described as "the wisest and most upright of the cardinals," and assuming this was true he must have felt sorry indeed for the old man who was so lost in a world he didn't understand . . . or perhaps understood too well. Gaetani said yes, a resignation was possible, but he advised against it: the people might be scandalized and now was a bad time for something like that. Celestine said things might only be worse if he stayed. When the word got around to the other cardinals they too tried to discourage the Pope from quitting, each for his own reason, and when Celestine refused to be diverted they discussed the legality of his decision. Celestine's own monks did not want to lose the honors which his election had brought to the Order. They went among the people, stirring them up, and one day a huge crowd gathered outside the palace, singing hymns, reciting litanies, calling to Celestine not to resign.

On the morning of December 13, all the cardinals were summoned to the great hall of the palace. They entered in a group. There on the throne, fully dressed in all his pontifical robes, sat Celestine. He waited until the cardinals were gathered in front of him; then he began to read his resignation in a loud firm voice. A cardinal tried to interrupt, but Celestine silenced him with a glance. Finished, Celestine stood and began to disrobe, removing the beautiful garments one by one until he stood before the cardinals only in the long white alb. The cardinals watched him silently, some with quiet incredulity, some in soft amazement, some in tears. He left the room for a moment and when he returned he was dressed in the simple robe of a monk. He went to the throne, bowed to it, then sat on the lowest step.

He said, "Behold, my brothers, I have resigned from the honor of the papacy, and now I implore you by the Blood of Jesus and by His Holy Mother quickly to provide for the Church a man who will be useful for it, for the whole human race, and for the Holy Land."

As yet they were not sure that all this could be done. Cardinal Matteo Orsini suggested that Celestine decree that it was possible for a pope to resign. He did, the document was prepared, and he signed it. He was Peter again.

Ten days later the cardinals elected Cardinal Gaetani to be Pope Boniface VIII. This wise and upright man was worried about Peter. After paying homage to Boniface by kissing his foot, Peter said he would like to return to his cave. Boniface knew many people still opposed Peter's resignation, and he was afraid these people might rally to Peter and thus start a schism. He asked Peter to stay around for a while. Though no longer pope, Peter received deference wherever he went; he was discomfited by it. Also, he heard rumors that Boniface planned to make a palace prisoner of him to prevent a change of heart that might erupt in a schism. Disturbed, Peter left Naples without a word to Boniface and returned to the mountains.

Boniface took Peter's flight as a danger signal and sent troops to fetch him. Warned by villagers, Peter made his way to the sea and boarded a ship bound for Greece. Bad storms forced the ship back and Peter was captured. Told why he was taken prisoner, he said, "Far be it from me to cause dissension in the Church. I did not give up the papacy to take it back again, and I am still of the same mind, come what may."

He was sent to a fortress at Fumone and consigned to a small room on the top floor. He was allowed no visitors, except two monks to share in his prayers. The room was so tiny that the monks couldn't stand the tight quarters and had to be replaced. Peter said, "I have longed for a cell and a cell I have got." Ten months later he died there. Ten years later he was canonized.

2

Pope Boniface VIII ennobled the cardinalate further by awarding the red cassock as well as the red hat. This was his way of expressing what he considered the unchallengeable dignity of the high Church officials. Among the fourteen upon whom he bestowed the dignity were three of his nephews, a cousin, and several adherents to the Orsini faction of which he was a member.

It was Boniface's ill luck to be pope at a time when Europe was growing up. Nationalism had taken root. Men who ruled wanted more to say in their own domains. A resentment gradually appeared against the rights of popes to intrude in local affairs. Actually the rights were questionable, evolving out of the old idea that the head of the state was the head of the religion and the subsequent partnership of the Holy Roman Empire. The extent to which the rights were applied depended on each pope himself. Most popes discovered that the less they had to do with political matters the better off they were. But by now many princes of the Church were also princes of the realm, and this meant a hopeless involvement in both. Also, some popes—Boniface among them —figured that God owned the world, the head of the Church was God's vicar on earth, therefore the Church ranked higher than any political division, and all political divisions were subject to the Church. As neat as such reasoning was, it was not entirely proper. By custom, however, it was generally practiced.

The test case came from France, where Philip the Fair was king. Impoverished by wars, he sought to raise money by

additional taxes on the clergy. Nearly a hundred years earlier an agreement had been reached that no ruler could tax
any of the local clergy without the permission of the popes;
Philip disregarded the agreement. When Boniface criticized
him for it he reacted by declaring that not only did he have
the right to tax the clergy, who had received so many benefits from the government, but henceforth any clergyman who
broke civil laws would be adjudged by government courts
instead of ecclesiastical tribunals. This was another outright
violation of an old agreement. Boniface issued two bulls
condemning Philip's conduct, to which Philip responded
with a letter that began:

"Philip, by the grace of God King of France, to Boniface,
who calls himself pope, few or no greetings. It is important
that your great stupidity know that we are not subject to
your person in matters pertaining to the temporal order."

Rude, it was nevertheless right. But Boniface, with his
exalted opinion of his own position, said: "God has set us
over kings, to build, plant, weed and destroy." The exchange
became bitter and more vitriolic with each day. Philip was
soon accusing Boniface of atheism, heresy, and the murder
of Celestine. The Pope took steps to excommunicate the
King. Boldly, Philip sent troops to the Pope's summer house
at Anagni, and when they burst into the throne room they
found Boniface sitting there, ready for them, fully robed in
his pontificals. He rose and shouted at them: "Here is my
neck, here is my head!" His own awesome dignity prevented
them from killing him. They held him prisoner for three
days, until Cardinal Nicholas Boccasini arrived with four
hundred Roman soldiers who routed the French. Now Boniface was set for full attack against Philip, and he was kept
from it only by sudden illness which in a few months caused
his death.

The cardinals were torn between revenge and fear. Not
for centuries had the Church been so insulted as it was by

Philip's troops, and if a man dared assault the papacy as Philip had there was no telling where he would stop. In electing Cardinal Boccasini to succeed Boniface the cardinals hoped they had chosen a man who could handle the situation with both force and tact. As Benedict XI, the new pope displayed a strange blend of both traits. First he condemned all those who had taken part in the Anagni affair, then he forgave them. Some cardinals felt the forgiveness should have been tempered with a severe penance, and thus when Benedict died mysteriously after a year as pope there were suspicions that a clique of cardinals had done away with him.

3

Whatever influence the clique possessed faded in the election of the archbishop of Bordeaux as Clement V. He was not present at the Perugia conclave that elected him, which gave the impression that he was a compromise choice. Bordeaux, although part of France, was then in the hands of the English; thus Clement was French but not under French domination. At any rate, he refused to become a Roman by moving there. Notified of his election, he announced that he would be consecrated at Lyons and the College of Cardinals had to go there.

With Clement, the papacy left Rome for almost seventy years. The new pope was a friend of Philip the Fair, and when the King suggested that it might not be safe for a Frenchman to try to rule the Church from Rome Clement settled down at Avignon. This too was a compromise. Situated in southeastern France, Avignon belonged to the Kingdom of Naples and bordered on the papal state of Venaissin. The compromise, then, became a three-way split: the Church was existing under the protection of France, with headquarters munificently provided by Neapolitans within walking distance of Church property.

Clement's reign in Avignon opened what became known as the Babylonian Captivity of the Church. There were indications that he intended to move the Church back to Rome some day, but he never did. A clue to his inclinations might well have been in the fact that of the twenty-four cardinals he created between 1305 and 1314, twenty-three were French. It seemed that the Church of Rome had become the Church of France. During the Avignon residence of seven French popes, 113 of the 134 cardinals created were French.

The Church virtually was a nationalized institution, and therefore it was not surprising that abuses should appear. When Clement died there were over a million gold florin in the treasury. The cardinals wrangled for two years to select the next pope, John XXII, and when he examined the treasury he found only seventy thousand florin. The culprits were the Curial cardinals. To be sure, the Church was cut off from its patrimonial income and financially suffered greatly because of this, but nevertheless regular maintenance expenses were not so enormous that so much money should have disappeared. Some of it went to support propaganda campaigns against Church enemies, and there were a lot of enemies. But undoubtedly most of the missing money filtered through the ranks of the cardinalate to friends and relatives. There were kickbacks. Without the leadership of a pope, in full control, the cardinals were accountable to no one. They sold benefices and privileges wholesale. During this period one man was able to have himself made bishop of eight different dioceses at the same time, and with each benefice the cardinal who arranged the acquisition was well rewarded.

Contributing to the chaos was a series of weak popes. Clement got himself involved in a fight between Philip the Fair and the Knights Templars. The Knights had been organized in Palestine as military guards of holy places there.

Forced out by the failures of the Crusades, they set themselves up in Europe as guardians of monasteries and in this
position received control of large amounts of money. Philip
wanted the money. To get it, he accused the Knights of
heresy, simony and homosexuality and drew confessions
from them by savage torture. Though the confessions were
subsequently withdrawn and the Knights swore innocence
to the Pope he nevertheless disbanded them, weakening his
defenses still further.

The next Avignon pope, John XXII, was so inept a theologian that he proclaimed that the dead were not immediately
judged by God and given their just rewards but that they
had to wait until the end of the world for the judgment.
Catholics everywhere roared their resentment at the obvious
heresy, and John modified his statement by saying it was his
private opinion and was not to be accepted by others as an
article of faith. Before he died, he changed his mind completely.

So allied with France and French Naples, it was inescapable that the Church should suffer in its relations with Germany, England, Spain and Ireland. In Rome the Church
was represented by a committee of cardinals who had little
authority, and the Romans were annoyed that their bishops,
the popes, gave so little attention to their city. The situation
grew entirely hopeless when Pope Clement VI (1342-1352)
bought Avignon from the Naples rulers and built a gorgeous
palace. Papal families literally took over the Church. In
such hands it was scarcely possible that the Church could
produce any men of note. Strength, so necessary, came instead from women.

The most outstanding woman was Catherine of Siena, a
Dominican nun, one of the most remarkable figures of the
Church. Of low birth and uneducated, she was probably the
only woman outside of royalty ever to push a pope around.
Unable to write, she dictated long letters to the Avignon

popes, urging them back to Rome. She went to Avignon where, ignoring protocol, she made her way to the popes, assuring them that each day they remained out of Rome was another wound from which the Church might not recover. She cared nothing for politics, only for souls, and she warned the popes that they would be responsible before God for any souls lost by the vacuum their absence from Rome created.

Due to her, Urban V actually visited Rome briefly. But the Orsinis and the Romans were fighting; the city's population had dropped to 10,000; there was poverty, the plague, and crime everywhere. Urban went back to Avignon.

There was another problem. With Rome in decline, business moved to Florence. Florentine bankers wanted to keep Rome down; they had designs on the lush province of Tuscany and they sought some means of freeing the country from French domination without giving the Church a chance to restore Rome. French-influenced Gregory XI, convinced by Catherine that he should return to Rome, found the way blocked by the Florentines. He placed Florence under interdict. Catherine argued that this was a foolish thing to do. Bewildered, the Pope appointed her papal legate to Florence with the hope of working out something else. The amazing power of Catherine was evidenced in the fact that, despite great pressure from the French and the cardinals to remain at Avignon, she actually did get Gregory to move back to Rome and she arranged an armistice council at Florence at which a peace was to be worked out.

Gregory was in Rome only a short time when he died. For the first time in seventy years, a conclave was held there. Incensed Romans stormed the Vatican, shouting, "Elect an Italian or you die!"

Terror-stricken, the cardinals didn't know what to do. Of the sixteen at the conclave, four were Italians. The majority being French, they preferred a Frenchman, but they knew

what would happen to them if they chose one. As a compromise, they went outside their own group and picked Barthol-
omew Prignano, the Archbishop of Bari, an Italian in that he
was a native of Naples but a Francophile because he was
Neapolitan.

The cardinals had just agreed when Romans broke into
the conclave and wanted to know who was being favored.
Stunned and afraid, the cardinals grabbed Cardinal Tibald-
eschi, an elderly Roman, and pushed him onto the throne,
saying "Him."

The calmed Romans departed, and when they were gone
the cardinals had to decide what to do next. They waited a
day, then sent out an announcement that a mistake had been
made: they were electing Prignano. At least he was an Italian; the Romans were satisfied. The Florentines weren't sure.

As Urban VI, the new pope turned out to be a wild man.
There were some doubts that he was completely sane. He
whipped out at the cardinals until none of them dared enter
his presence. He swore to end the French influence, which
he did by appointing a majority of Italian cardinals. He
tossed bishops out of their dioceses as if they were pawns. He
refused to see delegations from countries or duchies he disliked. It was impossible to reason with him; it was impossible
even to talk to him. Catherine of Siena wrote him: "Those
devils in human form have made an election. They have not
elected a vicar of Christ but an anti-Christ!"

And yet when the crisis came she stood by him.

Within weeks after Urban's consecration, the cardinals
who had put him on the throne began to leave town. Dissension was deep and irreparable. Urban had been pope for
about five months when the irked cardinals met at Fondi
and proclaimed that his election was illegal because it had
been forced upon them by the riotous Romans. This wasn't
true, but it was an excuse to depose him. Declaring him
deposed, they elected the French Cardinal Robert, Count of

Geneva, to replace him. If they expected this to be enough to send Urban packing they were unrealistic. When he refused to give up his throne, the insurgent cardinals with their pope went off to Avignon.

The Catholic world took sides. France, Scotland, Naples and Spain went over to the antipope, Clement VII. Italy, England, Poland, Hungary and the Empire supported Urban. Knowing the details of Urban's election and confident that the election was valid, Catherine sided with Urban though she couldn't stand him.

Never in Western history had the Church been in such a mess, and it was a mess that was to last forty years. In that period, Rome had four popes, all claiming *bona fide* election. Avignon had two bishops, two tax bills were sent to the same ecclesiastic divisions, and the two bishops tried to impose their plans upon the European rulers.

Affairs worsened when, in 1409, cardinals in Rome and at Avignon called a council in Pisa for the purpose of determining which pope should actually head the Church. Both reigning popes—Gregory XII in Rome and Benedict XIII at Avignon—agreed to attend the council but neither did. The cardinals then went ahead and elected their own pope, Alexander V. When he died they elected another pope they called John XXIII. Five hundred years later, when Cardinal Roncalli of Venice was elected pope in 1958 he felt free to take the name of John XXIII on the grounds that the first holder of the title had been the Pisan antipope.

In the absence of consolidated spiritual authority, heresy was a constant threat. Theological discipline, which had held the Church together for 1400 years, could not be exerted as a single force when there were three popes competing for jurisdiction. Church division was to take its toll: a world deprived of spiritual leadership was ripe for spiritual multiplicity.

There lived in the fourteenth century an English Franciscan called William of Ockham, described by some as the first Protestant. In the theological realm, William was completely opposite Thomas Aquinas. Aquinas maintained that theological tenets such as immorality, the existence of God, and the existence of the soul could be explained by logic and reason in terms comprehensible to the human intellect. William said these were beyond the human mind's grasp and that salvation depended on vague intuitive convictions he defined as faith. In this, William gave far more credit to conscience than conscience deserved, far more honor to animal instincts than animal instincts deserved. The end result of William's ideas was to devalue the Church as interpreter and protector of theology and to exaggerate the individual's right and ability to make private judgments. In an era marked with prideful nationalism and egocentric individuality, Ockhamism won many followers. Summoned to Avignon, Ockham was imprisoned, but his ideas already had a reckless freedom.

On Ockham's heels came John Wyclif, another Englishman, who believed that the Church, guided by Christ, didn't need any hierarchal leadership at all. Popes weren't necessary. Any decisions that had to be made could be made at councils, which by their representations were superior to papal decrees. Wyclif's disciples, who like him believed in predestination, wanted laymen included in the councils. Wyclif, on the basis of his predestination convictions, said the Sacraments were worthless, confession of sins superfluous, and that Holy Communion involved only the moral presence of Jesus—not the actual—in the substances of bread and wine. Most of Wyclif's ideas were picked up by John Huss, a Czech priest, who spread them through Central Europe. Huss became a factor in the pre-Reformation period due to a disagreement with Pisan Pope John XXIII.

The antipope was having troubles with the Kingdom of Naples, and to marshal an army he offered indulgences to anybody who would fight for him. This was unquestionably an abuse of indulgences. Simplified, an indulgence was—and is—a period of time, in purely relative terms, subtractable from the purgatorial punishment required for sins already forgiven and was earned by special prayers, visitations and pious acts. For centuries popes had granted indulgences in return for various spiritual demonstrations, but since the Church was in such disparate shape at this particular time it was inevitable that somebody would abuse indulgences by putting a price tag on them or granting them in return for support.

Huss's first complaint was based on his belief in predestination. If the future in Heaven or Hell of each person was already determined, then indulgences in any guise were fraudulent. Why say or do anything to hasten your entrance into Heaven if you were already doomed to Hell? Using this as a starter, Huss sent broadsides to all the popes, wherever they were.

Divided from within and besieged by Huss from without, the Church was facing a terrible crisis. The only hope lay with Emperor-elect Sigismund, since by tradition the emperor was to rule the Church in the event of a long vacancy. Previous emperors had not been called upon during the election battles among cardinals, but the situation now was more serious than that. Expecting favorable treatment from Sigismund, John XXIII turned to him for help. Sigismund called a council at Constance. John went; the pope in Rome and the pope in Avignon sent cardinal representatives.

Actually, the Constance council was illegal because only the pope could call such an assembly, and the Pope—the one in Rome—hadn't. Nevertheless there was a tacit agreement among several popes to accept its decision. John soon detected that he didn't rate as high as he thought, and he left. The council ruled that all three men should dismiss their claims to the papacy and that a new pope should be elected. Gregory XII in Rome renounced his claim, but John and Benedict XIII refused. John eventually accepted his deposition by the council. Benedict did not, but as a result of the council all but three of his cardinals left him. Without support, there was nothing he could do.

The council elected Cardinal Oddone Colonna, of the important Roman family, who took the name Martin V. The council also denounced John Huss and turned him over to the civil authorities. During his trial he recanted and would have been freed, but he was then charged with heresies he had not preached and therefore, he said, could not discard. He was burned at the stake. Most of his followers eventually withdrew from the heretical teachings, but there were some who didn't. Seeking safety, they made for the Alps, and there they encountered the Waldenses, the French heretics who had taken refuge in the mountains three hundred years earlier, and the two groups settled down together.

Pope Martin was in an awkward position. He had been elected by the Constance council, a council which declared itself to be superior to popes, and now he was expected to approve the decisions of the council. Doing so, he would have placed all subsequent popes in the position of being subordinate to councils; instead of being the supreme authority of the Church the popes would have become something like chairmen of the board. Aware of this, Martin repeatedly postponed signing the minutes of the council until they were rewritten in a tone that did not reflect the council's self-exalted superiority. They required him to call further councils at regular periods. The next one was scheduled for 1423, and only a fatal attack of the plague saved him from having to face it.

To Pope Eugene IV therefore fell the delicate task of permitting a council in 1439. To test his personal strength, Eugene transferred the site of the council from Basel to Ferrara. Only one cardinal and four bishops refused to go to Ferrara and there was a brief schism. At Ferrara, Eugene enjoyed complete success, brought on by the unexpected arrival of the Eastern Emperor John VII who, accompanied by an impressive entourage of Eastern bishops, announced that the Constantinople church wanted to return to Rome and submit itself to the popes. The gesture enormously enhanced the papacy; nobody at the council was moved to diminish the glory of the moment by insisting on the powers of the council over the popes. The great schism was over and the papacy at Rome was restored.

Beneath the triumphs, however, lurked new dangers. On becoming pope, Eugene faced violent opposition from the Colonna family which, having recaptured the papacy by the election of Martin, disliked losing out so soon by the election of the next pope. To hold off the Colonnas, Eugene had to turn to Florence for help. The most important family in Florence was the Medici. The Medici didn't do anything for anybody without getting something in return: now they wanted a few cardinals in the family. In Spain, an important family was the Borgias. One of them, Alfonso Borgia, had already risen in the Church. Avignon Antipope Benedict XIII had made him a canon, but when the Church was reestablished at Rome Alfonso turned to it and later refused to attend the council at Basel called by the short-lived schism against Eugene. For this, Eugene made him a cardinal and appointed him to the Curia. And in Saxony, in the village of Eisleben, was another family—not very important at the time but marked by destiny. It was the Luther family, and they were soon to have a son. They would name him Martin.

IX

*I*t is said that Napoleon Bonaparte, so often at odds with the Vatican, once told a cardinal, "The Church is my enemy. I will destroy her." The cardinal replied, "I don't think you will. We cardinals have been trying to destroy her for centuries and haven't been able to do it."

Apocryphal or not, the story contains a sad truth. No heresy, no schism, no lay intruder did as much harm to the Church through the centuries as many cardinals. They were like company vice presidents suspicious of each other because all were competing for the presidency. To strengthen their own positions, they formed factions and cliques in and out of the Church. They stopped at nothing to make their personal power felt wherever they could. Some of them, whatever their conduct, undoubtedly felt they were acting for the good of the Church; but unquestionably most of them acted for the good of themselves. Fortunately, most cardinals when they became popes ceased these activities, aware that they no longer had reasons to connive, aware too that they now had to keep all the other cardinals in line.

One reason for this situation was that the ordinary common man had small chance to reach ecclesiastical heights. In Rome, the Church was for years controlled by noble families who kept the city in endless civil war. Outside Rome the nobility likewise ran the Church, but with less chaos because the European thrones were more secure and there was a slower turnover.

There was another factor, in addition to class, that shared responsibility for producing the existing situation both in and out of Rome. That was the availability of education. In medieval Europe, education was a luxury possible only to the rich. The poor merely served apprenticeships to learn an occupation. Even so, practically everybody of noble birth who learned more than how to read and write was destined for the Church, by his own inclination or his family's. The existing schools were in monasteries or Church-sponsored universities, and the curriculum was almost entirely ecclesiastic. The student bodies were always small: only the rich or men already in the Church could afford the time for higher schooling. Thus it was inevitable that most of the educated men who rose to high positions in the Church should come from noble families with backgrounds steeped in the political intrigue which flourished at the time, and since the majority of such men were practically consigned to the Church by their wealthy families as though the Church were a family holding, it should be no surprise that they used the Church for family profit. This explains why so many of the early popes were related to each other, and such close family ties were even more prevalent among cardinals, arch-bishops, bishops and abbots throughout Europe.

Even worse was the fact that educated men comprised a tiny portion of the clergy. There were two ways of life open to priests: in monasteries or out among the people. Those in monasteries, devoted to prayer, meditation and study, had more of a chance to adhere to their vows—unless they had an abbot who allowed them to grow lax in their spiritual duties, which sometimes happened. Separated from the world, the monks used their knowledge mostly to train future monks, and thus they had little intellectual influence on the surrounding communities unless they had facilities to take in a deserving local boy for a few years. Therefore, important though monks were in preserving knowledge, they did not do much to disseminate it.

Secular priests—those who worked among the people and under the bishop's jurisdiction—were in a more demanding position. The young man who felt called to the priesthood, whose family thought he was called, or who simply chose it as a livelihood, did his studies under his local curate, a man who had become a priest the same way. Often the length of studies depended on the young man's intelligence more than his spirituality. If he proved outstanding, he might come to the attention of his bishop and be sent to a university, but this was rare. It was, then, up to the local curate to decide when the applicant was ready to pass through minor orders to the priesthood, a circumstance that sent many young priests to their altars with shaky spiritual foundations and skimpy theological knowledge. It was amazing that more of them didn't preach heresies; it was astounding that more of them didn't break their vows.

The Church had some security in the friendship of kings, but it was a wavering security because kings died and were replaced. Therefore it was not as valuable as the internal strength that came from good priests, for when the priests were good the people were. Realizing the need for this internal strength, various popes acted to improve the clergy. The twenty-four-year age minimum was intended to guarantee a maturity in new priests. The theologians appointed to cathedrals were there as advisors to the priests as well as the people. Lay groups, like Milan's Pataria, received Vatican cooperation because they aimed at keeping the clergy in line. And papal envoys who worked against abuses among the hierarchy gave equal attention to the country priests who, isolated and unguided, faced the risk of moral decay. Yet all this was not enough. The best assurances for a good priesthood could come only in the training period. Even in the fifteenth century the Church was too big and unwieldy an organization for the men at the top to keep their eyes on all the men entering at the bottom. Periodically, some kind of reform became necessary.

Reform of the priesthood occurred during the reign of Eugene IV (1431-1447), who established the Church's first seminary for secular priests, at Florence. From then on, all men preparing for the Florence secular clergy had to enter the seminary where, for a specified number of years, they studied, prayed, meditated and, in general, equipped themselves for the tasks ahead. This was the turning point for the priesthood. In the years that followed, other seminaries were opened throughout Europe. Their importance could not be exaggerated. More than anything the Church needed an enlightened clergy, since it was from such priests that enlightenment would pass to the people. With the coming of the Renaissance, the Industrial Revolution, and political revolutions such enlightenment was increasingly vital: as society moved toward new ways, there was a good deal of turning against established authority, and it was natural that many people should also turn against the Church. Some did so, violently. That the Church survived the upheavals as well as it did was directly attributable to the increase in spiritual enlightenment that preceded the social and economic upheavals. The enlightenment endured and was subsequently enhanced by those churchmen closest to the people, their priests.

It was ironic that Florence, the city that gave the Catholic world its first diocesan seminary, should also have given the Church one of its worst influences: the Medici.

2

The election of Pope Nicholas V (1447-1455) was evidence of the Medici influence on Rome. Born Thomas Parentucelli, he took two years off from his studies at the University of Bologna to tutor the children of the prominent Florence banking family, and from them he acquired a taste for luxury he never lost. Upon ordination he immediately became personal assistant to the bishop of Bologna, and eventually succeeded the bishop in 1444. In 1446 he was made a cardinal, and two and a half months later he was elected pope. Significantly, he never broke his contacts in Florence, returning there often on Church business or for visits. Also, he was not the popular choice at the conclave that elected him. Once again the Orsinis and the Colonnas competed to get their own men through, but when the third scrutiny ended in a deadlock the majority of the cardinals turned to Parentucelli as a compromise. His election so surprised other cardinals that they demanded to see the ballots to find out who had voted for him. Those who knew of his friendship with the Medici weren't sure whether or not to be relieved that the new pope was at least free of any Roman entanglements.

The Medici family had begun to rise in financial influ-

ence in the mid-fourteenth century, when Giovanni di Bicci
di Medici became the leading merchant-banker of Florence.
As such, he had more power than kings. As the result of
several wars with surrounding principalities, Florence became
a city-state with the Medici in control. Enormously rich, the
Medici made Florence the heart of the Italian Renaissance,
attracting men like Michelangelo, da Vinci, Raphael, Dona-
tello, Fra Angelico, Lippi, Cellini, Bernini, Dante and many
others. Most of them derived their income from commis-
sions by the Medici. The Medici reign at first was tolerant
enough and within the city's democratic constitution, but
the Medici remained benign only as long as they got their
own way; when opposition arose, even within the family,
they resorted to trickery, bribery, persecution, blackmail
and murder. They were able to control Florence even when
they did not hold public office, and they had a similar influence in the Church.

There was almost nothing in the world they couldn't buy.
They literally bought Florence, and they came near buying
the Church (they produced three popes and a string of
cardinals); they bought creative genius, they bought politicians, and those politicians they could not buy they paid
others to eliminate. Three times during their two-century
control of Florence they were chased out of the city, only to
be welcomed back. Their presence meant profits and glory
for the city. Furthermore, each time they returned they
promised to behave, and they did—as long as things went
their way.

The election of Nicholas V was definitely in their favor.

One of the cardinals who voted for Nicholas was Alfonso
de Borgia, cardinal-archbishop of Valencia, who had received his red hat ostensibly because he refused to side with
the schismatic popes at Avignon after the Church had returned to Rome. But there was more to it than that. The

Borgias were the Medici of Spain, rich, powerful, influential. Like the Medici, the Borgias had so much money
that their only interest in the papacy was the additional
power and influence it represented. Thus in the 1447 conclave, Cardinal Alfonso de Borgia welcomed the chance to
cast his vote for a man who would remove the papacy from
the Orsini and Colonna factions, for once the papacy was
out of Rome it would be simpler for him to get it to Spain.
It was easier for him to be friendly with Nicholas than with
either the Orsinis or the Colonnas, and so during Nicholas'
eight-year reign Borgia spent more time in Rome than he
did in Valencia, where he belonged.

Nicholas proved to be a pope of many hues, none of them
particularly brilliant. He had no relatives to favor, which at
least freed him from nepotism. He was a well-read man,
but he was no scholar. In Florence he had seen rich men
gather poets and artists around them, thus creating a schol-
arly atmosphere; in Rome Nicholas adopted the habit,
bringing into his circle men like Lorenzo Valla, Pozzio, and
Filelfo. But he also adopted several writers who were nothing more than popular pornographers, and their presence in
the papal court made people wonder if the Pope really knew
what he was doing. He was trying to inject into the Church
some of the Renaissance humanism then sweeping the continent, which was not an unmitigated blessing. He managed
to hire Fra Angelico to paint majestic frescoes on the Vatican walls, he had the architect Alberti at work on the Vatican museum, and he spent a fortune acquiring manuscripts
for the Vatican library. But at the same time as he was encouraging a humanism which had its source more in ancient
Greece than in the Early Church, he was letting a kind of
cultural materialism seep into the Church. In time humanism, which put sophistication above spirituality, became a
contributing factor to the Protestant Reformation. Though

this occurred much later, it had roots in the reign of Nicholas V who overemphasized the Church's role in the realm of culture.

In other spheres, however, Nicholas showed good judgment. He had inherited several serious problems, one of which pertained to the authority of councils over popes. The Council of Constance, which had ended the great schism and put Martin V on the papal throne, had adjourned with the delusion that henceforth councils rated above papal decrees and the College of Cardinals. Since the council was preponderantly German, this idea was prevalent throughout Germany. Martin tried to squelch it by side-stepping the Council of Basel, which actually was supposed to be a follow-up to the Council of Constance. Indignant, the few prelates who went to Basel anyway had elected their own pope, Felix V, who had the support of many German princes. Pope Eugene IV, who succeeded Martin, had done little to clear up the situation, so the problem fell on Nicholas' shoulders. What he did was complicated, almost Machiavellian, yet effective and far-reaching.

Emperor Frederick III had been King of Germany, head of the House of Hapsburg, and consequently emperor of the Holy Roman Empire, for almost ten years without having much to do with the Vatican. At the time of the Basel schism he had taken no stand. At Basel was a man named Aeneas Sylvius Piccolomini, humanist, opportunist, and first-class scoundrel. Born to a poor but noble family near Siena, he studied at Florence and Bologna, becoming an expert at canon law. He worked as an assistant to several cardinals and it was expected that he would enter the priesthood, but his personal life was so utterly immoral that he knew better than to take vows. His conduct forced one cardinal after the other to discharge him, but he was very clever and so there was always someone ready to give him another chance. When the Basel schism occurred, he supported Antipope

Felix V. He then proceeded to write filthy tracts and poetry against the popes. As years passed and Felix didn't seem to be getting anywhere, Piccolomini toned down his poetry and restricted its content to humanist subjects. As he wished, this brought him to the attention of Emperor Frederick. Frederick fancied himself a patron of the arts and hired Piccolomini as court poet, then advanced him to court secretary. Sensitive to popular trends, Piccolomini underwent a sudden change of heart. He perceived that Rome was going to win out over Basel and he advised Frederick to come out officially against the antipope.

This done, he resigned his secretariat, put aside his humanism and fast life, went to Rome, obtained an audience with Pope Eugene, renounced his flamboyant past, pledged support of the papacy, and asked permission to become a priest. With unusual generosity, Eugene forgave him and approved his ordination. That was in 1445. In 1446, Piccolomini was a priest, in 1447 he was the Bishop of Trieste, in 1450 he was the Bishop of Siena.

Frederick's declaration for Rome meant the end for the Basel schism. Antipope Felix, however, had been a man of some renown, which his claim to the papacy had enhanced, and he was reluctant to give it all up. As long as he persisted he was a thorn in the side of Rome. Nicholas decided to devise a way for Felix to withdraw gracefully. He offered Felix an estate and a life pension, with the understanding that Felix would give up any claims to the papacy and that upon his death no effort would be made to replace him as antipope. Felix agreed.

But there was still Germany, and in Germany there was still resentment among certain bishops and noblemen against Vatican attempts to keep councils subordinate to popes. Nicholas decided to overcome this by bringing Frederick closer to the Vatican. For ten years Frederick had been king in fact and emperor in theory, but he had never been crowned by a pope. Due to the circumstances, however, Nicholas could not simply come out and invite Frederick to Rome for coronation. Church relations with Germany needed adjustments. Looking around, Nicholas discovered the perfect man to correct the situation: Frederick's old friend Piccolomini. The Pope appointed Piccolomini to work out a concordat with Germany and Piccolomini subsequently conferred in Vienna with representatives of the emperor. Knowing the Germans so well, Piccolomini was highly successful. He managed to regain confiscated Church properties and revenues; he granted Frederick the right to approve freely elected bishops, but he retained for the popes the privilege of rejecting the elected bishop and appointing another man if necessary. In March, 1452, Frederick arrived in Rome to be crowned by the Pope, the last emperor to do so.

But the day had passed when agreements of emperors were likewise binding on bishops and noblemen. Aware of this, Nicholas had to find another way of dealing with them. A council was out of the question; the work would have to be done by personal contact with individuals and regional groups. He chose his man, then announced that he was sending a legate to Germany for consultations. Immediately the recalcitrant Germans, prepared for a domineering Italian to arrive in their midst and start giving orders in Latin, let it be known in Rome that they would have absolutely none of it.

The Pope surprised them. The legate he appointed was Cardinal Nicholas of Cusa, in Luxembourg, a holy, wise, and brilliant man, who spoke German fluently and understood the German mentality. The Cardinal had himself won a few votes at the conclave that elected Pope Nicholas, losing out because he was more concerned with prayer than he was with politics.

The Cardinal did a fantastic job. He spent over a year touring Germany, and wherever he went he made a profound impression. Whenever he arrived at a town or a monastery, he went first to the chapel to pray, a sincere gesture that convinced his observers that he was truly a man of God. In monasteries, he asked to be allowed to follow the daily schedule of prayer and meditation with the monks, and the sight of this important personage conducting himself as the monks did quickly melted resentment. In the palaces of prelates and princes, he declined the obeisance that rightfully should have been shown him; entering a house with the authority of a papal legate he behaved like a grateful guest. When the time came for him to get down to business the major hurdles were already removed, and men who had prepared themselves to fight him found themselves listening reverently. He could discuss papal prerogatives both spiritual and temporal, he could stress the importance of obedience, he could sternly point out moral abuses. Always he was gentle, patient, tolerant. With a skillful diplomacy that had its roots in his personal sincerity he achieved everywhere what he set out to do. He was particularly effective among the Augustinians, a strong religious order in Germany. In their strength was a weakness that came with popularity and favor: they were inclined to be lax in their monastic life and presumptuous in their public life. Cardinal Nicholas devoted much time to them in order that their popularity might be used for the spiritual benefit of the country.

When the Cardinal's work was finished there was no doubt of his success. There no longer was a German problem. His achievements reflected well upon himself and upon Pope Nicholas. Sadly, the good he did was to be short-lived.

3

Cardinal Nicholas of Cusa was not able to get to Rome for
the conclave following the death of Pope Nicholas in 1455,
and in his absence was an omen of things to come. His absence did not preclude his being elected, but the presence
of such a holy man might have blocked the path of the man
who was.

Fifteen cardinals attended the conclave—seven Italians,
two Greeks, two Frenchmen, and four Spaniards. The Italians
were split between the Orsini and Colonna factions: the
Colonnas wanted an Italian pope; Cardinal Orsini was prepared to settle for a Frenchman if he couldn't get the papacy
for himself. Pope Nicholas had been ill for several months,
during which both the Orsini and Colonna parties poli-
ticked among the cardinals. The Colonnas used a gentle,
subtle approach; the Orsinis came right out with campaign
promises. Had Pope Nicholas died sooner, it is likely the
Orsinis would have captured the throne, but his lingering
illness served to divide the cardinals deeply and to open the
door for a dark horse who was quietly working for himself:
Alfonso de Borgia.

The conclave began on Good Friday, and over the week-
end three ballots were taken. The foreign cardinals seemed
to ally themselves against the Italians. The leading candidate was not an Italian at all, but Cardinal Bessarion, a
Greek, serving as legate to Bologna. He had eight votes—
the four Spanish votes, the vote of the other Greek, and the
votes of three of the Orsini group which had switched from
the French when it was seen that a Frenchman was not going
to be elected. Of the remaining seven votes, one was Bessarion's, and he could not vote for himself. The four Colonna party cardinals kept their votes among themselves. As

a result, the two crucial votes, which would have made
Bessarion pope, were French. But the French refused to vote
for a Greek. Although Bessarion had lived at Rome a long
time and served on many important legations, he was Greek
born, he wore his beard in the Greek fashion, and his election would have shed honor, however indirectly, on the
schismatic Greek church. The French could not abide any of
this.

There was only one man who had the political perception
to foresee that a Greek candidate would lead to this kind of
stalemate: Borgia, the cardinal of Valencia. All he had to
do now was wait until somebody suggested a compromise:
sooner or later it would become evident that if the new pope
was not going to be Italian, French or Greek there was only
one other possible nationality—Spanish. Cardinal Alain of
Avignon was the first to deduce the inevitable and point it
out. The other cardinals evaluated the situation and realized
that Alain was right. On the conclave's fifth day another
ballot was taken and there was little doubt about the outcome. As pope, Borgia took the name Calixtus III.

He proved troublesome from the very beginning. First
off, he disliked the humanists and cleared the Vatican of
the artists and quasi-intellectuals who had looked to Pope
Nicholas for patronage. The housecleaning stirred indigna-
tion among humanists throughout Europe, who saw in the
wholesale eviction a Church return to dogmatism. Calixtus
found himself with clusters of enemies in the intellectual
centers of Europe, but he couldn't have cared less.

His primary concern was the increase of Moslem aggression in the East. From the start of his papacy, he called
for a crusade against the Moslems—in this case, the Turks,
who were sending armies into southeastern Europe and conquering parts of Bulgaria. Actually, Calixtus' concern was
deeper and more personal. His own country, Spain, was
overrun by Moslems in the south. It would have been too

much even for a Borgia to ask European kings to fight
Moslems in the land where the Pope's family had great holdings. However, it was clear that defeating Moslems on the
opposite side of the continent would also weaken Moslems
wherever they were.

Calixtus' call for help against the Moslems went unanswered. He offered indulgences to anyone who would take
up arms, but nobody seemed anxious for them. Then he imposed new taxes on all dioceses for funds to support an army
he planned to raise himself. The reaction was violent. German bishops especially complained against the tax and all
the good work Cardinal Nicholas of Cusa had done to rally
the German bishops to Rome began to fade. Complaints
came, too, from England where prelates said they simply
did not have the money. Only the Albanians were ready to
fight, and this was understandable because the Moslems were
at their doorsteps. To get money to help the Albanians,
Calixtus sold precious manuscripts Pope Nicholas had purchased, he sold paintings and jewels, and he said he was
ready to pawn his tiara if there was no other way to get the
funds.

Calixtus was of the opinion that Emperor Frederick III
should have come to his aid. At least in theory Frederick was
his partner in the rule over the Holy Roman Empire. But
whatever his personal sentiments may have been, Frederick
was not free to move. A change was coming over Europe.
With the stirring of nationalism, men of different countries
no longer looked upon each other as brothers united by a
common religion. Germans were Germans, French were
French, English were English, and out of the growing nationalism grew international distrust, jealousy and suspicion.
National self-concern was becoming the dominant factor in
Europe. Although there was a war in the southeast, a war
that threatened Bulgaria and Albania and Christianity itself,

the Western powers could not get too upset about it as long
as they were not personally involved. Even if Frederick
wanted to help the Pope, he would have had a great deal of
trouble rallying his princes and barons to join with him.

As the months passed, delegations from various countries
arrived at the Vatican to pay national respects to the new
Pope, to give him gifts and pledge their obedience. In view
of what was going on, the meetings were strained, often
abrupt. With the Germans, the situation was most ticklish:
the German government had not responded to the papal
call to arms, the German bishops were annoyed by the new
taxes, the German intellectuals resented Calixtus' eviction
of humanists from the Vatican. There had even been talk in
Germany of adopting the French pragmatic sanctions, by
which French courts claimed superiority over Church courts
in matters involving Church personnel and properties.

There were two German cardinals, Nicholas of Cusa and
Peter von Schaumburg of Augsburg, neither of them much
involved in Vatican intrigue and neither particularly
friendly with the new pope. It seemed unlikely that either
man could properly appear before Calixtus to offer German
obeisance. But to do nothing would have been an inexcus-
able affront: the Concordat of Vienna and Frederick's coronation by a pope supposedly indicated the existence of
amicable relations between the Vatican and Germany.
Frederick got around the problem by a most unusual maneuver. To present his respects to the Pope he chose not a
German but an Italian: his old friend, Bishop Piccolomini of
Siena.

Now Piccolomini was on the spot. He certainly wanted to
sustain his friendship with the Emperor, so he couldn't refuse the assignment Frederick gave him. But he also wanted
a red hat for himself, and he realized there was slim chance
of it if he did anything to get Calixtus mad at him. Arriv-

ing in Rome to perform his delicate mission, Piccolomini needed all his unique abilities as a poet, a politician and a bit of a shyster.

Probably no other man could have handled the situation as well. In presenting Frederick's tribute to the Pope, Piccolomini spoke glowingly about the wonders of both men. As evidence of Frederick's love for the Church and the Holy Father, Piccolomini pointed to the Vienna concordat which so clearly and generously had outlined the prerogatives of both the Church and the State. Calixtus observed that his only concern about the concordat was that Frederick not consider confiscating Church properties or revenues. Piccolomini quickly moved on to the Pope's favorite subject: a crusade against the Moslems. For more than an hour he discussed the importance of the crusade, hinting that surely Frederick would come to the Pope's aid as soon as the situation allowed.

Later Piccolomini wrote Frederick: "We were placed in no small perplexity, but as we saw that nothing else could be done and that it would only cause scandal if we were to depart without making profession of obedience we decided on doing this."

The Bishop of Siena had acted wisely. After making his favorable impression he remained in Rome for several weeks—to make himself useful in any way, as he explained it—before returning to his own diocese. A year later he had his red hat.

The general feeling toward Calixtus was revealed in a letter Antonious, the Archbishop of Florence, sent to a Pisa friend. The mixed fears prevalent at the time seep through the Archbishop's carefully chosen and charitable words:

The election of Calixtus III at first gave little satisfaction to the Italians, and this for two reasons. First, inasmuch as he was a Valencian or Catalan, they felt some apprehension lest he might seek to transfer the Papal Court to another country.

Secondly, they feared that he might confide strongholds of the Church to Catalans and it might eventually be difficult to recover possession of them. But now the minds of men have been reassured by more mature reflection and the reputation which he bears for goodness, penetration and impartiality. Moreover, he has bound himself by a solemn promise—a copy of which I have seen—to devote all his powers, with the advice of the cardinals, to the war against the Turks and the conquest of Constantinople. It is not believed or said that he is more attached to one nation than to another but rather that as a prudent and just man he will give to everyone his due. The Lord alone, whose providence rules the world, and especially the Church, and who in His infinite mercy brings good for her out of evil, knows what will happen. Meanwhile we must always think well of the Holy Father and judge his actions favorably, even more so than those of any other living being, and not be frightened by every little shock. Christ guides the bark of Peter, which therefore can never sink. Sometimes He seems to slumber in the storm: then must we wake Him with prayers and good works, of which there is much need.

There were many "little shocks," some of them actually severe. The very thing Italians feared—the infiltration of Catalans—occurred when the Spaniards swarmed into the Vatican. Awaiting them were numerous vacancies caused by the resignations of other nationals who did not like Calixtus, mostly for his anti-humanist sentiments. Though the Pope showed no tendencies to move the Church to Spain, he certainly opened the door for Spain to move to Rome. Contemporaries reported that Spanish was heard more in Rome than Italian. Inescapably there were serious sociological effects. The time soon came when hourly gang fighting in the streets was common. Lawlessness broke out everywhere, and there was a startling increase in sexual promiscuity and its companion vices. All this was bound to make itself known throughout Europe, with the result of widespread disgust toward the city.

It was said that Calixtus, an old man preoccupied with the Turks, really didn't know how bad the situation was. But he could not have been equally unaware of the effects his own conduct was having. Other popes had practiced nepotism, but none quite as outrageously as Calixtus. Borgias in Spain reaped amazing benefits from their loving uncle on the papal throne—bishoprics, estates, titles, art objects. Three of his nephews who moved to Rome practically took over the peninsula. Two—Rodrigo and Luis—were made cardinals while still in their twenties, when neither of them was a priest. A third nephew, Don Pedro, was appointed governor of the papal states, commander of papal armies, overseer of foreign investments, and civil authority over Rome. Rodrigo became vice-chancellor of the Church, a position second only to the papacy. Luis was made governor of Bologna. The three young men were described as being irresistibly good-looking, which brought on all sorts of problems. A contemporary said of Rodrigo: "He is handsome, of a pleasant and cheerful countenance, with a sweet and persuasive manner. With a single glance he can fascinate women and attract them to himself more strongly than a magnet draws iron." One result of Rodrigo's charm was six illegitimate children, some born after he eventually became a priest.

Everybody knew about Rodrigo's escapades except, apparently, his uncle. When rumors appeared that Calixtus might make him a cardinal, other cardinals voiced their objections. The Pope waited until mid-summer heat and pestilence sent most of the cardinals out of Rome. Then he called a secret consistory at which he gave the red hat to his two nephews. The resentment of the cardinals became plain some months later when Calixtus called another consistory for the purpose of nominating cardinals. The cardinals attended in a mood of blunt resistance. One of them wrote with piercing metaphor: "Never had cardinals more difficulty in entering the sacred college. The hinges had become so rusty that they would not turn. The Pope had to use battering-rams and all kinds of engines to burst open the door."

But the door was opened, and those of the six new cardinals who weren't Spanish were, like Piccolomini, men whose appointments were intended to win foreign support for Calixtus' war against the Turks. The maneuver didn't work.

By the night Calixtus died Rome had sunk to a moral level unseen since the days of pagan emperors. His death unleashed an Italian fury that sent Spanish blood flowing. Rodrigo and Luis took to the hills. Once again the city passed into Colonna hands, hands which actually had never surrendered their grip. Although opposed to Calixtus at first, the Colonnas had quickly perceived what kind of man they had and shrewdly offered him their support when they realized they were not going to have much conflict with him. Upon his death, the Colonna cardinals felt they had seen the last of the Spanish influence, and they were therefore astonished to discover, on Calixtus' last night, that Rodrigo had secretly returned to the city, made his way to the old man's deathbed and knelt there, apparently awaiting what he presumed to be his inheritance.

X

There was an avalanche over Rome. The tragedy had begun, and there was no stopping it. A bad pope here, a weak pope there, a nest of conniving cardinals—blended with growing nationalism, materialism, and greed among the laity—produced a complicated mixture that could give rise only to chaos. There were, to be sure, men who saw the danger coming, but the cancer of corruption was too deep to be removed by morality's sharp blade. There would have to be a great death before there could be a resurrection.

The Roman predicament must have been alarming indeed, since even the men most responsible for it tried to make corrections after the death of the Borgia pope. Eighteen cardinals attended the conclave following Calixtus' funeral: eight Italians, five Spaniards, two Frenchmen, one Portuguese, and two Greeks. Although the foreigners out-numbered the Italians, this was no guarantee for a safe choice of a successor. The cardinals seemed justly concerned about the internal disorder of the Church. Before getting down to the business of an election they spent three days composing a document of capitulation intended to restrict papal powers and extend the rights of the Sacred College, and they agreed among themselves that whoever was chosen pope would abide by it. At first it seemed a workable idea. But in a monarchical structure, which the Church was, issues of dogma, morality, and discipline could not be expected to be resolved by conference and compromise. What was needed was a strong pope, and the fault lay not in the method but the spirit with which the popes were being selected.

The Duke of Milan and the King of Naples were both afraid that a French cardinal might be elected. Although France was at odds with the Church, the French cardinals were influential men both in Rome and in their homeland. They were, moreover, shrewd politicians, ready to make deals in return for votes. Furthermore, the French King Charles VII had designs on Italian territory, and to make his private campaign easier he was willing to back up any arrangements his cardinals made with other cardinals who might otherwise oppose his plans. Aware of all this, the Italian rulers were anxious for a pope whose loyalty was to them as well as the Church. But the old conflict between the Colonna and Orsini houses was threatening to divide the Italian cardinals as usual. The Duke of Milan cleverly arranged a marriage between a Colonna and an Orsini, thereby uniting the two factions and assuring both that any future pope chosen from either clan would nevertheless be in the family.

But there was the immediate future to consider as well.

The only Italian cardinal at the 1458 conclave who was acceptable to other Italians was Piccolomini, and he was far from an outstanding candidate. The Duke of Milan wrote his friends at the conclave that, in the circumstances, it was clearly a choice between Piccolomini and a foreigner.

When talk of Piccolomini began to circulate in the conclave the powerful French Cardinal d'Estouteville remarked viciously, "How can Piccolomini be thought fit for the papacy? He suffers from the gout and is absolutely penniless. How can he succor the impoverished Church or, infirm as he is, heal her sickness? He has but lately come from Germany; we do not know him; perhaps he will move the Church there. Look at his devotion to the heathen Muses. Shall we raise a poet to the Chair of Peter and let the Church be governed by pagan principles?"

It was a weak argument, a selfish argument, but a typical argument.

The Venetian Cardinal Pietro Barbo had hoped to win the election himself, but when he saw there was no chance of it he called a separate meeting of the Italian cardinals with the exception of Prospero Colonna who favored the Frenchman. In no uncertain terms Barbo enlightened the Italians to the dangers implicit in the election of a Frenchman. It was for their own good as well as the Church's that the new pope should be Italian. When the next scrutiny was taken, Piccolomini had nine votes, d'Estouteville had six.

After the count the cardinals sat around staring at each other. Piccolomini needed twelve votes to be elected, and not having captured the necessary majority right on the heels of the Italian conference there was every likelihood that he would lose support instead of gain it.

Suddenly Cardinal Rodrigo Borgia stood up and announced, "I change my vote to the Cardinal of Siena." Ten for Piccolomini.

Spanish Cardinal Juan Torquemada, wary of the Borgia

influence, quickly said, "I move this scrutiny be adjourned."
But before a second Spanish cardinal could support the mo-
tion, a third sided quickly with Borgia, giving Piccolomini
eleven votes.

The next voice came as a surprise. Perhaps it was inspired
by nationalism, perhaps to save face, perhaps a desire to
join the bandwagon. In any event, Prospero Colonna, who
had opposed Piccolomini so openly that he had been excluded from the Italian meeting, got up and said, "I also
vote for the Cardinal of Siena, and I make him Pope." Then
the Greek Cardinal Bessarion, who previously had voted
French, made a speech extolling the attributes of the new
pontiff—a man who had joined a schism, written obscene
poems about the popes, cavorted in the German court, and
then found God.

As Pius II, Piccolomini tried to live down his reputation.
He asked people to forget Piccolomini and remember Pius.
The humanists, remembering his past, expected Pius to
restore them to influence in the Vatican, but he didn't. In
fact, he issued a bull denouncing all his early writings and
conduct, including humanism, and to all appearances he sincerely tried to be a good pope. But he was not quite the man
for it. Also, he was limited by the capitulation document
he had signed at the conclave, as a consequence of which any
radical changes he might have made inside the Vatican would
be prevented by the cardinals.

One good thing he did was to appoint Cardinal Nicholas
of Cusa to be vicar-general of Rome. By going outside the
city to find a man for the important position, Pius was
able to elude local intrigues, and in Nicholas he had an ex-
ceptionally qualified personage. Soon after taking office,
Nicholas proposed what was known as the Rule of Visitors
—three-man committees appointed to examine the condition of the Church from top to bottom. They were to be
authorized to detect and correct pluralities of bishoprics,

abuses in monasteries and convents, immorality in the clergy, simony and bribery, misuse of indulgences and privileges, general laxity, and specific misconduct. Some committees were actually put to work and achieved a degree of success, but in Rome the situation was so hopelessly involved that it was difficult to know where to start.

Pius tried to help by increasing the College of Cardinals, but he faced a unique problem. In the first place, the capitulation act gave the existing cardinals the right to approve appointments, and the existing cardinals were divided into two schools: the Gallicans, who preferred to exercise controls on the popes, and the Ultramonatists, who felt the popes should have supreme authority. To get any cardinals appointed at all, Pius had to balance the number between the two conflicting ideas, and so in increasing the college he was unable to give either school dominance. Also, he was not above nepotism. He gave the red hat to his sister's twenty-year-old son, then just a seminarian, and upon the death of Nicholas of Cusa the Pope appointed his nephew into the royal family at Naples, thus hoping to achieve a little more harmony with King Ferrante.

There was a distinct lack of harmony with France. The Pragmatic Sanction had been in effect for many years and its mere existence weakened papal authority over the French clergy. This was the root of Gallicanism, and Pius hoped that by getting rid of the sanction he could restore some of the papal dignity in France. King Charles VII had proved wholly uncompromising, but when the dauphin became King Louis XI in 1461 Pius felt he had more of a chance. He assigned Bishop Jean Jouffroy of Aras to negotiate with the new king, unaware that the Bishop, despite his good reputation, had ambitions of his own. During the negotiations, King Louis informed the Pope that the Pragmatic Sanction would be repealed provided Jouffroy and Prince d'Albert were made cardinals. Louis also held the opinion that since the kingdom of Naples had once been Aragonese he, as the King of France, ought to have some say in its administration. Although the Neapolitan King Ferrante was impoverished, existing mostly on loans from the Duke of Milan, he was not about to permit any encroachments by France. Pope Pius considered the Naples issue to be an added proviso by France for repeal of the Pragmatic Sanction which could be compromised in some way, and in responding to Louis he hinted that perhaps the matter of Naples should be left to the future. The cardinals were strongly adverse to adding to the Sacred College, and particularly to the addition of Frenchmen. Louis knew this, and he realized Pius would have job enough getting through the appointments without attempting to settle the Naples problem at the same time. Eager for action, Pius appointed Jouffroy and d'Albert to the college over fierce objections from the cardinals. In a short time the sanction was repealed; for the first time in years France recognized the Pope as the head of the Church with no strings attached. And yet there was a string. Cardinal Jouffroy and King Louis became great friends, and when the question of Naples arose again it was the Cardinal who informed the Pope that unless something was done the Pragmatic Sanction would be reimposed.

For a while Germany seemed likely to adopt similar restrictions of its own. Having lived at the German court, having worked out the Vienna concordat, and having honored Germany by choosing a German cardinal as his vicar, Pius expected to have better relations with the Germans than he had. As Bishop of Siena, he had represented Emperor Frederick to Calixtus, diplomatically conceding that Frederick should send troops against the Turks. War against the Turks was an important papal aim; Pius confronted Frederick with the idea. The German princes went as far as to hold a council about the war and agreed that something should be done, but when they adjourned and went home they apparently forgot all about it. Pius' efforts to remind them, through letters, bulls and proffered indulgences, represented to the princes the kind of pressure they were trying to escape and, along with certain bishops, they thought very seriously of adopting the French sanctions.

There were two other circumstances which made new enemies for Pius. One was the African slave trade, then just starting. The Portuguese, Dutch and British were in the business, capturing or buying Africans on the continent's west coast and selling them along the Mediterranean. On Africa's east coast, the Moslems of the Middle East carried on their own trade. Pope Pius denounced the slave traffic, threatening excommunication on those engaged in it, but this was an era when the Pope's voice didn't carry far and the warnings were ignored.

The second matter concerned Jews in Spain. Over the centuries Jews were periodically persecuted by various European rulers, and the excuse given was that Jews living hundreds of years after Christ were responsible for His crucifixion. Only in Rome and under good popes did Jews have much of a chance. Now Spain was turning against them. Spanish kings, growing steadily stronger and richer, were beginning to push the Moslems out of the country, and in their senseless fanaticism they declared that only Christians could live in Spain. If Jews wanted to stay in Spain—often if they merely wanted to stay alive—they had to become Christians. Here was the beginning of the Spanish Inquisition.

Pius foresaw the terror ahead. He wrote bishops that they must do all they could to stop the persecution of Jews. He decreed that conversions under duress were not conversions at all because the convert had not acted of his own free will, and he specified that no Jewish children under twelve could be accepted into the Church without the written permission of their parents. Also, he let it be known in the Jewish settlements in Spain that if any Jews wanted to escape Spain they would be welcome in Rome under his protection. Just as the slave traders resented papal intrusion into their business, so did the Spanish kings complain that the Pope had no right to tell them how to run their country, especially in view of the fact that, so they claimed, they were acting for the sake of the Church.

Thus even when Pius tried to do good he ran into trouble. The next ten popes were to have the same experience, and unfortunately much of the trouble they faced was caused by themselves.

2

The next ten popes included another Borgia, another Piccolomini, and two Medici, and during their reigns occurred such events as the Protestant Reformation, the Anglican schism, the Savonarola rebellion, the Spanish Inquisition, the final expulsion of Moslems from Spain, the discovery of America, and the architectural reconstruction of the Vatican. This was a lot to happen to ten men. There were, of course, many other men involved, and the responsibility, as well as the credit, for all that happened must be widely distributed. One thing was certain: in the short span of fifty years the world Pope Pius II knew when he died in 1464 was drastically changed. It would never be the same.

There was a general feeling among the cardinals that Pius had let them down. Although he had signed the Act of Capitulation, he had made appointments, especially to the cardinalate, without their approval, and they didn't like this. Most of them were of the opinion that a pope, instead of being the supreme authority of the Church, should serve merely as the president of their own consultative body. To press their point, they prepared another document at the next conclave that reiterated all the restrictions of the first act and then added more. It is an indication of the regard they had for each other that they agreed that the new pope could not appoint relatives to command the papal armies or occupy a fortress within the patrimony. Obviously they didn't want to put anyone in a position to use forceful persuasion on them.

They elected Cardinal Pietro Barbo, the wealthy Venetian who had strongly influenced the election of Pius II. The nephew of Pope Eugene IV, Barbo had been made a cardinal at the age of twenty-three. He was now forty-seven, young compared to his immediate predecessors. Even so, it was felt that the older cardinals were responsible for his election. Pius had been a cardinal only a few months when he was elected; the older cardinals said that such a novice could not have proper respect for the cardinalate. Barbo, at least, was a senior member of the club.

But he soon revealed what he thought of it. As Pope Paul II, he was expected to sign the new capitulation act within three days after his consecration, but weeks passed before he got around to it. During that time, he turned the document over to Vatican lawyers to determine whether he was obliged to sign it. The lawyers said no. In compromise, he watered the document down, returning to the cardinals an act that had lost its teeth.

Despite their original sentiment toward him, the cardinals denounced Paul as a traitor. One said, "You have spent twenty-four years as a cardinal awaiting this chance to destroy us!" The accusation was a bit silly.

For that matter, the College itself had become picayune. On his election, Barbo had first chosen the name Formosus, but the cardinals told him that the word "formosus" meant handsome and people might think he had taken the name because he was good-looking. Barbo then suggested the name Mark. This was rejected because Mark was the war-cry used by Venetian soldiers. There were no objections to Paul.

Paul consoled the cardinals by beautifying their costume. They had worn the red hat since 1244; in 1295, Pope Boniface VIII had given them a red cassock. Paul gave them a red biretta, a white miter of silk damask and bordered with pearls—which had previously been worn only by popes—a purple coat, and a scarlet saddle-cloth to be used when they were on horseback. They were getting to be a colorful group, in appearance as well as in conduct.

Paul had few friends, surprising in view of his soft-hearted nature. He could not stand violence. Repeatedly he commuted death sentences of criminals; often when he sat down to eat he would visualize the butchering of the meat placed before him and he would become so upset by the thought of violence that he left the table. He initiated the custom of pre-Lenten carnivals in Rome and he used to enjoy standing at a palace window to watch the people reveling in the streets. Not a humanist, he was however a patron of the arts and kept several painters and sculptors busy at the Vatican. His friendlessness stemmed from two sources, one being the dislike of the cardinals. Secondly, he had no use for the humanist writers who previously crowded around many a papal table, brightening the room with their wit and charm. The writers, in turn, produced satirical poems about him, picturing him as a simple-minded pontiff who peeked through windows at merrymakers in the streets. Practically exiled in his own palace, he diluted whatever moral influence the existence of the papacy in Rome could have.

The city was one big, endless carnival when the Sacred College met to choose Paul's successor in 1471. Paul had appointed fourteen new cardinals, including three of his nephews, and eighteen members of the College managed to reach Rome in time to participate in the election. By now the foreigners were a shallow minority; only three were present at the conclave—Borgia, Bessarion, and d'Estouteville. Surprisingly, the foreigners fared remarkably well against such odds. As the scrutinies were taken, Borgia and d'Estouteville both got as many as six and seven votes—impressive but not enough.

The politicking was confused. The usual aspirants resorted to their usual promises and the usual compromises were made, and yet there was a steadily growing sentiment as the conclave dragged on that it might be a good idea to go beyond the usual factionism and pick a man whose record was clean and above suspicion. The only man present who met that requirement was Francesco Della Rovere, a leading Franciscan, who had received his red hat from Pope Paul four years earlier. A respected theologian, Rovere had never lived like a cardinal; after his appointment he returned to a monastery and existed like a monk, donning his brilliant cardinal's robes only when summoned to Rome for consultation. There could be no argument against him, and even ambitious cardinals indicated, "If not me, then Rovere."

He turned out to be one of the big disappointments of all times. He simply did not have the capacity for the job. If his record was clean it was because his slate was blank. As a cardinal he had done nothing; as pope practically everything he did was wrong. A holy man, he was nevertheless a hollow man, unable to foresee the results of anything he did. Also, he came from an enormous family, and immediately upon his election the whole clan moved from Liguria to Rome to take advantage of the honor bestowed upon Uncle Francesco. In time, he appointed some thirty-four cardinals, three his nephews. One nephew received so many benefices in the form of dioceses and estates that he had a private income of over half a million dollars a year. The Pope's relatives swarmed into every Church crevice. Those for whom jobs couldn't be found were simply put on the Vatican budget: sisters received palaces, brothers took over villas, nephews were given civil appointments that had no duties, nieces acquired huge dowries in order to marry well.

The fantastic nepotism of Pope Sixtus IV appalled the Romans and alarmed the cardinals, all of whom were ready for some of it but none of whom had ever seen anything like this. As difficult as it might be to believe, the Pope had no idea that he was causing scandal. In matters of money, appointments, and character evaluation he was incredibly naive. If his harmful innocence had been restricted to his own family, affairs would have been bad enough, but he displayed the same well-meaning ignorance in other appointments. Some of his choices of cardinals were men who hadn't seen the inside of a church since they were baptized. Several were young men so worldly and so lascivious that when they heard of their appointment they thought it was a joke. This was the irreparable damage: these were the men who would elect future popes and become popes themselves. At a moment of history when the Church needed strong men to withstand the landslide of criticism soon to fall, the presence of such men in the Sacred College could only be a disaster.

In Spain, King Ferdinand and Queen Isabella had been enriched in many ways for having financed Christopher Columbus' journey to the New World. Like most European rulers, they kept an eye on the Church in their country, aware of both its influence on the people and its wealth. On several occasions when Pope Sixtus appointed bishops in Spain, King Ferdinand rejected the appointments and put in his own men. Sixtus criticized the King only to the extent of saying he ought not do such things. Victorious over the Moslems and triumphant over the New World which they thought would forever and entirely be theirs, the Spaniards were in an arrogant mood. The papal complaints were ig-

nored. There was talk for a while of an ecclesiastical council
in Spain to loosen the ties with Rome. Anxious to avoid that,
Sixtus retreated.

The Spanish Inquisition was beginning to take shape. It
was directed primarily against the Marranos—Jews who had
nominally become Christians in order to remain in the country but who secretly continued to practice their own faith.
In the eyes of the ruling Spaniards, this was heresy. It was
also a good excuse to confiscate the businesses and properties which some Jews had acquired during the many years
their families had lived in Spain. The very basis of the Spanish Inquisition was invalid: the Jews could not be considered
heretics for not practicing a religion they had been forced
to adopt. In other lands, heretics had frequently been anarchists, against the State as well as the Church, and perhaps
there was some justification for the treatment received by
such groups. But this was not the case in Spain.

The Spanish situation had its roots in the popular fantasy
that pops up from time to time: rich Jews were supposed to
be taking over the country. This was hardly likely. Moslems
had dominated the Spanish peninsula for many years, and
they certainly would not have permitted a Jew to get far. The
expulsion of the Moslems by united Spaniards was accompanied by an increase in anti-Semitism, which again precluded any Jewish *coup d'état*. So there was no reason to
fear Jews. In fact, many Jews, having lived in Spain for generations, were more Spanish than Ferdinand, who was an
Aragonese before he married Isabella and thereby adopted
Spanish nationality.

Jews in Europe were traditionally the scapegoats for national economic or military frustrations. Since the Crusades,
they were forbidden to own land in most European countries and the majority of them were forced to live in ghettos.
They were banned from most businesses other than small
shops and moneylending but it was inevitable that over the

years those with talent should achieve a certain wealth and influence if they had the luck to be able to remain in one place long enough.

Ferdinand and Isabella, who were enthroned in 1479, called themselves the Catholic Monarchs, and with the support of other Spanish kings, they initiated a campaign to convert everybody in the country. Moslems who remained at Granada and Jews throughout Spain had a choice of submitting to baptism or leaving. Those who submitted were, of course, immediately suspected of insincerity.

Undoubtedly many of the forced converts were nominal Christians only, but under the circumstances this was understandable. To the Catholic Monarchs, however, it was unforgivable, and they created the Spanish Inquisition. The ground rules were the same as in the earlier inquisitions in Central Europe: those deemed guilty who would not recant could be deprived of their possessions, imprisoned or killed. As before, guilt could be established by circumstantial evidence and the testimony of informers.

It was unfortunate that a man like Sixtus IV was pope at the time. When the Spanish delegation to the Vatican told him in 1482 that the Inquisition was ready to go to work they presented the request of Isabella and Ferdinand that he name the Grand Inquisitor. All Sixtus knew of the Spanish situation was that the Spaniards told him there were heretics in the country: heretics ought to be investigated. Isabella's personal confessor was a Dominican prior named Tomas de Torquemada; Sixtus appointed him to be Grand Inquisitor. From then on the Spanish Inquisition was a purely Spanish affair.

Under a strong pope, the Spanish Inquisition might have been brought to an early halt. But Sixtus was not a strong pope, and because of him the Catholic Church was blamed for a reign of terror in which its only official participation was the appointment of the Grand Inquisitor. When Sixtus received first reports of Torquemada's madness he wrote the Spaniard, instructing him to adhere to traditional inquisition justice: the accused was to be released if he could name his accuser; a penitent heretic was to be immediately released and left alone thereafter; the death penalty was to be imposed only upon those who, freed after paying a fine or serving a reasonable imprisonment, might endanger the faith of others.

But Torquemada ignored the instructions and turned Spain into an abbatoir. He prosecuted not only "insincere converts" but anybody he personally suspected. Nobody was safe from him. Among his victims were many Spaniards whose only crime was that they were on the wrong side of the political fence. Estimates on the number of people who died because of him range as high as 8,800, but it is believed that the figure was closer to 2,000. The entire Spanish Church was in his hands. He even banned books that had already been approved by the Vatican.

The Inquisition continued after Torquemada's death in 1498, but not without opposition. Bishops in the Spanish Netherlands refused to cooperate with the inquisitors when they arrived and thus investigations there never amounted to much. While Spain held Naples in 1510, the people themselves ran the inquisitors out of the city, reportedly at the urging of Pope Julius II, who was, of all people, a nephew of Sixtus IV.

It would seem that at least one of the popes of this era could have forced the Spanish Inquisition to an end by means of interdicts and excommunications, but this was not done. In the first place, half a dozen popes were to come and go before one appeared who might have the fortitude for such aggression. Secondly, the Renaissance, humanism and foreshadows of the Protestant Reformation had weakened the impact of such measures: people who had lost their spirituality were not likely to be distraught by being deprived of the sacraments. Also, this was the great age for Spain and, like Germany and France before her and soon afterward England, she considered herself beyond moral criticism. Indeed, what had the Vatican to complain about? Wasn't the Spanish Inquisition initiated to help the Church?

On the contrary, it did a great harm.

3

The death of Sixtus IV in August, 1484, touched off riots in the city. The victims were the mass of Ligurians who had followed Sixtus IV to Rome and practically taken over the city. Members of the Pope's family were attacked in the street, their homes were burned and their businesses ransacked. Many didn't wait for the Pope's funeral, but fled Rome in the middle of the night. Soldiers in the papal armies under the late Pope's relatives and friends put down their arms and refused to serve. Cardinals, too, were attacked. Several hired guards, turning their homes into fortresses. For over a week, Rome was at war with itself. There was talk that the people, dissatisfied with the cardinals, intended to hold their own papal election, and it was only after Sixtus was buried and his clan was out of the city that some semblance of order was restored.

On August 25, twenty-five cardinals, the largest number in years, went into conclave. Only four were foreigners: two Spaniards, a Portuguese, and a Frenchman. This seemed to preclude the election of a foreigner, but it didn't stop Cardinal Rodrigo Borgia from campaigning. He offered Cardinal Giovanni d'Aragona the post of vice-chancellor and a palace for his vote; he bribed Cardinal Prospero Colonna with an

offer of twenty-five thousand ducats and the Abbey of Subiaco. And Borgia was not the only cardinal casting out such
tempting bait.

Before getting down to the business at hand, the cardinals
prepared another capitulation act, this one the worst of all.
They stipulated, first, that the papacy would no longer comprise a monarchy but an aristocracy, and that the personal
interests of the cardinals, as electors, were to be of primary
consideration. The document clearly specified that every
cardinal who did not have an income of four thousand ducats a year from his benefices was to receive one hundred ducats a month from the papal treasury. Furthermore, if any
cardinal was deprived of any part of his income by a secular
prince who disapproved of his vote in the election, the new
pope would have to reimburse him completely. This was a
dismal atmosphere in which to choose a new vicar of Christ
on Earth.

The conclave lasted four days. Even before the first ballot,
the session was torn by so many factions that it looked as if
nobody would ever gain a majority. When Borgia realized
he could muster only five or six votes, all purchased, he got
behind his countryman, Cardinal Moles, figuring that the
old man wouldn't last long and Borgia would have another
chance at the next conclave. But Moles's age was enough to
discourage other cardinals from considering him as a compromise choice. Detecting this, Borgia then threw his weight
behind Giovanni Battista Cibo, the fifty-two-year-old son of
a Roman senator.

Cibo had little to offer. He had been a wild youth, the fa-
ther of two illegitimate children. Appointed cardinal by
Sixtus IV, he was a close friend of Sixtus' nephew, Cardinal
Giuliano della Rovere. Easy-going and fun-loving, Cibo had
been among those surprised to find themselves cardinals.
The fact that he was a frequent house guest of Lorenzo de'

Medici in Florence might well have had something to do with his appointment.

In the first scrutiny, Cibo was far behind. The greatest number of votes—twelve—went to Cardinal Barbo. Afraid that Barbo, making such an impressive first showing, might sweep into office on the oral assents of others, Rovere moved quickly to have the balloting closed, then came out strong for Cibo. One by one, the cardinals came around; then Borgia swung his influence to Cibo. As each man agreed to vote for him, Cibo signed agreements for payoffs to be made after his possible consecration. Negotiations went on around the clock, and each time the opposition demanded a scrutiny Rovere thought of some excuse for a delay. It was early in the morning of August 29 when the cardinals finally voted again. Rovere had been successful: Cibo got eighteen votes, one more than the two-thirds he needed.

With that, the Church resumed its steady decline. Roveres trickled back to Rome, now that they had a kinsman close to the new pope; Rodrigo Borgia, due to his support, was again a man of power; and the Medici were more influential in the Church than they had ever been before. Example: Cibo, as Pope Innocent VIII, gave the red hat to the thirteen-year-old son of Lorenzo de' Medici. It was Cardinal Rovere's hope to be the power behind the papal throne, but he soon found that Innocent had no desire to be involved in any way in politics. To everybody's consternation, he invited his two illegitimate children to move into the Vatican, then seemed to dimiss the fact that he was the holder of the most important office in the world. When he needed advice on matters he couldn't elude he turned not to Rovere but to Lorenzo de' Medici.

The moral state of the cardinalate was now at its nadir. Of those living at Rome, Sforza, Riario, Orsini, Sclafenatus, Balue, Rovere, and Borgia were known to have mistresses.

They were a fast crowd, devoted more to parties, luxury, supporting humanists and selling papal bulls than to their ecclesiastic duties. The Pope's bastard son was in the midst of it all. Gambling was a popular pastime. Franschetto Cibo complained to his father that Cardinal Riario took him for fourteen ducats one night—by cheating. Cardinal de la Balue lost eight thousand to Riario on another night. The money had come from taxations on the benefices the cardinals held.

The Medici influence would be difficult to exaggerate. The family was incredibly rich. There was scarcely a business deal of any kind in Europe that they were not a part of. They spent lavishly on their own pleasures and the most expensive pleasure of the time was art. To the Medici must go credit for most of the Italian paintings and sculpture that is treasured today. The bulk of the work—paintings, statuary, or poetry—produced with their support, however, was in questionable taste, and much of this was responsible for the moral decay that swamped the country. Another factor making for widespread immorality was the spreading worship of success. To be at the top, to be rich, to live luxuriously, to have achieved something no matter how—this was the new credo. A worthwhile person was a successful person, in any field whatsoever, and so the time came when people who considered themselves on the way up were ready to pay anything to smooth the road, and the price was dishonesty, deception, and decadence.

It was no surprise, then, that the next man upon the papal throne should be he who had connived for the papacy for forty years: Rodrigo Borgia.

Pope Innocent VIII, never in good health, began to fail in the winter of 1491. Ambitious cardinals moved into Rome and, as patient as spiders, took up the death watch. The Pope hung on through the winter and the spring; nobody believed he would last through the summer. Factions were formed. King Charles VIII of France deposited two hundred thousand ducats in a Rome bank to finance the candidacy of pro-French Cardinal Giuliano della Rovere; the Genovese nobility put up another hundred thousand for the same man. Behind this action was one thought: get rid of the Medici.

The difficulty was that the cardinals didn't like Rovere. His strong influence on Innocent VIII had cost them some of their own plans. Also, Innocent's switch to the Medici later on had been so much to their benefit that any man openly against the Florentines didn't stand much of a chance. Nevertheless, Rovere knew that if he couldn't make it himself he could use his campaign money to help the man who looked second-best to him.

There were several cardinals in second place, each there because of his harmlessness. Bringing up the rear were the serious contenders, and they were in the rear because the many factions blocked any of them from enough votes to be a threat. At the end of the line was Borgia.

Borgia, however, had more than money to make him attractive. He had received enormous benefices from his uncle, Calixtus III, and picked up more from the succession of popes. He owned towns, abbeys, farms and businesses in Italy and Spain; in Spain he held sixteen bishoprics and several abbeys, each with a good income. All these he was ready to distribute among those who would vote for him.

The conclave opened on August 6; by August 10 there had been three ballots. In the lead were Cardinal Carafa of Naples and Cardinal Costa of Portugal. Actually they were offered mostly as teasers, to see how the conclave would shape up behind them. By this, other cardinals could determine how they themselves rated.

The first man to realize he was out of the running was Ascanio Sforza, who had one of the worst reputations in Rome. He was ready now to listen to Borgia. The Spaniard offered him the vice-chancellorship, his palace, the Castle of Nepi and the bishopric of Erlau with a revenue of ten thousand ducats a year. That took care of Sforza and the votes he could win. Borgia soon found other ears bent his way. To Cardinal Orsini he offered the fortified towns of Monticelli and Soriano, the legation of the Marches and the bishopric of Carthagena. Cardinal Colonna got the Subiaco abbacy with the surrounding towns. To Cardinal Savelli went Civita Castellana and the bishopric of Majorca. Pallavicini received the bishopric of Pamplona; Cardinal Michiel took the suburbicarian diocese of Porto; Cardinals Sclafenati, Sanseverino, Riario and Domenico della Rovere were given abbacies.

On the next scrutiny Borgia had only one vote short of a majority.

The holdouts were either men who despised Borgia and would never vote for him or simply men who refused to abandon their losing favorites. In that condition, Borgia, coming closer than ever to the fulfillment of his forty-year ambition, would come no closer. His lone chance lay with Cardinal Gherardo, a man ninety-six years old, ill, senile and tired. Gherardo wanted to go home. On the night of August 10, Sforza went to Gherardo and pointed out to him that the election was stalemated and might well remain so for weeks. Gherardo knew this and was unhappy about it, but what he did not know was that he was about to become the victim of an unusual filibuster. Sforza kept talking to Gherardo, and the old man struggled to stay awake to listen. When Sforza tired, another Borgia supporter replaced him. All night the talking kept on. None of the cardinals pressured Gherardo to change his vote; he was too old to be moved by pressure or bribery. They just kept reminding him how sad it was that the conclave had reached an impasse. He agreed. Hour after hour he agreed. At last he could stand it no more. Puzzled by all the attention he was getting, he was too tired to figure it out. All he wanted was to go home and get some sleep. Near dawn it occurred to him how he could do it.

Just as the morning light fingered over the city, Cardinal Sforza, the new vice chancellor, opened a window in the room and announced to the people outside that the conclave was over. Cardinal Rodrigo Borgia had been elected and taken the name Alexander VI.

Miles away in Florence was a Dominican friar named Savonarola. Opinions were divided concerning this man. Some thought he was a saint; others considered him a devil. To all appearances he was a reformer—his criticism aimed at the State as well as the Church. Weeks before he had told a Florence crowd: "The wrath of God shall smite the earth, for the time of chastisement has arrived."

Indeed it had.

Strangely, the election of Alexander VI was heralded far and wide. Gifts came from everywhere. Kings, princes, foreign cardinals and foreign bishops behaved as if the Second Coming had taken place. Some of the conduct was, surely, part of the protocol that accompanied the election of a new pontiff, but a great deal of it was heartfelt. In view of Alexander's broad reputation, the joy could only have been relief. And it was boundless. One humanist poet wrote:

"Rome was great under Caesar, greater far under Alexander; The first was only a mortal, but the latter is a God."

4

Alexander VI had six illegitimate children, two born after he became pope. He was very fond of his children and heaped honors on them. His son Juan was made the duke of Gandia and given the duchy of Benevento. Caesar Borgia, the

Pope's third son, was made a cardinal and appointed to command the papal armies. Caesar's character was such that he later was used by Machiavelli as the inspiration for *The Prince*. Caesar never took religious vows, and during the height of his vicious political intrigue he gave up his cardinalate to marry the daughter of the King of Navarre. Lucretia Borgia, the Pope's only daughter, had three husbands. The Pope annulled her first marriage, to Giovanni Sforza, on the grounds that since no children had been born the marriage had not been consummated and he paid off Sforza to sign a paper to that effect. Lucretia then married Alfonso of Bisceglia, whom Caesar murdered to get his property. Caesar also murdered his brother Juan for the same reason. Lucretia next married Alfonso d'Este, son and heir of the Duke of Ferrara, whose fifteen-year-old son the Pope had made a cardinal. As depicted by Machiavelli, Caesar Borgia always got whatever he wanted, one way or the other. The Pope refused him nothing, approving any battles into which he led the papal armies to acquire more land for himself. What Caesar could not acquire by combat he acquired by treachery. A vile, conniving, unscrupulous man, he became the epitome of crookedness for all times.

His father was close behind him. Any friends he had in Rome at the time of consecration were soon lost. Suspicions were that four or five of the cardinals who died during Alexander's reign were poisoned, either by Caesar or on Alexander's orders. This was one way to get rid of enemies; others removed themselves in order to go on living. In their places, Alexander brought every Borgia from Spain well enough to travel and gave them Vatican appointments. He created a preponderance of Spanish cardinals, and the only reason they were not a greater factor in subsequent conclaves was the distance that prevented them from arriving in Rome in time to vote.

Some of Alexander's enemies dared to fight back. Cardinal Giuliano della Rovere openly accused him of simoniacal tactics at the conclave. This was no surprise to anybody, but it was annoying to the Pope to be reminded of it for years afterward. Cardinal Orsini, who had accepted Alexander's simony, turned on him because of his outrageous generosity toward Caesar. In time, Rovere had to move to France, and Orsini was poisoned.

The most persistent of Alexander's opponents was Savonarola. Born in Ferrara of a good but poor family, Girolamo Savonarola entered the religious life while still a youth. Devout and withdrawn, he was an extraordinary recluse even for a monk. He was about thirty when he was assigned to the Dominican convent at Florence, and he continued his studies there in a library donated by the Medici. He remained obscure for almost ten years, when his superiors appointed him to preach in Florence churches. He proved to be a stern, fiery, eloquent speaker and he was soon very popular.

He believed that God was soon to punish the world and his warning was: repent or be damned. In view of the storm of immorality in Florence, Savonarola was amazingly effective. He managed to put an end to the annual carnival, he packed churches, many rich people obeyed his admonitions to give their wealth to the poor and enter monasteries. He dared to criticize the Medici for both their personal and business conduct; he loudly denounced Pope Alexander and the laxity in the Vatican. He was convinced that Italy was lost, and he urged the new French King Charles VIII to take over the country and save it. He called Charles "the new Cyrus," comparing him to the Persian king who freed the exiled Jews in Babylonia.

Charles responded, but not wholly out of a desire to save Italy from self-destruction. France had long felt that Naples belonged to her, and if it was now possible to go to Naples via Florence the French welcomed the detour. Charles led troops to Florence, took the city, ousted the Medici and put

Savonarola in charge. This was a remarkable thing to have happened. Under Savonarola, Florence entered a perpetual Lent. Political leader of the city-state, he made himself spiritual leader, and the combination gave him more authority than any man had previously had in Florence. A false piety of severe extremes struck the people. There were public burnings of obscene humanist books, paintings and sculpture; flagellants marched through the streets whipping themselves and shrieking for God's mercy; men and women stood up in churches and shouted their confessions in the most intimate detail; processions passed endlessly from one church to another; monasteries and convents were jammed. There arose a loud regret for past sins that was both horrendous and a little sick.

Pope Alexander tried to put a stop to it. He summoned Savonarola to Rome, but the friar excused himself on the grounds of ill health. The Pope then wrote Savonarola, ordering him to desist, but the friar replied that the Pope, in view of his own life and the circumstances of his election, was in no position to condemn what had become the holy city of Florence. Alexander retaliated by excommunicating Savonarola. Savonarola ignored the order and went on saying Mass. In the eyes of the Church, this was his great mistake. By his disobedience, Savonarola became not a reformer but an anarchist.

When all else failed, Alexander displayed his own lack of values by offering Savonarola a red hat if he would recant. The gesture served only to stir Savonarola further. If he had been fierce before, now he was violent. He left nothing untouched. In what he considered justice, he ordered banks to decrease their interest rate on loans until moneylending, a major business in Florence, was almost reduced to charity. Not surprisingly, this aroused some ill-feelings against him.

The fever that Savonarola caused in Florence inevitably began to cool, and as it did the existing city government tolerated less and less of his intrusion into political affairs. Seemingly fearful that he was losing out, he became all the more defiant. Roman attempts at conciliation were crudely rejected; Savonarola insisted that he would submit himself only to a Church council, which he considered to have more authority than a pope. Alexander sent some Franciscans to reason with him, and the outcome of the talks was a challenge. A Savonarola aide said the friar was so convinced he was acting in accordance with God's designs that he would submit to an ordeal by fire: let a Franciscan and Savonarola walk together through a fire: God would protect the one who was right.

The Florentines grabbed at the idea. On the day scheduled for the test a heavy rain fell upon the city. Savonarola did not show up, and the people took this to mean that he had backed off. Now anti-Savonarola sentiments grew deeper. A trial was demanded; the city government made the arrangements to determine whether or not Savonarola was indeed acting for the welfare of the people. Two Franciscans were put on the board of inquiry: the Church as well as the city-state was to judge the man. There was little doubt that the infuriated Alexander instructed his delegates how to vote. Under torture, Savonarola reportedly admitted that he was a false prophet and that he had led the people astray. He was found guilty, and the papal commissioners approved the verdict. On May 23, 1498, he and two aides were hanged, then burned and their ashes were thrown into the Arno River.

He left no disciples. When he died, his crusade died with him. There was no one around to carry on what he had started. Subsequent popes studied his writings and found nothing in them contrary to doctrine. He was not a heretic, but simply a man who did not know how to perform the good he might have done. He was certainly right in one thing: the time of chastisement was nigh.

XI

*I*n 1510, Father Martin Luther, an Augustinian monk and professor at the University of Wittenberg, went to Rome on business for his order. In later years he said that this event proved to be the turning point of his life. Seldom, however, does a life turn on a single point. Possibly the importance he attached to his Rome visit, during which he was amazed at the abuses he saw, was a matter of hindsight. But the letters he wrote from Rome had a far different tone: he had inspected hospitals and orphanages and was deeply impressed by their efficiency. He suggested incorporating certain aspects of the Roman system into similar institutions in Germany.

His shock at Roman immorality was somewhat surprising. In 1510, he was twenty-eight years old and had been a priest for three years. He was an intelligent, clever, well-read young man, and extremely capable. Although he was of peasant stock, his family could afford to educate him; his schooling began when he was five. His goal was law. He attended excellent schools and won good grades. On receiving his degree he astounded his parents by announcing that he was going on into the priesthood. His father was strongly against it; he didn't feel young Luther was intended for the Church and after struggling for years to put the boy through school he resented being deprived of having his son take care of him in his old age.

Martin Luther chose to enter the monastery of the Observant Augustinians, a group that had evolved from the house-cleaning mission of Cardinal Nicholas of Cusa. The Cardinal had found several Augustinian houses lax in their practices; the Observant Augustinians were one order that reacted sharply. Their life was austere, the rules severe. It was perhaps significant that Luther should enter this particular group.

He was a solemn young man, given to deep brooding and preoccupied with death. He was haunted by the fear that he might go to hell. In the monastery he took on a far more rigorous regimen than was required of him. He was always in the chapel at prayers. For a while he was a flagellant. He often fasted for days without taking a bite of food. He went to confession every day, spending hours in relentless self-examination. Despising himself, he was intolerant of others.

But it was hardly likely that, having spent his young manhood in the sophisticated atmosphere of universities, he had not acquired some notion of the abuses prevalent in the Church, and he must indeed have been ignorant of the ways of the world if, on his trip to Rome, he was so scandalized by what he claimed to have seen there that he never got over it. The greatest irregularities were to be found among the cardinals and, even on business for his order, he would scarcely have penetrated their realm. But he was a German and perhaps unable to comprehend the Latin ways of the men with whom he transacted his affairs.

But Luther was to experience an intellectual disillusionment as well. As a Catholic, he had been taught about the spiritual efficacy of good works in terms of the achievement of grace. Prayers, the sacraments, spiritual exercises, pious acts, charity—these were the avenues on which the soul approached God and became enriched. Well, he had prayed and done all the rest but he was not aware of any spiritual enrichment, any keener perception of God, any confidence of His nearness. Also, Luther did not fully comprehend the Church's conception of predestination: knowing all things, God knows how each individual will act in every situation in his life and whether, in the end, he will go to heaven or hell. But what is predestined is not preordained: God knows, but man decides. Luther, however, saw only half of this; seeing only God's knowledge, and thus concluding that the free will of the individual meant nothing and had no responsibilities, he therefore looked upon Him as a capricious being who arbitrarily decided the eternal fates of His creatures. Luther wrote that he often found himself loathing God for this.

At Erfurt University, Luther had studied the writings of William Ockham, the English philosopher who maintained that the truths of Christianity, being beyond the scope of human intellect, had to be accepted on faith in the accuracy of the Bible and the authority of the Church. Although Luther read in Thomas Aquinas how such truths could be explained by reason, he nevertheless sided with Ockham—except the part regarding the Church. As far as the Church was concerned, he was more in agreement with Huss, Waldo, and Wyclif, accusing the Church of having no actual spiritual authority, of distorting the sacraments and misleading people in matters of good works, indulgences, reverence of the Blessed Virgin and the saints, and in the nature of the Mass.

In St. Paul's Letters to the Romans, Luther came upon a line that became the basis of his doctrine. Paul had written that "the just shall live by faith." Luther interpreted this as meaning that an individual becomes just—*i.e.*, worthy of God—by faith, and he defined faith as full confidence in God. Such faith alone, he said, was all that was required for salvation. Having faith, one could be confident that God wouldn't predestine him to hell.

The possession of faith, Luther maintained, made every man a priest, and thus the priesthood as it existed in the Catholic Church was not only unnecessary but, as he saw it, was an immoral spiritual segregation that put priests above the people. Just as the Holy Ghost had inspired the Apostles on the first Christian Pentecost, so did Lutherian faith bring the Holy Ghost into the mind of each believer, empowering him with the ability to interpret the Bible, and even though interpretation might vary from man to man, each man, acting in accordance with his conscience, was right. His critics pointed out the Biblical fact that on the first Christian Pentecost it was to the Apostles that the Holy Ghost gave the gift of tongues and the power to heal, not to all the people out in the street, but Luther did not accept this.

Many people found Luther's ideas attractive. Humanists found in it permission to call themselves Christians without being bound by Catholic restrictions. Certain intellectuals relished the intellectual labyrinths it opened. Anti-clerics—and for numerous reasons these were in the majority—grabbed at the chance to escape from clerical authority. And although Luther denied that the authority of the Church was God-given, he nevertheless claimed that the authority of political government was of divine origin and that therefore the head of the state should be the head of the religion and that temporal rulers had the right to decide which religion should be practiced in their domains. As precedent for this, Luther cited the Council of Nicaea, which had been called by Emperor Constantine and presided over by him and which produced the Nicene Creed. Actually, the Nicene Council was summoned with the political intent of ending the doctrinal conflict between Rome and Constantinople which had given rise to open battle.

The German rulers faced a similar concern. For almost five hundred years they had objected to Church intrusion into what they considered their private affairs. Many had objected violently, some with good cause. The opportunity of having a Christian church in which every prince would be a pope was obviously attractive to them. Now there would be no problems about lay investitures, civil control over church properties, absentee bishops, Church taxation, and foreign interference.

Martin Luther was to be a thorny problem for many years. And yet he was the best thing that could have happened to the Catholic Church, in terms of the internal changes he indirectly effected.

2

Martin Luther was still a student at Erfurt University when Pope Alexander VI died in 1503. Within days all Europe knew that fighting had broken out in Rome against the Spaniards. The Pope's son Caesar, who held the rank of Captain-General of the papal armies, was in the city. He considered sending his troops against the populace, but he held back only because he hoped another Spanish cardinal would be elected and was therefore reluctant to do anything that would infuriate the people more. The eleven Spanish cardinals were dominated by Caesar; despite their desire to flee to save their own skins, they could not move because of the solid block of votes they would take into the next conclave.

Once again, the vital issue before the conclave was the nationality of the new pope. The critical matter was Naples. France wanted it, Italy wanted it, and Spain had it. Typically, Caesar had accepted money from both France and Spain to fight on their opposite sides over the city. Actually he was for neither country; he was for himself.

Thirty-seven cardinals took part in the conclave. Before they would begin, they insisted that Caesar Borgia withdraw his army from Rome. His presence, they said, created excessive pressure and endangered a free election. France and Spain, both confident of victory, both agreed to a cessation of hostilities. Eager to appear cooperative, Caesar moved his soldiers ten miles out of town. Distrustful of him, the cardinals held their conclave in the Castel Sant' Angelo, behind whose fortress walls they hoped to protect their peace.

The twenty-two Italian cardinals were superior in number, but as always they were divided into family parties. The French were the weakest, and yet Cardinal Charles d'Amboise, archbishop of Rouen, was a leading contender. His friendship with the French King Louis XII gave him considerable power, which he enhanced with politics of his own.

It was important for Caesar Borgia's plans that Cardinal Giuliano della Rovere should not attend the conclave. Rovere had fought Alexander's election and had not, even for the appearance of unanimity, surrendered his vote to him. He was a bold critic of Alexander from the start, and as a result he had been forced into exile for ten years. Determined to attend the conclave, he waited until Caesar had pulled back from Rome, then entered the city by night from the opposite direction.

Despite Caesar's hopes, the Spanish cardinals knew that none of them stood much chance to win the election. With him out of the city, they did not even campaign. One thing was sure: they would not vote for a Frenchman, out of loyalty to their king. Also, Rovere's fight with Alexander put them against him. Rovere wanted the papacy for himself; if that weren't possible, then he wanted an Italian—a free Italian. There weren't many of these around.

D'Amboise remarked to a Venetian assisting at the conclave, "I have heard that several cardinals have bound themselves by an oath not to elect any cardinal who is a Frenchman or a friend of the King of France. This has greatly incensed me. I see no reason why the French nation should be shut out from the papacy, and if my King, who is the first-born son of the Apostolic See, is trying to promote the election of a French pope I don't think he should be blamed, when he has seen how unworthily one Spaniard and two Italians have ruled her. Our generals are aware of these intrigues and will not patiently endure such a slight to their King."

D'Amboise was no fool. Some anti-French cardinals started rumors that the election of a Frenchman meant that the papacy would be moved to France again. This was not likely, and it was not the question. The question was Naples, and d'Amboise's reference to French generals was a hint at how serious the question was.

The balloting began. No one achieved a majority. Rovere got as many as fifteen votes; d'Amboise at one time captured thirteen. Cardinal Carafa of Naples got fourteen in one scrutiny. It was the split vote of the Spaniards among backfield Italians that precluded a majority for any leading candidate. D'Amboise wondered if feelings against him personally were blocking the French efforts, so he withdrew as a candidate and began to work for other French cardinals. But this too proved fruitless. Then d'Amboise resorted to a familiar tactic: choose a man who obviously wouldn't last long and hope for a happier atmosphere at the next conclave.

The cardinal who best fitted this bill was Francesco Piccolomini, nephew of Pope Pius II.

Appointed a cardinal at twenty, Piccolomini had spent most of his forty-four years as a cardinal out of Rome, which he always found uncomfortable. His experience was mostly with papal legates. He was now an old man with a clean but uninspiring record, and he had a bad case of gout. Rallying Cardinals Ascanio Sforza, Soderini, and the youthful Medici to his side, d'Amboise proposed Piccolomini to the Spaniards. The Spaniards agreed to support him. The next scrutiny was held and Piccolomini won, chose the name Pius III, was ordained a priest and consecrated Bishop of Rome and Supreme Pontiff of the Holy Catholic Church, and in a month he was dead.

Mourners were still filing past his coffin when the cardinals returned to their intrigue. This time there was no stopping Rovere. He proved to be more Machiavellian than Caesar Borgia; despite his feud with the Borgias, he won Caesar over. On Sunday, October 29, he invited Caesar and the Spanish cardinals to his palace and made an offer. If elected pope, he would appoint Caesar to be standard-bearer to the Church. Caesar would be allowed to keep all the benefices his father had given him, provided he supported Rovere in all things. As for the Spanish cardinals, they would be appropriately rewarded in bishoprics and abbeys in their own land and Italy.

On Tuesday evening, all the cardinals entered the conclave room to settle down for what many thought would be a long fight. Before they retired they began to sound each other out. Several Romans had already decided for Rovere; the Venetians had orders from their government to support him; the Spaniards were all set. The uncertain voters were so bewildered by the frequency with which they heard Rovere's name that they concluded that either there had been a tremendous fix or the Holy Ghost had been very busy. Even the French saw the light. Early the next morning the crowds had yet to gather outside when the vote was taken. To nobody's surprise, Rovere won on the first ballot.

His uncle had been Pope Sixtus IV, the generous Franciscan with the big family. Sixtus had been a weak man; his nephew, sharpened by twenty years in the cardinalate, was shrewd. As Julius II, he epitomized the political power that the Church could wield. With astonishing cunning, he managed to be on both sides of a conflict at the same time, and European powers never knew from one day to the next whether they were his allies or his enemies. He used Caesar Borgia to reclaim papal lands that had fallen into the hands of unfriendly Italian noblemen. That done, he offered to side with Spain regarding Naples if Caesar could be evicted from Italy, and the Spaniards removed him by force, taking him home. That done, the Pope personally led papal armies against other Italians who held papal estates. He won, then made peace among the noblemen by arranging marriages among various factions. The Venetians turned against him. He formed an alliance with German Emperor Maximillian and King Louis XII to put down the Venetians. That done, he got the Venetians to join with Spain to get Louis out of Milan, which he had occupied. In just a few years he restored to the Church vast areas that had been slipping away for decades. In the eyes of many, this made him a great pope.

King Louis hoped to get even by starting a schism. The King called a council at Pisa for the purpose of deposing him and demanding reforms. Only six cardinals took part—two Spaniards (one a Borgia), three Frenchmen, and an Italian. Julius excommunicated four of them and threatened the remaining two with the same; the schism fizzled before it got started.

With a Rovere on the papal throne, the humanists flocked back to Rome. Most were third-rate in their arts, but there were geniuses among them. It was Julius who commissioned Michelangelo to work on the Sistine Chapel and Fra Angelico to paint in the Vatican. Julius also assigned Donato Bramante to plan the new St. Peter's Basilica, and it was this project that created the situation that was to ignite Martin Luther's outrage.

3

At first nobody took Martin Luther seriously. Even he did not realize what he was starting. But once the start was made there was no stopping.

A prime figure in the coming storm was the man who would follow Julius to the papal throne: Giovanni de' Medici, who had received his red hat at the age of thirteen. As a cardinal-deacon, he subsequently served the Church in Florence and Romagna dutifully but without distinction. He was just thirty-eight at the time of the 1513 conclave, and the improbability of his election was indicated in the first scrutiny. But in the next, held a day later, he had more than two-thirds. His sudden popularity resulted from the skillful campaign management of the Florentine aide he brought into the conclave. His campaign was reportedly free of simony; its support came from two types of men: young cardinals who expected liberality in so youthful a candidate, and any cardinal who desired the kind of a pope a Medici would make.

A true Medici and therefore a flamboyant humanist, Leo X turned the Vatican into a playhouse. The place was overrun with artists of all kinds, and plays and ballets were performed nightly. Leo also liked to hunt, and he was out in the fields after game more than he was on his throne. He was anxious for progress on St. Peter's and commissioned the great Raphael Sanzio to work on it, expanding the design in beauty and majesty far beyond anything even Julius had had in mind.

All this cost money, much more than the Vatican's normal income provided. Fresh funds had to be found somewhere. Leo made some bishoprics available—for a price. Then he remembered a fund-raising campaign Julius had started for St. Peter's. To encourage contributions, Julius had granted an indulgence to all those who donated. There was, actually, nothing wrong with this. Contributing to build a church— whether St. Peter's or a jungle chapel—certainly constituted a good work, and if a pope saw fit to apply an indulgence to such a charitable gesture it was proper for him to do so.

Julius had appointed the Franciscans to carry out the program, but in a restricted area away from the trouble spots in the north countries. It was Leo who opened the floodgates.

There was considerable discontent, particularly in Germany, with the covetousness of Rome. Taxation and tithe demands had mounted steadily, until the people felt they could bear no more of it. Also, much of the German hierarchy was no better morally than the Romans. Some of the prelates were very rich, and when they pressured further for funds to meet the Rome appeals the people began to writhe impatiently. Strangely, churchmen in high places seemed ignorant of the public sentiment. Only a few voices were raised in warning of what might happen if the fundraisers hit the people too hard. But the warnings went unheeded.

The Archbishop of Mayence, Magdeburg and Halberstadt was the Elector Albert of Brandenburg. That one man should hold three such important dioceses at one time was in itself an occasion for scandal. Worse, he had paid twenty-four thousand ducats to the Roman Curia to get them, and now he was badly in debt. When Leo suggested that the St.

Peter's Indulgence be extended to Albert's three dioceses the Archbishop approved—with the proviso that half the money raised would go to him to pay off his bills to the bank which had advanced him the money to buy his titles. Leo agreed.

Before this, the St. Peter's campaign had been carried on without much fuss; nobody expected to raise all the money for St. Peter's for many years; it would take many years to build the church. But Albert now had a personal reason to bear down on his people to get the money. To head the work he appointed a Dominican preacher named Johann Tetzel.

Over the centuries theologians had analyzed the subject of indulgences, and arrived at this interpretation: Holy personages, such as the Blessed Virgin and the saints, had received abundant merits from God as a result of their good deeds. These merits were endowed, among other attributes, with the faculty of satisfying for the temporal punishment due to sins which had been absolved by a priest in confession. In other words, confession removed the sin, but the individual was still responsible for it, and the responsibility was met in Purgatory where the soul was cleansed to prepare it for Heaven. The Virgin and the saints, because of the way they had lived, were ennobled with much more satisfactory merit than they needed to achieve Heaven. These merits, by their nature, could not simply evaporate. Instead the superabundant satisfaction of the Blessed Virgin and of the saints, together with the infinite satisfaction of Christ, accumulated in what the theologians called the Treasury of Merit, and the Popes, as vicars of Christ, were empowered to draw upon this treasury for the spiritual welfare of the people. An indulgence, then, was the remission of the temporal punishment due to sins already forgiven and was granted by the Church for pious acts, prayers, and reception of the sacraments. An indulgence could either be plenary—complete remission of responsibility—or partial—a remission of responsibility for a specified period in terms of time as measured in this world and applied relatively in whatever terms of time may be used in the next world. But for an indulgence to be effective the recipient had to be truly contrite and go to confession. However, an indulgence earned by the living could be consigned to the dead already in Purgatory to shorten their stay there, and in this instance the living person who earned the indulgence did not have to go to confession. Indulgences had been traditional in the Church since its first days; in elucidating on them theologians drew on the writings of St. Paul, who had indicated the existence of this kind of spiritual experience.

Unquestionably, the practice of indulgences had been abused. Granting them in return for funds to promote specifically Church efforts was all right; but some popes offered indulgences for money which they intended either for political purposes or for themselves, and this obviously was all wrong. The intention of Archbishop Albert to use half the money raised by the St. Peter's Indulgence to get himself out of debt could not be interpreted any other way but as a serious wrong. Pope Leo's willingness to go along with Albert was equally serious.

Their conduct provided fatal ammunition for Martin Luther.

Johann Tetzel's energy as a fund-raiser was equal to his energy as a preacher. For efficiency and thoroughness, he built up a small and well-organized team of men to assist him, and together they began their intense canvass of Albert's dioceses. If they seemed overly fervent, it was because Tetzel was a good businessman. They entered every church, every rich home, every office. On their schedule was the Wittenberg church where Martin Luther would hear them.

In years to come, there would be a great discussion on whether or not Tetzel preached heresy, and he would have to face serious cross-examination to determine whether he had given the wrong impression about the indulgence. He was able to clear himself, but some of his men were possibly not so innocent. In any event, the impression spread that to benefit spiritually from the St. Peter's Indulgence people had only to give the money; they did not have to go to confession. This implied, then, that people could buy their way into Heaven without resorting to the often embarrassing, humiliating and nerve-rending sacrament of confession. To some, this might have been attractive; to most, it was a shocking distortion of dogma.

Martin Luther continued to search for his personal justification. Prayers brought him no peace, the sacraments seemed worthless to him, good works were empty gestures, and he was beginning to believe there was really nothing to any of them. He was not the first frustrated man to feel this way and he would not be the last, but circumstances put him in a position to do the most damage. Faith was all that mattered to him—the declaration that God existed and deserved to be loved above all things. On the night of October 31, 1517, he nailed to the door of the Wittenberg church a list of ninety-five theses, criticizing the St. Peter's Indulgence, indulgences in general, and other doctrinal precepts with which he was no longer in accord.

The act itself was not unusal. It was common, particularly at universities, for students to invite debates in this manner. With Luther, the timing and the subject made the difference. The next day was the Feast of All Saints, when everybody would go to church and thus see the list on the door. And the basic subject was one on everybody's mind at the moment: Rome's persistent demands for money.

Overnight Luther was a sensation. His theses were printed and circulated throughout Germany, then Europe. If Luther thought he was alone in his protesting, he soon found that he had thousands of adherents.

Rome at first was not distressed. This sort of thing had happened before. When Luther sent a copy of his theses to

Pope Leo X, the paper was read and then filed. Leo wrote Luther's religious superiors and ordered them to silence the man. But Luther would not be silenced.

The following summer, Leo summoned Luther to Rome on charges of heresy and disobedience. The Saxon Elector Frederick, who sympathized with Luther, asked Leo to transfer the inquiry to Augsburg. Leo agreed, and he appointed Cardinal Cajetan, an Italian Dominican, and Cardinal Matthew Lang, a German, to represent him at the hearing. Both men were extremely capable theologians; Lang's only failing was that he was too friendly with Emperor Maximillian and thus not untouched by politics. Cajetan, aware of the needs for reform, hoped to rid Luther's insurrection of its heresies and then use his popularity as a means to effect corrections. But Luther, now a celebrity, was not about to let himself be used.

Tetzel tried to set things straight in a sermon at the University of Frankfort on the Oder, in which he pointed out Luther's errors regarding indulgences. Tetzel's remarks were published, and when copies reached Luther he burned them in the Wittenberg public square. He declared, "If I am called a heretic by those whose purses will suffer from my truths, I care not much for their bawling: for only those say this whose dark understanding has never known the Bible." Accusing Tetzel of being concerned only about money met with great acclaim among Luther's followers. As for the Bible, Luther's emphasis on private interpretation convinced farmers, shopkeepers and barely literate noblemen that they now understood better than theologians.

In reply, Tetzel brushed confusion aside. The question, he said, was not a matter of indulgences and it would be deceptive to pretend any longer that it was. The basic question was the authority of the Church. Either this authority was accepted or it was not. With the issue thus crystallized the next move was up to Luther: he had either to accept Church authority or be responsible for a schism.

At Augsburg, Cardinals Cajetan and Lang were given a cool reception. Before getting down to the matter at hand, the civil leaders present complained about the steady stream of Germany money that flowed over the Alps into Roman hands. Another complaint, its roots in growing nationalism, was against the appointment of Italians to German bishoprics and the Church's demand to approve the choice of any German prelates. In effect, what the Germans wanted was not a catholic church but a German church. Luther was offering them one.

At last the two cardinals were able to get around to the reason they were in Augsburg. Their criticism of Luther fell on prejudiced ears. Instead of replying immediately, Luther asked for a few days to prepare his rebuttal. When he presented it, it was a strange statement. He conceded that the Catholic Church was the true church and that it had accurately preserved the faith over the centuries, but then he added that he felt the Church had no right to do what he had just finished praising and he refused to retract any of his critical statements. Then, fearing he might be arrested and killed, he asked the Elector Frederick for safe travel back to Wittenberg. Frederick provided it. He also gave Luther a palace in which to hide out from the Church—an unnecessary precaution because Pope Leo, eager to keep affairs calm, had no intention of anything drastic. Instead, the Pope issued a bull explaining indulgences, and then he told the Dominican superiors to recall Tetzel to a monastery to preclude further debate between him and Luther.

But it was too late for diplomacy. In the palace Frederick had given him, Luther was busy at his writing. Over the next few months he produced a half dozen tracts that were bitter and vitriolic. He gnawed at every pillar of the Church—

the primacy of Rome, papal authority, reverence to Mary and the saints, the Mass, traditional celibacy for the clergy, grace, the sacraments. He translated the New Testament into German, editing according to his precepts.

By June, 1520, Leo realized the breach could not be repaired. He declared the excommunication of Luther in a bull titled *Exurge Domine,* which began: "Arise, Lord, and judge Thy cause. A wild boar has invaded Thy vineyard." The bull listed forty-one doctrinal errors in Luther's writings, ordered the burning of his books, and gave him sixty days to recant. The cardinals assisted the Pope in preparing this bull. Great care was taken to defend the Church's position in language that would explain her authority without irritating those Germans whose Lutheran sympathies were more political than theological. Pressure came from Spain, France, England, the Low Countries, and Italy for Church action against Luther. In London, King Henry VIII wrote a treatise against Luther that won for him the title of Defender of the Faith.

But all this was in vain. When Luther received a copy of the bull he burned it.

What had begun as the melodramatics of a totally unknown German monk whose inner turmoil was quite evident in his personal spiritual life now became the crucial issue on the entire continent. No heretic in centuries had won such attention, but no heretic had ever appeared at a moment when moral abuses, both in and out of the Church, created such vulnerability.

4

It was impossible to move fast. There was too much at stake. There was, also, a confusion of heart among those who knew best the great need for reform. The cardinals, seeing the Church deteriorate all around them, realized the urgency for corrections, and yet the cardinals stood to lose the most should corrections be made. Any reform that did not include the cardinalate would have been futile, indeed. The slow pace of progress toward reform was therefore inevitable.

Pope Leo X died on December 1, 1521. Thirty-nine cardinals were able to reach Rome in time for the conclave, two of them so ill that they had to be carried into the conclave on stretchers. Despite the furor of the past three years that should have bound the princes of the Church closer together, they were more divided by politics than before. The most ambitious candidate was Giulio de' Medici, cousin of the late pope. Several of the cardinals were for him: his election would have secured the extension of the Medici humanism in Rome and leniency toward reform within the cardinalate. But there were others who felt that the election of one Medici after another would look as if the papacy had become an inheritable office. The Orsinis were against him. In recent years the Orsinis had developed French leanings, and Giulio was known to be anti-French. From England, Cardinal Thomas Wolsey, appointed by Leo X on the insistence of King Henry VIII, campaigned by long distance. He had one hundred thousand ducats to invest in his efforts and he had convinced the King to send troops to Rome to force his election if early scrutinies gave him half a chance.

The many poets Leo had supported took over two weeks to read their poems about him, so it was December 17 before Leo was considered officially buried and the cardinals could get on with their work. The actual voting was to take place in the Sistine Chapel; just beyond a large room was divided into tiny cubicles for living quarters. More than two hundred aides, servants and conclave officials were locked up with the cardinals.

The first scrutiny was not held for several days, to give

the cardinals time to sound each other out. Traditionally, the Colonnas and Orsinis were in opposite camps, with Medici in his own. There was further division by age; the older cardinals reminded their confreres of the old law that the pope must be at least fifty years old, hoping thus to block the election of another youngster like Leo X. When the voting began, the first ballots gave nobody any advantage. Wolsey was out of the running from the start. By the sixth and seventh scrutiny Medici was still unable to get half the votes he needed. In hopes of supporting someone else who would be favorable toward him, he suggested other candidates, but because he had named them none got much support from the conclave. The Orsini faction worked on for France, but theirs was a losing battle: relations between England and France were already strained, and Cardinal Wolsey was working to bring Germany around to England's side. Spain, too, was cool to France.

A month passed. Eleven scrutinies were taken. There was talk of adjourning the conclave to give the cardinals a few days of fresh air. One cardinal asked to be released from the session on grounds of ill health; others suspected that he actually felt ill will because he wasn't going to be elected and they let him go.

Finally Cardinal Medici suggested, "I see that from among us who are here assembled no pope can be chosen. I have proposed three or four, but they have been rejected. Candidates recommended by the other side I cannot accept for many reasons. Therefore we must look around us for one against whom nothing can be said, but he must be a cardinal and a man of good character."

Someone asked, "Whom do you suggest?"

Medici thought a moment, then said, "The Cardinal of Tortosa."

There was an uneasy murmur; few of his fellow cardinals had even heard of the man.

The Cardinal of Tortosa (a Spanish coastal city) was a Dutchman named Adrian. He was an old man, sixty-three years of age. His ascendance came about in this way: Years before a marriage had been arranged between the daughter of the Spanish monarchs and the son of the German emperor. The couple lived in the Spanish Netherlands, where their son Charles was born. In time, Charles inherited both the Spanish and German domains. His parents died while he was still young, and he was raised by his aunt, Margaret of Austria, and educated by Adrian, then a professor at Utrecht. The young Emperor Charles V returned to Spain in 1517; distrusted as a foreigner, he didn't like much of what he found in Spain. Raised in the land where the Spanish Inquisition had failed, he was displeased to see the investigation still active in Spain itself. He dismissed the man then serving as Grand Inquisitor and appointed Adrian to the position. At the same time, he named Adrian his viceroy in Spain. In the next five years Adrian also became bishop of Tortosa, then cardinal. This was the work he was doing the day his name was mentioned in the Sistine Chapel.

It was Cardinal Cajetan who took the floor from Medici and gave a long, glowing report on Adrian, whom he had met previously in Germany. He also suggested that it might be a good idea, especially at this time, to have as pope a man who was so friendly with the Emperor. One by one the cardinals came around. Only Cardinal Orsini himself was adamant. When he saw how things were going, he jumped up and shouted, "Blockheads, do you not see that this is the ruin of France?" But the votes mounted for Adrian by accession until he had twenty-five. Then Cardinal Cupis, a Roman, announced, "I also am for the Cardinal of Tortosa, and I make him Pope."

The fact was that the cardinals didn't know what they were doing. Only days later did they begin to wonder what kind of mistake they had made. They knew little, almost nothing, about Adrian. Fears arose that he might move the Vatican to Spain, even to Germany. Because he was a stranger in Rome, no cardinals could confidently expect favoritism from him. The hundreds of laymen Leo had packed into the Curial offices wondered if, as under the Borgias, they would lose their jobs to Spaniards. Humanist artists on the Vatican payroll worried that, being Dutch, Adrian might not want them around.

When, in Spain, Adrian learned of the cardinals' decision he remarked softly, "They can't be serious."

If they weren't, he was. Because of the complications of his resigning the viceroyship, Adrian was not free to leave Spain for five months, but Rome felt his presence even when he was hundreds of miles away. It would be unrealistic to credit the cardinals for making a wise choice; if they had known him better they wouldn't have elected him. Before the year was out, people were saying, "Rome isn't Rome anymore. Adrian has turned it into a monastery."

The great regret was that Adrian—the first pope in five hundred years to keep his own name—sat on the papal throne about one year. Had he been younger or lived longer, the course of history might have been changed. He was a good and wise man. Stern, aloof, almost anti-social, he brought a sober atmosphere to Rome. Because of the tension that existed between Spain and the Church on one hand and France on the other, Adrian was faced with the problem of how he was going to get to Rome. The land route went through French territory, and this could be dangerous. When French King Francis I offered to permit him to pass under royal protection and even invited him to stay a while, the problem changed. If Adrian accepted, the rest of Europe would get the impression that he was regarding France sympathetically, and in Europe such impressions always meant a great deal. And yet to refuse Francis was not a good idea. Then Henry VIII invited Adrian to visit London, suggesting that he travel on to Rome via the Netherlands and Germany. This route was preferable in that it allowed the new pope to meet many more people en route. But it also provided Adrian with the chance to handle the French situation delicately. He refused both invitations and announced he would travel to Rome by sea.

A plain, soft-spoken, reserved man, Adrian alarmed Rome with the quiet way he made sweeping changes. Within his first weeks at Rome he pared the Curia payroll to the bone. People wondered if he meant to make Spanish replacements, since his entourage had been entirely Spanish. After allowing his traveling companions time to visit the Roman shrines, he ordered them home. He was brief, almost rude, with Dutchmen who rushed to him, refusing to see most of them. His own nephew wrote him from the University of Siena, pointing out how near he was and offering to do anything for his uncle he might want. Adrian replied that all he wanted his nephew to do was get good grades.

He dismissed practically all of the poets, painters and artists who had become Vatican leeches under Leo, retaining only those required for the work on St. Peter's. He ousted the many laymen in the Curia who, not being on a payroll, worked for whatever they could get out of people who wanted things done in the Vatican offices, and he ordered that fees for Vatican services—notarizations, transcriptions, legal transfers, etc.—would be limited to two ducats. Any employees who, because of their connections, had received a house or land in addition to a salary were informed that if they wanted to keep their extra benefits they would have to pay rent for them. When complaints reached him about his severity, he replied, "I am only trying to economize in order to pay the bills of my predecessor."

He restricted the cardinals to an income of six thousand ducats a year and indicated an intention of breaking up the multiple holdings most of them had. A cardinal told him one day, "I feel you should allot me two thousand ducats annually."

"Why?" asked Adrian.

"You said we should get six thousand a year, but I'm only getting four."

Adrian said, "When I was a cardinal I only got three thousand a year. You're better off than I ever was."

His personal piety, which should have edified, bewildered even the cardinals. He kept the canonical hours, arising in the middle of the night to read his breviary prayers at the designated time, and the only time he left the Vatican was to go to a shrine to pray. He had no use for pomp. He lived simply, ate like a monk, seldom donned his gorgeous robes except when religious ceremony required; he had few guests at mealtimes, and when he did they were astonished by the plain menu.

One day the Neapolitan delegation arrived with their city's annual tax and, as always, they brought along a big parade. As it approached the Vatican, a cardinal in Adrian's office went to the window to watch. "Here are the Neapolitans," he said.

"I hear," said Adrian.

"The parade is beautiful."

"I'm sure." Adrian did not move from his desk.

The cardinal glanced over his shoulder. "Aren't you going to look at it? They expect you to."

"Don't bother me," said Adrian. "I've got work to do."

He had hoped to do a lot. He had just informed the cardinals that he wanted to examine their books when the plague hit Rome again and the cardinals fled. Advisors urged the Pope to leave, but he said, "I am not afraid. I trust to God." It had been a long time since a Bishop of Rome had said anything like that—and meant it.

The cardinals were away six months. Adrian worked on without them. He wrote to Emperor Charles that he was sure both of them felt the same way about reforms in the Church, and he suggested this was the best time for it. He asked Charles not to put great pressure on Martin Luther to quell his schism but rather to use the public discontent to enforce corrections inside the Church itself. Had this been done, perhaps the embryonic Protestantism might have gone the way of earlier disruptions but Adrian was an old man, weary from overwork. Within a few days after the cardinals straggled back to Rome he died. There was dancing in the streets.

The conclave to choose a new pope lasted fifty days—the longest in many years. The thirty-nine cardinals present were split into three factions of equal strength. Emperor Charles backed Cardinal Giulio de' Medici, the cousin of Pope Leo X; Henry VIII again supported Cardinal Wolsey; Francis I wanted a French pope, and so did the Orsini party. The unity of the Church was about to suffer a severe blow, and instead of being concerned about it the cardinals were once again preoccupied with their personal welfare. As evidence, the capitulation act composed at the start of the conclave stipulated that the new pope would have to divide his benefices among the cardinals, a requirement that gave the vote-getting advantage to the man who had the most to give away.

All traditional conclave rules were disregarded. Instead of being isolated, the cardinals kept up a flood of letters and messages with outsiders who had an interest in the outcome. Four cardinals arrived weeks late, causing fresh onslaughts of politicking and promises. Despite agreements against simony, men fell asleep nights adding up the price tags on their votes.

Wolsey was the first to lose out. Even his strongest supporters wondered if, because of his intimacy with the English king, Wolsey might move Rome to London, and when at last it became apparent that Wolsey was giving up the fight there was a sigh of relief among those who had voted for him.

His withdrawal did not give either the Medici or the French group the necessary majority, and if either group had an effective weapon it was the order Medici's campaign leaders gave their followers: don't panic, don't worry, don't waver. The Franco-Italian faction lacked that control; gradually, one man at a time, the conclave moved to Medici. The process was so slow that people outside wondered if the cardinals intended to remain locked up for the entire winter. The conclave might have gone on much longer, had the French not made a serious mistake. In an effort to hang on to their votes and perhaps to win back men who went over to Medici, the French proposed one cardinal after another as their candidate, and then they proposed Cardinal Orsini himself. This was too much for Cardinal Pompeo Colonna, whose family had always been enemies with the Orsinis. Colonna entered a protest vote for Medici. Cardinal Medici then offered a hard cash prize if Colonna could convert some of his friends, and at the next scrutiny Medici was declared pope.

The Romans were overjoyed. Again they had a Medici for pope, and they expected a quick return to the typical Medici-type reign. As Clement VII, the new pope lived up to much of the expectation. It was said that he doled out more gifts, grants and benefices in one day than Pope Adrian VI had in a year, and this was the sort of thing the Romans liked. For himself, however, Clement adopted a comparatively simple life. There was, to be sure, much more gaiety in the Vatican than there had been for over a year, but not nearly as much as the humanists had hoped for. In flamboyant terms, Clement was something of a disappointment.

He was a disappointment in another, more serious, way. Clement proved to have the gift of elusion: he was incapable of taking a stand or making a decision. He could answer pointed questions floridly, but still say nothing. He was a poor judge of men because he was not much of a man himself. His conclave campaign had been clever and forceful, but now it seemed that his efforts might have been in the hands of other men because once he acquired papal power it was soon evident that he lacked any papal talent. Unlike the other Medici, he was not an immoral man, but he wasn't very holy either. He was a priest—indeed, the ranking priest of the world—and yet he seldom said Mass or displayed any special piety outside of important ceremonies. Men who thought they were his friends found him unapproachable, not because he was haughty or busy but simply because he was vague. Had this been an era of golf or fishing, he might have spent much time away from the Vatican at such pleasures; instead he remained at his palace, hidden behind a fog of indecision and ineptness, surrounding himself with men of equal mediocrity.

Emperor Charles expected great things from Clement, especially since the Emperor had been greatly responsible for his election. But, presumably fearing that Charles intended to dominate him, Clement, to wide consternation, signed a treaty with the King of France. Thus Clement became an ally of the very man who had connived for fifty days to prevent his becoming pope. In effect, the French lost the papal election, but they won the pope. The result was war and revolution. Imperial troops, judged by some to be in mutiny, stormed Rome and sacked the city. In the end, Clement had to turn back to Charles for help and eventually humble himself to the extent of traveling to Bologna to crown Charles as temporal head of the Holy Roman Empire.

Clement, then, was scarcely the man to solve the internal problems of the Church, and it was not surprising that during his eleven-year reign the Church began to crumble.

5

For almost three years Martin Luther remained at the palace near Wittenberg which the Elector Frederick had loaned him and he occupied himself with his writing. Repeatedly he insisted that he had not instigated a schism and he denied that he intended to start a new church. His writings gave quite the contrary impression; his attacks on the Catholic tradition left little hope for any reconciliation. Men near him took firm steps toward a new church. The Mass was pared to a brief ceremony; the new religion put its spiritual emphasis on sermons and hymn-singing. Whether he wanted it or not, a new denomination was appearing, and when it seemed to be passing into other hands Luther decided to assure control of it by writing devotionals and hymns and prescribing religious ceremonies. In 1525, he met Katherine von Bora, a nun who had left her convent after reading his works; they married and subsequently had six children. Luther urged all his friends, particularly apostate priests, to marry nuns, which in view of the moral climate of Germany was not difficult to do.

Emperor Charles still hoped Luther's damage could be repaired. With Pope Clement's approval, he summoned a conference at Augsburg to determine whether any of Luther's complaints, which weren't outright heresy, could be modified in a way that would return the Protestants to Rome. There had been long discussions among the cardinals about the Augsburg session. Some of them considered it a waste of time. Luther had claimed that councils were greater than popes, but that the individual was greater than councils, so it seemed fruitless to concede to another council when obviously Luther would ignore its results unless they were favorable to him. Nevertheless, Clement went along with the idea in order to placate Charles and he appointed Cardinal Lorenzo Campeggio to represent him. Luther assigned Peter Melanchthon, an extreme humanist who taught Greek at Wittenberg University and had changed his German name, Schwarzend, to its Greek form. It was Melanchthon who did most to organize Luther's ideas into a sect; it was he who tried to reconcile the humanists and the puritans by trying to retain some church decorations, and it was he who struggled futilely to prevent other Protestant leaders from protesting so much against some of Luther's precepts that they threatened to start fresh heresies within his heresy.

Cardinal Campeggio found the Augsburg atmosphere definitely unfriendly. At early sessions when he tried to explain the position of the Church he was seldom able to finish a sentence without interruptions by hecklers. More anxious than the Protestants for Church reforms, Campeggio was prepared to discuss corrections, even extreme changes, and he was confident that he could convince Clement to approve modifications which, in the long run, would serve to benefit the Church. But he was not given much of a chance by the German clergy and noblemen.

Melanchthon's remarks to the council were much calmer than anybody expected. Speaking for Luther, he showed an unusual willingness to conform to many Vatican attitudes which previously had been points of contention. Campeggio would have been the first to agree that mismanagement by weak popes and abuses by ambitious cardinals had caused scandal and that reform was necessary. The same was true about absentee bishops, excessive taxation, and misuse of indulgences. If anything, the Lutheran complaints were to be credited with making all this a continental issue which had to be cleaned up.

There were, however, three points in Melanchthon's remarks that went much deeper. The first pertained to the sacrament of Holy Communion. Luther agreed that the sacrament contained the Actual Presence of Jesus, as He had indicated when He instituted it at the Last Supper. In the first centuries of the Church, the laity received both the bread and wine, as they had been presented at the Last Supper. Theologians subsequently defined that the bread—the Communion wafer—in itself contained the True Presence and it was sufficient for the laity to receive it alone while the priest, filling at Mass the role of Jesus at the Last Supper, should receive the wine as well. Now Luther wanted the laity to take both the bread and wine. Melanchthon's second point concerned the celibacy of the clergy. Traditional for centuries and then made law by the popes, celibacy among the clergy was a vital precept of the Roman Church. Luther wanted priests to be able to marry. As his third point, Luther wanted changes in the Mass and other ecclesiastical ceremonies which he personally disliked.

Having expected much more, Campeggio was relieved by Luther's demands and optimistically forwarded them to the Vatican. Pope Clement wasn't too sure what to do. Empowered to reach decisions himself, he was unwilling to do so. Of the three points, he felt the matter of marriage for the clergy was the simplest to resolve. In the Greek rite, priests could marry before ordination but not after. If granting the same prerogative to the Germans meant holding the Church together, Clement was ready to comply. Nevertheless, he did not feel it within himself to move ahead on his own. Instead, he called a consistory and submitted the issues to the cardinals. Their reaction was a blunt refusal to all three points, and Clement accepted their decision.

The outcome of it all was that the Augsburg council achieved nothing, except to provide Lutherans with a definition of their creed which they have since referred to as the Augsburg Confession. Other denominations were to reject parts of it, the most important of which was the denial of the True Presence in the Communion sacrament. This and other differences eventually put the Protestants against each other and soon, despite their insistence on private interpretation of doctrine, they were in open conflict and resorted to the kinds of pressure they resented from the Catholic Church, even to the extent of executing heretics.

Crystallized at Augsburg was the growing attitude of, in Latin, *Cujus regio, illius religio:* As is the ruler, so is the religion. This was the beginning of the Lutheran State Church, which spread from Germany to Denmark, Sweden, Norway, Iceland and the Baltic. In all these countries, Catholics in Lutheran spheres had a rough time. Priests and bishops loyal to Rome had to leave the country and their properties passed into the hands of the ruling power. That much of the clergy quickly sided with the new religion indicated how far removed they already were from Rome. Anti-Catholic laws were imposed, turning Catholics into steerage-class citizens. Many years were to pass, years of persecution, tribulation and bloodshed, before priests would be allowed to return to meet the spiritual needs of Catholics who did not leave the country. Undoubtedly there were sincere people on both sides, or else fewer would have been willing to die for what they believed, but it should be pointed out that just as cardinals and popes were guilty of effecting the shocking conditions which erupted into the German schism the German nobles, bishops and priests had a guilt of their own in depriving thousands of the Church for no other reasons but money, safety and power. To convert by persuasion would have been one thing; to convert by royal edict was quite another. Overnight entire Catholic states found themselves Lutheran: what was doctrinal truth yesterday was not true today, and the verdict had not been reached by theology but by politics. In lands where apostate priests harped on the importance of individual interpretation of spiritual precepts the interpretation of spiritual precepts became the domain of the individual who ruled. The moral responsibility for this was far more serious than the misconduct in the Vatican. The damage done could not be as easily repaired.

6

English difficulties with the Church had a decidedly different hue. As on the continent, there was an old discontent in England toward Church prerogatives, going back three hundred years to the Barons' War and the Magna Carta. Forerunners of Protestantism, like Wyclif and William of Ockham, had planted the idea that perhaps the laity was not quite as responsible to the Church, even in moral issues, as had been maintained, and the growth of nationalism stirred resentment against what was considered foreign intervention. Furthermore, as in Europe, England had undergone a spiritual decay: in over a hundred years there were only six new monasteries. The desire for the absolute religious life was withering. Certainly the moral climate in Rome contributed somewhat to this, but other factors of weight were Renaissance humanism, wars, the new emphasis on personal success, the ambitions of the nobility for more wealth and power, and the increasing poverty in the lower classes. In England, however, the explosion occurred at the top.

In 1501, King Henry VII, eager to improve his position among European royal families, arranged a marriage between his son Arthur, then fourteen, and Catherine of Aragon, the sixteen-year-old daughter of Ferdinand and Isabella of Spain. When Arthur died six months later, Henry, afraid of losing the important connection with Spain, offered to marry Catherine himself, but this was not acceptable to the Spaniards. The King then suggested his son Prince Henry as Catherine's new husband. Church law forbade a man to marry his brother's widow, and Prince Henry, then eleven years old, was scarcely a man in the first place. A papal dispensation was necessary, and in 1504 it was granted by Pope Julius II. Even then young Henry was unwilling to proceed with the marriage. It was in 1509, when the Prince had become king and reached the age of nineteen, that the ceremony was performed.

Present at it was Thomas Wolsey. After a brilliant career at Oxford, Wolsey had become a professor at Magdalen College while still a young man, and he was ordained a priest in 1498 at the age of twenty-six. His patron was Thomas Grey, marquess of Dorset, who opened many doors to the young priest, and in 1506 he was appointed chaplain to Henry VII. He served the King well on various diplomatic missions and took care to ingratiate himself with the young prince. When the prince became King Henry VIII he appointed Wolsey the royal almoner in 1509, then privy councilor in 1511. On the young king's insistence, Wolsey was made a cardinal in 1514 by Pope Leo X and received the archbishopric of York. The next year Henry made him lord chancellor, the second most important position in the country. Wolsey was a master at power politics and was probably more responsible for England's rise in world affairs than the king. From his positions in both the Church and the government he acquired a great deal of money, building several palaces and maintaining a very elaborate personal court.

The trouble began some twelve years later. Catherine had borne several children, but only one—a daughter—survived infancy, and Henry began to complain that he wanted a son. Actually, Catherine and Henry had never really cared much for each other; Henry had a series of mistresses and he was particularly enamored of his latest—Anne Boleyn, daughter of the earl of Wiltshire, who was one of Catherine's ladies-in-waiting. Henry wanted to get a divorce from Catherine so he could marry Anne, but he knew that this would be difficult to obtain from Rome. He instructed Cardinal Wolsey to see what could be done.

Wolsey had twice failed to win a papal election for himself, but he felt nevertheless that he had friends in Rome who could help him with the impossible task Henry had tossed at him. Wolsey had been surprised by Henry's decision; he had no idea how far the affair with Anne Boleyn had gone. When Henry finally confided in him in June of 1527 the Cardinal was so stunned that he was unable to think of any way to help for over a month. Henry accused him of stalling, and thus began the rift between the two men. Also, the King complicated matters further by ordering Catherine out of his bedchamber. With that, the situation had gone too far to retrieve and Wolsey realized he would have to do something to save his own neck as well as Henry's.

A divorce was out of the question. Wolsey's only chance was to establish that the papal bull permitting the marriage was illegal or that certain circumstances existed which made the marriage invalid. In either case, an annulment was then possible, although after eighteen years of living together as man and wife the annulment of the royal marriage would seem strange indeed. Furthermore, with Catherine now living apart from Henry and Anne practically living in, attempts to mask the situation could not be effective.

In the fall of 1527, Wolsey had his delegate to Rome present to Pope Clement VII a declaration to the effect that the marriage between Catherine and Henry was invalid on the grounds that Pope Julius II had had no authority to grant the dispensation which permitted it and that for eighteen years the English royal couple had been living in sin. Clement almost went into shock. He put Vatican experts to work studying the dispensation and it was soon clear that the Church lawyers who had prepared it had done so thorough a job in establishing precedents for it that there could be no question of its validity.

Now it was time for Wolsey and Henry to suffer a shock of their own. Catherine announced that her marriage to fourteen-year-old Arthur had not been consummated during the six months it existed; it was, therefore, not a true marriage. Consequently no dispensation had been necessary for her marriage to her first husband's brother. This changed the entire picture. Even before Clement had time to reply to Wolsey's first document, the Cardinal prepared another and rushed it off to Rome. The new document was in the form of a papal bull which Wolsey wanted Clement to sign, and it provided for an annulment on the grounds that the marriage had been arranged without Henry's knowledge, at a time when he was too young to marry, and that he had subsequently been forced into the marriage against his free will and consent. The fact that Henry had waited eighteen years to declare his position was overlooked.

The problem could not have hit Clement at a worse time. Still reeling from the Lutheran uprising in Germany and wars in Italy, Clement was ill-prepared to deal with what he knew perfectly well was Henry's desire to switch wives. Henry had defended the Church against Luther; there were not many rulers around willing to do that. To reject Henry's request as the outrage that it was would have been extremely indelicate.

In any event, a trial would have to be held, and by rights it should have been held in Rome, but because a king was involved Clement conceded to Wolsey's request that it be conducted in England. He then appointed Cardinal Campeggio to represent him and when the Cardinal left for England months later he was armed with two documents. The first permitted the investigation into the marriage to be made. The second, prepared after long discussion with the cardinals and then without their knowledge, was a concession to Wolsey, in that, depending on the outcome of the trial, it authorized Campeggio and Wolsey to declare the marriage annulled, subject to Clement's approval. Clement was afraid of this document because he knew how easily misused it could be by the wrong people, but he had issued it on pleas from Wolsey that without some indication of the Pope's sympathy for Henry the entire Church was threatened in England. Clement authorized Campeggio to show and to read the second bull to Henry and Wolsey but never to let it out of his hands until he was convinced that grounds for annulment existed. If such grounds failed to appear or if anyone tried to take the document from Campeggio by force, he was to destroy it.

Wolsey did all he could to push the annulment through; his own career depended on it. He went so far as to get French King Francis I to write Clement, urging the papal approval. He tried every trick to convince Campeggio to accept false evidence that might invalidate the marriage, even resorting to bribery. But Campeggio would not be convinced. He realized there was no sense in going on, but he knew he could not simply pack up and go home. Instead, he invoked a Roman law which closed Church courts during the summer months. It would have been awkward for Henry to object; doing so, he would have revealed that he was not as anxious to end his presumably sinful life with Catherine as he was to start a new one with Anne. He permitted Campeggio to leave London. At Dover, Campeggio's luggage was searched, obviously for the papal document that Clement had unwisely written too soon. But Campeggio, expecting trouble, had already burned it.

Wolsey's career was over before Campeggio reached Rome. He was dismissed as lord chancellor, deprived of all his titles and lands except those of the Church, and banned from the royal court. A short time later he was accused of high treason and summoned to London for trial, but he died before he could reach the city. Near his end, he said of himself, "If I had served God as diligently as I have done my King, He would not have given me over in my gray hairs. But this is the just reward I must receive, for in my diligent pains and studies to serve the King, I looked not to my duty towards God but only to the gratification of the King's wishes."

The cardinals in Rome then took the marriage problem into their own hands. At a consistory held while Campeggio was traveling across France, the cardinals voted that future hearings of the trial would be held before the Church tribunals in Rome. Their announcement put the emphasis not on Henry's position, but on Catherine's. Since she had long insisted that the marriage was valid, with or without the dispensation, there was little doubt how the Rome trial would decide.

Henry did not intend to quit. Rising in popularity in England was a priest named Thomas Cranmer. Destined for the clergy by his family, Cranmer had married while at college, then resumed his seminary studies after his wife's death. A few years younger than Martin Luther, Cranmer had been impressed by the German's ninety-five theses when copies of them arrived in England. Protestant emissaries visiting England found Cranmer interested in what they had to say. With Wolsey out of the way, the door was open for Cranmer to move into royal company and he awaited the moment when he could get close enough to the King to suggest an idea that had occurred to him as a result of reading Luther's theory regarding the role of temporal rulers in religion. If, Cranmer told Henry, the head of the state was the head of the Church, couldn't the clergy subject to the King decide certain ecclesiastic matters, such as divorce, without intervention from Rome? Ought not the leaders of the English clergy get together to take a stand on something like that? This was exactly what Henry wanted to hear.

Leaders of the English clergy were, for the most part, associated with universities which depended upon Henry for their budgets. In January, 1531, these men adjudged that Henry was indeed the head of the Church in England. Henry then turned on the clergy by summoning a convocation in Canterbury and accusing that, in accepting Wolsey to be a papal legate to sit in judgment of him, they had broken an old and forgotten law prohibiting recourse to Rome on matters pertinent to England itself. As punishment, the clergy were to pay the King a fine and recognize him as head of the Church in the country. They did both.

Then things began to move fast. Under pressure from Henry, Parliament passed laws against annates to Rome and the Peter's Pence collection. Another law proclaimed that England no longer was subject to Rome in determining cases regarding marriages. In a surprising show of weakness, Pope Clement approved Henry's request for Cranmer to be made a bishop, then the King appointed him archbishop, second in Church authority only to himself. Cranmer in turn appointed a committee to hear—secretly, to avoid public complaint—divorce evidence on Henry's case, and the divorce was granted. On January 25, 1533, Henry and Anne were secretly married by Cranmer. Anne was several months pregnant with her daughter who was to become Queen Elizabeth I.

At first Henry tried to keep the Church in England as Roman as possible. Although some changes were introduced in worship, doctrine remained untouched. Cranmer was displeased with this, because he hoped to adopt many of the ideas popular in Germany, especially regarding Communion, confession, and celibacy for the clergy. To prepare the way, he encouraged Henry to have all references to Rome and the popes erased from devotionals and replaced by his name as supreme head of the English Church. Henry actually didn't intend to spend much time at the new role he adopted, and he appointed Thomas Cromwell, a member of the House of Commons, to supervise the Church for him. Under Cromwell, monasteries were confiscated and convents closed, the manner of Communion and confession was changed, priests were allowed to marry, and about three hundred people who opposed Henry's religious leadership were beheaded.

At a consistory in Rome, Pope Clement pronounced the excommunication of both Henry and Anne. But the King and Queen of England were not disturbed. They had a church of their own.

XII

*L*ong before Luther there had been men who saw the need for reforms in the Catholic Church. With the Vatican itself a battleground for Roman nobles, there was little chance for dramatic corrections at the root of the trouble, but outside of Rome, in every nation, men and women at every level of the religious life dedicated themselves to the immense chore of rectifying abuses. In Spain, Ignatius de Loyola and Teresa of Avila were so energetic in their efforts that both were suspected by the Inquisition of schismatic plots against the Church they were merely trying to cleanse. Loyola's militant Jesuits were literally an army against corruption, exercising such blatant force that time and again they were to be expelled from countries where they had turned their moral guns on evil.

In Italy, new orders of priests appeared. The Oratory of Divine Love concentrated on reformation of the secular clergy. The Theatines and the Barnabites, organized in Chieti and Milan, fanned out across the continent to reach people who seldom saw a priest and never saw their bishop. Many bishops, too, participated in such activities. Bishop Gaetano dei Conti di Tiene resigned from the diocese of Chieti to join the work of the Theatines. Bishop Giberti of Verona ceaselessly toured his diocese to enforce discipline upon the clergy and stir piety in the people. It was Giberti who instituted the ringing of bells when the Host was elevated during the Mass, now a universal custom, and it was also he who first had the Blessed Sacrament reserved on the high altar for adoration at all times, another practice now followed in every church. Cardinal Charles Borromeo of Milan was particularly outstanding. He founded seminaries, reorganized monasteries, opened elementary schools for the poor, started houses for beggars, solved labor disputes, and set up a legal aid society for those who could not afford lawyers. When an epidemic struck Milan, he sold all his household effects to provide medicine for the poor and even had his draperies made into clothing for those who had lost everything.

Several members of the Sacred College of Cardinals were great scholars, profound theologians and truly saintly men; the trouble was that they were outnumbered by another type. At the six conclaves that took place at the beginning of the sixteenth century the devout cardinals insisted that a pledge for reforms be written into the acts of capitulation; consequently, if the pledge was not fulfilled, the fault lay with the men who were elected. Since the councils of Basel and Constance at which such conferences were acclaimed superior in authority to popes, the occupants of the Vatican were afraid to encourage further sessions of this kind. Only Adrian II gave serious thought to a council, but he didn't live long enough to do anything about it.

The Lutheran heresy and the English schism had both served to spotlight the deplorable state of Church affairs, and it was soon evident that corrective measures must be taken promptly. This conviction became apparent at the conclave following the death of Clement VII in 1534. For the first time in years, age and nationality were not important factors for the thirty-five cardinals present, and even political connections in Rome seemed to make little difference. French King Francis I and Emperor Charles V had both notified their cardinals of their personal preferences, but even they conceded that a neutral pope who was concerned primarily with reforms would be acceptable.

Even before the conclave began the cardinals agreed that their obvious choice was Alessandro Farnese, dean of the College, who, while Clement was still alive, had frequently said that a council ought to be held to resolve the many issues facing the Church. If any cardinal seemed equipped to accomplish reform, Farnese was it. When he was appointed cardinal by Alexander VI in 1503 he matched the Borgia pope for wild living. His own sister had been one of Alexander's mistresses and he himself had an equally promiscuous record. He continued at it after becoming cardinal for almost sixteen years, but when he was ordained a priest in 1519 he reformed completely.

The morning the 1534 conclave opened there was such agreement on Farnese that nobody suggested an act of capitulation because there was nothing to fear. Even before the first scrutiny could be taken, the cardinals appointed a committee to inform Farnese that he had been elected, and it was only for the sake of the record that a vote was actually taken. There hadn't been so clean, so quick, an election since Hildebrand, five hundred years before. But this did not guarantee that the new pope would have an easy time of it.

As Paul III, the new pope turned his reform attentions on the Curia itself. This came as a shock to several cardinals, who had hoped that Paul would start a little farther from home. To them, it seemed a general council was the best approach, if only because it would take a long time to organize. The Pope felt, however, that it would be unwise to submit the Church to a continental conference of bishops when the Curia, the Church's executive department, was the source of most of the abuses people were complaining about. Ignoring the cardinals' criticisms, Paul appointed cardinals to reorganize the Curial departments: the Rota, the Cancelleria, the Penitentiaria, the Dataria, and the Courts of Justice. In making the appointments—two men to each investigation committee—Paul was careful not to assign cardinals to reform departments with which they already had any affiliations. As a further safeguard, the Pope chose a dozen new cardinals, among whom were some outstanding men as eager for reforms as he; four of Paul's appointments subsequently became popes during the reformation period on which the Church had now embarked.

But it proved extremely difficult to get the Curial reorganization off the ground. Left alone for hundreds of years, it had developed its own social hierarchy. Important jobs remained in the same family—often the family of a cardinal or a pope—for generations. This was the sort of thing that had contributed heavily to the mismanagement of the Curia: men swindled, pilfered, and accepted payoffs, knowing their grandfathers had done so and believing that was the way things were supposed to be. Now to have a committee of cardinals examine accounts and records and treasuries was more insulting than embarrassing. The cardinals had to be careful. They never knew when they would expose as an outright criminal a man whose uncle or cousin was an examiner on another committee, or when the finger would be pointed at a relative of theirs. The investigation, therefore, proceeded slowly. Pope Paul was on his throne five years before a dent was made in the chore.

He trimmed staffs on all sides, unmindful of whose head must roll. Noblemen lost their soft berths as swiftly as an inept clerk, and in time most of the best families of Rome had reason to despise the Pope. He ordered a double-check system by which no individual could acquire enough unquestioned authority for bribes or favoritism to pass undetected. He had manuals prepared for people who weren't sure what their jobs were, and this was the predicament in a surprising number of cases. He insisted on a careful accounting of all funds, coming in and going out, and if any of it seemed to be disappearing along the way he wanted to know where it went. This was unheard of in Roman economy, in or out of the Church; the popular attitude was that any employee who didn't steal at least a little was definitely a man to be watched because he was probably out for bigger game.

Living in Rome were eighty bishops who held sees elsewhere; some had never seen the dioceses they ruled but simply used their income to live well in Rome. One day the Pope called them all together, reminded them that a shepherd's place was with his flock and told them to go home. A few of them were actually startled enough to go.

2

That was the trouble with it all. The reformation was so long overdue that those who wanted it most couldn't believe it and those who needed it most didn't believe it. Since Paul had been sixty-nine years old when he was elected, some of the culprits were hopeful that he would not last long. But he hung on for fifteen years, occupied principally with house-cleaning. Each step he took was blocked by indifference, lethargy, hopelessness and opposition. To many, his efforts were a joke. Roman dramatists wrote plays ridiculing him. But he would not stop. Ten years after his election he could say that things were running more smoothly in the Vatican, if not as happily.

His major concern was to hold a general council. With this, too, he ran into trouble. Cardinals who had elected him had wanted a council, but now that they had seen how Paul conducted himself they were not so sure. Other factors were involved. Europe had become a powder keg, filled with Protestant noblemen ready to explode on the slightest provo-cation by their Catholic emperor. Emperor Charles, dur-ing one of his friendly meetings with the Pope, said he, too, wanted a council, but he wanted the Protestants to be there and he didn't want anything discussed that might offend them. Pope Paul pointed out to Charles that the purpose of the council was to strengthen the Church, not dilute it.

Protestant sensitivities even affected the site of the coun-cil. Charles suggested Basel or Constance, scarcely wise choices in view of the setbacks the papacy had suffered at councils previously held in both cities. The Pope suggested Mantua, but the duke of Mantua refused: he didn't want any Protestant-Catholic debate to break out into war in his duchy. The rulers of Venice used the same reason to avoid having a council held there. Spain was too inaccessible, France was not too friendly, and Germany was such a hodge-podge of bitterly denominational principalities that one step in the wrong direction could put a Catholic or Protestant into enemy territory. The Pope proposed Trent, an in-dependent city-state bordering both Germany and Italy, and everybody agreed.

On December 13, 1545, the Council of Trent was opened

by three cardinals assigned to act as presidents. One other cardinal was present to take part in the proceedings. Of the hundreds of bishops in Europe, only thirty went to Trent. No Protestants were there, so the hope of restoring unity seemed slim. And yet this was destined to be the most important council in the history of the Catholic Church.

The Council of Trent extended over a period of eighteen years, during which twenty-five one-day sessions were held to receive, discuss and vote on definitions prepared at long and turbulent committee meetings. Like the Curial reformations, the council was slow to start, mostly because of the apprehensions of the men who were there. Opinions on several matters were sharply divided. Cardinals Giovanni del Monte and Marcello Cervini, both eventually to become popes, sternly rejected any concessions to the Protestants. English Cardinal Reginald Pole, assigned to the Curia, felt the Protestants had a point or two, especially in the matter of justification by faith. The two Italians accused Pole of latent heresy, whereas Pole was guilty only of being over-anxious to attract the Protestants back to the Church. In appointing three such men as council presidents, Pope Paul sought not compromise but balance, something so emotional a convention needed.

Another divisive feature of the opening sessions concerned subjects to be discussed. Bishops submissive to Emperor Charles wished to restrict the disciplinary measures intended to correct the abuses Protestants had criticized. The Emperor feared that any name-calling or finger-pointing might incite his Protestant nobles to further conflict. But the two Italian cardinals would not hear of such limitations. Reflecting the Pope's attitude, they said the Church had no intention of conciliating the Protestants. Dogma had been attacked; dogma would now be defended.

In such an atmosphere, the first sessions could do little more than prepare an agenda. Subsequent sessions were endangered by offers from Protestant princes to recapture the Piedmont which Charles had lost to France, provided he would denounce the council and sever his alliance with the Pope. It was a tempting offer, particularly since the council was not going as Charles had instructed, but Charles had already committed himself to go to battle against the Protestants, whenever necessary, so he could not enter into such an agreement with them. Instead, he invited Protestant leaders to a religious discussion at Ratisbon, at which he hoped enough harmony would be achieved to encourage them to go to Trent, but the talks at Ratisbon were such a dismal failure that the Protestants left the city even before Charles could get there. The Protestant affront ruined any chance of achieving the compromise wanted by the Emperor.

The Protestants were not ignoring the council. Philip Melanchthon, a close associate of and important influence on Luther, wrote two pamphlets, long and vitriolic diatribes on why Protestants rejected the council. A disconcerting aspect of the council was that so few bishops were there; to a mere handful went the responsibility of defining dogma which all loyal bishops would have to accept and preach. This was part of the Protestant objection to the Church itself: a few men decided what all men, at least all Catholics, would be bound to believe. But in this instance the situation couldn't be helped. Certainly more bishops could have gone to Trent. Some didn't because they did not think much would come of the council. Others were not free to travel: to reach Trent they would have had to pass through the territory of unfriendly Protestant rulers who understandably would give neither permission to do so nor guarantees of safe travel.

Nevertheless, a great deal was accomplished at the ten sessions held between 1545 and 1547. The council decreed that the only *bona fide* Bible was the Latin Vulgate, which the Church alone had the authority to interpret. This was tantamount to a denunciation of the vernacular translations of the Bible being produced in Germany and England, and it was also a rejection of the Protestant idea of private interpretation. The council also defined the Church's position on original sin, baptism, confirmation, and free will, and clarified the Catholic attitude that good works were necessary to earn spiritual graces.

One subject came up that the bishops could not resolve: bishops. The three cardinals proposed that a bishop should hold only one diocese and that he should live in that diocese, supporting himself and his work as well as he could on funds available in the diocese. The bishops had a hard time putting such restrictions on themselves, and when the subject came up in a general session the discussion became so heated that Pope Paul suggested it be dropped for the time being.

In March, 1547, an epidemic of plague broke out in Trent. The council was hastily adjourned and the bishops hurried out of the city. The Pope tried to reconvene the council at Mantua, but again the duke rejected the plan. The bishops, too, were against changing the site of the council, now that it had been started.

Pope Paul died in November, 1549, and was succeeded by Cardinal del Monte. Experienced at the council, the new pope, as Julius III, was anxious to get on with it. He managed to reconvene the council at Trent in the fall of 1551. This time there were about fifty bishops attending. There had been considerable haggling at the first session among the three cardinals acting as presidents; to avoid that, Julius appointed one cardinal-president: Marcello Crescenzi, the Bishop of Marsico.

The new meetings were just getting under way when exciting news arrived: the Protestants were coming. A dozen princes and barons, with a staff of theologians, had asked Emperor Charles for a promise of safe passage through Catholic states, of which he quickly assured them. Council leaders hoped for the best. Pope Julius ordered Crescenzi to welcome the Protestants in good faith and to give them every opportunity to speak their minds at council meetings. He added, however, that although the Protestants should be accepted as friends they were not to be given the impression that they were entering the council as conquerors: there was to be no compromise on basic tenets of the Church.

The Protestants lost no time in stating their position. Protocol and ordinary good manners required them to present themselves and their credentials to Crescenzi, but they refused to go anywhere near him. Instead, they declared their official presence to the Emperor's ambassadors and let it go at that. They avoided the Solemn Mass which opened each day's proceedings, and at the first session they attended they neglected to acknowledge their presence to Crescenzi. It was the Cardinal who acknowledged them, and he thereupon reported to the assembly the Pope's instructions for the spirit with which the Protestants were to be welcomed. He then asked the Protestant spokesman if he cared to make any remarks.

The man had much to say. First, the council must put aside any decisions reached at previous meetings and reopen all subjects to new discussion. Second, the bishops and cardinals present must disavow themselves of any oath of obedience to the Pope, the council must be disassociated from the Church, and the Pope deprived of his right to disapprove any conclusions reached. Third, the Protestants were ready to discuss any subject with the Catholics, providing the judges of the debates were not Catholic clergymen but a committee on which the Protestants would be equally represented.

The Catholics recognized they had been handed a stiff ultimatum, but they were eager to keep the Protestants at Trent because they believed they could win any debates on doctrinal matters. They therefore agreed to annul their past decisions and to compromise on a committee of lay judges. But they were all clergymen and, as such, could not break their oaths of obedience to the Pope, nor would they agree to have the council's decisions rated above the papal prerogatives. In that case, said the Protestants, there could be no discussions at all, and they left.

3

The council went on with its work. Two general sessions were held in the next two months, at which sub-committees presented in beautiful Latin that was lucid and incontrovertible a series of definitions on the Actual Presence of Jesus in the Communion Host, the importance of penance, the efficacy of Extreme Unction, the role and duties of bishops, and the responsibility of the clergy to lead pure lives.

Among Catholics the council was beginning to take on great importance. People were surprised and pleased by the vivid language of the decrees, the sharp definitions of Catholic beliefs, the conduct and spirituality of the council members and the speed with which the council decisions received papal approval and were put into action. Things went so well that Emperor Charles felt the 1551-52 sessions would bring an end to the council, which he wanted very much because of the thorn it was in the sides of the Protestants surrounding him. When the sessions adjourned with much work still undone, it was generally believed that the bishops would return to Trent in a few months. However, ten years were to pass before Council of Trent would meet again.

The principal reason for the long postponement was the change of popes. Julius III died in 1555 and was succeeded by Cardinal Cervini, who had served with him and Cardinal

Pole at the first meetings at Trent. Cervini was only fifty-four years old, but he had worked hard at Trent and his labors had cost him his health. Twenty-two days after his election as Marcellus II, he died in his sleep.

Forty-five cardinals participated in the conclave that elected Cardinal Gian Pietro Carafa after a month of deliberations. Seventy-nine years old, the new Pope had been Dean of the College of Cardinals. He was not well liked, but he was well respected. He had made no effort to win the papacy for himself; the men who campaigned for him considered him the best choice to carry on the reforms on which the Church was now embarked. He certainly was.

It was he who, as the Bishop of Chieti, had asked to be relieved of his diocese so he could join the Theatines in their reforms among the secular clergy, and he did such a good job of it that Pope Paul III had appointed him to the Vatican to supervise reforms in the Curia. He later served as the cardinal-archbishop of Naples, his home city, before his seniority among the cardinals brought him back to the Vatican. He was a stern man, crisp, almost rude, quick-tempered and about as diplomatic as a mule. As close advisor to Paul III, he was largely responsible for the Council of Trent and had suggested the three cardinals who acted as its presidents, but he could not abide committee-rule for long, and was probably responsible for having later council meetings conducted by one president. Because of his interest in the council, it was expected that he would quickly call it back into session, but he had greatly resented Emperor Charles's efforts to influence the council and wanted no more of it.

He took the name of Paul IV, and soon after his election he uttered striking evidence of the kind of pope he would be. When someone remarked that the Emperor was happy about his election, he replied, "Tell the Emperor not to think he had anything to do with my election, nor that his cardinals did, either. God chose me."

It was a choice made in a moment of wrath. The Church had not seen such a despot in years. Paul seemed oblivious to the changes in the world that had reduced the papacy from its absolute authority. He tried to rule like a pope of an earlier century, but fear of God had gone out of people and, with it, obedience to the Church. In being firm, Paul won nothing but many enemies. As a cardinal, he had urged the creation of a Roman Inquisition, but the office that was set up was far too ineffectual for him. He put scores of books on the Index and punished their authors as heretics. Jews who had come to look upon Rome as a haven saw the city turned into a hell for them and once again they were forced to wander the world's highways searching for a home.

Paul banned all merriment in Rome. Theaters were closed, festivals were prohibited, any gathering that was not specifically religious was virtually a crime. Laughter bordered on sin. The Vatican work day took on a monastic regimen. Staffs were greatly diminished, and people who managed to keep their jobs worked like slaves and for slave wages. Like all popes, Paul was besieged by his relatives and he gave a few of them important positions. But as soon as he detected that they were misusing their authority and indulging in undue luxury he slashed at them as he did everyone else.

It was impossible to get along with him, and dangerous to disagree with him. He refused to see important cardinals or ambassadors because he felt they had nothing worthwhile to say to him. Considering himself a supreme ruler, he saw no reason for consulting with anybody else. The few who did earn audiences with him departed hastily with the feeling that he was snapping at their heels. In time people stopped trying to discuss problems with him; the experience was humiliating and fruitless.

He turned his fury upon the most unlikely persons. When Mary, the daughter of Henry VIII and Catherine of Aragon, became queen in 1553, her Catholic upbringing led her to restore the Church in England. Cardinal Pole was sent to London by Julius III to make the restoration as painless as possible. By the time Paul became pope, Parliament was willing to go along with the idea to a modified degree. Anti-Catholic laws were repealed, ecclesiastical courts were re-opened and the Church of England returned to Rome. However, Parliament was reluctant to restore confiscated Church properties, and to Pole this was not so important a matter that it should be allowed to threaten the spiritual reunion of the country. But Pope Paul would not tolerate compromise of any kind. He recalled Pole on charges of heresy. Pole insisted on his innocence, but he was dismissed from his position as legate to England. Pole died before Paul could take serious steps against him.

Cardinal Giovanni Morone, the Bishop of Modena, was not that lucky. A brilliant man who led a blameless life and was loved by all, Morone got the shock of his life when Paul ordered him to be arrested for heresy. He was charged with reading books on the Index, of befriending the Lutherans at Trent, of sympathies toward justification by faith alone, and of discouraging the veneration of saints and their relics. Not mentioned were Paul's personal accusations: Morone was a friend of Pole's, he got along with Emperor Charles, and he felt kindly toward the Emperor's son, King Philip II of Spain—and Paul loathed Spain because it held his native city of Naples. Out of this hatred for Spain, Paul had actually instigated a war against the Spaniards; he lost it and thus despised the country even more.

Few people in Rome dared go to Morone's defense. He was called before a Vatican court to answer charges of heresy, and the members of the court were so embarrassed by their duties that they excused him with apologies. He just about reached the door on his way out when orders came from the Pope to arrest him. He was imprisoned in the Castel Sant' Angelo. He was permitted to have three aides with him; four soldiers were assigned to guard him, and he had to pay their salaries. He was stripped of all his offices and prohibited from celebrating Mass or attending the Masses of other priests.

Morone could not possibly be tried for political offenses; other cardinals agreed he had the right to hold any political convictions he chose, so he was tried on the trumped-up heresy charges.

The charges were basically false. Morone admitted that he had indeed read condemned books, but he pointed out that he did so in his capacity as a member of the Roman Inquisition, appointed by Paul to identify heretical books. Also, he had befriended the Lutherans at Trent; they were, after all, important men in their own rights and Morone considered it good manners to be polite to them. It was one thing to hate the heresy, but Morone did not take this to mean that he should also hate the heretics. The charges regarding justification by faith alone and the saints were nonsense. Morone had written on the importance of good works and in the churches he held veneration of the saints was encouraged.

Paul appointed four cardinals to try Morone. The judges knew Morone was innocent even before he defended himself brilliantly in their court, but they knew the Pope would not accept such a verdict so they gave no verdict at all. Paul, in a show of zeal, had said, "If I discovered that my own father was a heretic I would gather the wood to burn him." People wondered if this would be Morone's fate, and it might have been, had the four cardinals reached a verdict. Instead, they dragged on their discussions for months. Impatient, Paul decreed that any cardinal accused of heresy could not be elected pope. This was aimed directly at Morone. Paul knew how the cardinals felt about Morone and he suspected the judges were stalling on a verdict; Paul did not want Morone to be swept into the papacy on a wave of sentiments that might follow his death. The trial dragged on for two years, and when Paul died Morone was still a prisoner. The night Paul died the people of Rome stormed into the Vatican plaza and knocked over the statue of him that stood there and pulverized it.

That such a man should have been pope at this particular time was an extreme misfortune. Assuredly, he did some good, for a man like him was necessary to rock the Curia enough to effect the reforms other popes merely talked about. But Pope Paul IV was an intolerant puritan, who disregarded justice and mercy and tolerance itself, and in striving to perform his duties as he saw fit he drove men away from the very throne where they should have expected to find understanding, love, and forgiveness.

Chaos continued in Rome for several days after Paul's death. Enemies who had been driven into hiding or out of town returned and walked the streets amid great cheers. The Colonna family had lost many of its holdings; they were reclaimed by popular insistence. Morone was released from prison, exonerated by most of the cardinals and given the right to vote at the next conclave. As Paul had feared, strong public feelings made Morone a leading candidate for the papal tiara. Another eager candidate was Cardinal Ippolito d'Este, the Bishop of Ferrara, who had served as legate to France and whose relatives had been married to important French families. Pope Paul, after his election, had condemned Este for trying to buy the papacy during the 1555 conclave, which was true. Back in Rome again and with strong French support behind him, Este was boastfully ready for the same tactics. The city was in a joyous uproar.

Forty cardinals were in Rome for the new conclave at the end of August, 1559. Because of Este, there would be no new pope until Christmas Day.

The conclave was divided into three almost equal groups, with Italians in all of them. Those around Este favored a strong French influence in the Vatican; those preferring a

Spanish influence supported Cardinal Ascanio Sforza; the remainder rallied around the three Carafa cardinals, all relatives of Pope Paul. From the start, it was evident that no group had enough votes to win; victory could come only through alliances. There didn't seem to be much chance that alliances would be easily reached. Each group had cause— political, financial, and personal—to distrust the other. In the panic following Paul's death, the Carafas had suffered assaults upon themselves and their properties, and they wanted to keep the papacy in the family in order to recoup their losses. Este was out for power; he already had more money than he could spend. An Italian, he believed he could do better under a French pope, since his interests and connections were all French. Sforza was in the same position with the Spanish.

The conclave opened with a great deal of parrying. While the party leaders occupied themselves with bargaining, the candidates submitted for election were men who didn't stand the slimmest chances of winning. Everybody maneuvered for time. Among the first cardinals to make a good showing were Morone and Cardinal Gian Angelo Medici (no relation to the Florentine family). Both men had sided with the Spaniards; Morone, especially, had no intentions of backing the Carafas, since it had been a Carafa pope that put him in prison. After the first few scrutinies, Medici lost out, and in subsequent ballots he received no votes or at most two or three. Morone continued to win support. Then Este started rumors that the four cardinals who had adjudged heresy charges against Morone had not been entirely impartial and that a study he himself had made of the record showed that Morone was quite possibly guilty. Indignant, Morone announced that he was going to walk out of the conclave and he demanded that when the conclave ended Este must sit in judgment of him at a new trial at which, Morone was convinced, Este would have to eat his own words. Other cardinals begged Morone not to leave; the public would be scandalized if so admired a man walked out. Morone agreed to stay but he instructed that nobody should vote for him.

This was exactly what Este wanted. He was startled, however, when cardinals backing Morone indicated they might go over to Medici, but Medici ruined the movement when, at dinner one night, he happened to remark that he saw no objections, if it meant bringing back the Lutherans, to Communion of wine and wafer for the laity and marriage for priests. Este had the comment all over the conclave quarters in minutes, and that settled Medici, except for protest votes that later came his way when cardinals didn't know whom else to vote for.

Weeks fell away.

There was a great deal of interference from the outside. The Kings of Spain and France and the Emperor had all informed the conclave that they didn't care who was elected as long as it was a good man who would carry on reforms, but then they all kept up steady correspondence with friends in Rome, either in the conclave or accessible to it, nudging their favorites on. Philip II of Spain was the worst. His envoy to Rome practically lived at the conclave. On days when he couldn't get into the conclave he shouted through the window at the cardinals or sent notes in on their trays of food.

One cardinal after the other was proposed by the three parties, then rejected either by the cardinals or the outside powers. At times a candidate would seem to have all the votes he needed lined up, but when the scrutiny was taken enough minds had been changed to cause another checkmate. The three group leaders were all disliked men, but even they came out openly for themselves when all else failed, and this failed too. Bribes were offered and taken, but to no avail. Affairs reached the stage where a completely unexpecting cardinal found himself with almost enough votes to get elected, only to discover that the situation arose merely because another ballot had to be taken and the cardinals had voted for him because it was his birthday.

Pleas for a decision came from the Rome populace: the city was without a ruler and vandalism was rampant. At last the three leaders faced the fact that they would have to compromise. Deals began. Bargains with the Carafas were unthinkable; besides, they expected to win by sheer obstinacy. Thus the Spanish and French tried to reach an agreement among themselves. By now, however, King Philip had become such a factor in the conclave that he might just as well have been present. The most likely candidate, Cardinal Ercole Gonzaga of Mantua, was submitted to him. Philip wrote Gonzaga that he would be pleased to see him elected, then he wrote the Spanish cardinals and ordered them not to elect Gonzaga at any cost. Gonzaga, encouraged, campaigned strenuously for himself and was bewildered by the opposition coming from the King's own cardinals. He would ask why, the Spanish cardinals would agree to vote for him, but then they wouldn't.

Months fell away.

It got to be Christmas Eve. No seriously considered candidate gathered anywhere near enough votes. The cardinals thought of adjourning the conclave for the holidays, but then they realized that if they left there probably wouldn't be a pope for many more months. Instead, they asked that their confessors be brought into the conclave so that they could prepare for the Christmas holiday. It was one of the confessors, quickly deep in conclave gossip, who asked, "What's wrong with settling on Medici?"

There were many answers to that question. As secretive as he had been about it, it was known that Medici had a few illegitimate children around Rome. His brother was an important officer in Charles's army, which put him too close to the Emperor to please the French. He had moved so slowly up the ecclesiastical ladder that it was surmised he was either stupid, too honest, or too dishonest. He had a talent for being caught on the wrong side of the fence whenever popular opinion swerved. However, he was regarded as a good canon lawyer as well as a pliable diplomat, and he had taken loud objection to Pope Paul's war on Spain; these were good points.

The more the cardinals thought about it, the more convinced they became that Medici was about as well as they could hope to do. Talk about him increased all Christmas Day, but he was the only person who had no idea of it. Christmas evening he was in bed early and asleep when the decision about him was definite. The cardinals debated whether to awaken him to tell him the news and finally agreed upon it. He was dazed by the news and thought he was dreaming.

He turned out to be an excellent choice. As Pius IV, he quickly diminished the Roman Inquisition, he took many names off the Index, he called off the heretic hunt and he put an end to the anti-Semitism. He eased the tension in the Curia, where he had worked himself for many years, and he was able to carry on reforms without terror. He admitted that he was no theologian, which his remark during the conclave regarding Communion and marriage for priests had made clear, and so he appointed good theologians as his advisors. Without letting Rome revert to its pagan days, he encouraged the people to get a little fun out of life. His own entertainments were simple, but he enjoyed long dinner talk and was not against hiring an occasional jester to amuse his guests. Sometimes he invited authors to his table, enchanting them, especially the older ones, by reciting pages of their works. With similar charm, he was able to restore harmony with Spain, renew relations with France and strengthen friendship with the Emperor.

His one failing was his family. He had been one of four-

teen children and everybody related to him was equally pro-
ductive. When his relatives came to pay their respects it
looked like an invasion. He was generous with them in the
typical papal way, but because he was doing so admirably as
pope nobody in Rome objected.

One relative he helped was to become more famous than
he ever would. It was his nephew, Charles Borromeo. Then
twenty-two, Borromeo was already in the Church, having
spent some years in monasteries and become a deacon. He
had not seen his uncle for a long time, but upon one visit the
Pope asked him to move in. He was an unusual young man.
He was not good looking, witty, or bright, and hardly the
type to become a papal favorite, but he had one irresistible
trait: he was holy. Goodness came from him like music. He
was humble, pious, saintly and, as is often true of such people, it was impossible to escape loving him outrageously. He
was totally unaware of all this, unaffected by the adoration
that flooded him, and when others finally convinced him
how much his uncle loved him, Borromeo said this was not
a triumph but a responsibility.

Brought into the Vatican, he was made Church secretary
of state, the youngest in Church history. If he lacked the experience and capacity for the job, he made up for it by long
hours, careful study, and frequent consultation with older
men. He was the Pope's first cardinal appointment. He was
appointed legate to Bologna, Romagna and the March of
Ancona, and the protector of Portugal, the Low Countries
and the Catholic cantons of Switzerland, also protector of the
Franciscans, the Carmelites, the Knights of Malta and others.
His offices brought him an income of forty-nine thousand
scudi a year, a fortune; he gave almost all of it away to the
poor, and the remainder he used to help the impoverished
secular clergy of Italy.

He refused to pamper himself. One winter night he found
a Vatican servant trying to warm his bed with hot bricks and

he told the man not to bother with that anymore. "The best way not to go to a cold bed," he said, "is to go to bed colder than the bed is." On another occasion, he was traveling in the north, and a companion, about to retire, decided to check the Cardinal's room to see if there was anything he wanted. When the man entered, he saw Borromeo working by candlelight at his desk, wearing only a tattered cassock.

"The night is cold," the man said. "You ought to dress warmer."

Borromeo answered, "I have nothing else. By day I am forced to wear a cardinal's robes, but at night I can be myself, and this cassock is all I own, winter or summer." A man like Borromeo could make that observation without pride or false humility or self-concern.

He was saint enough to know he was human and therefore subject to temptations. He was uneasy in Rome because of the evil constantly simmering there, so whenever he could he got out of the city to spend time at his prayers. His desire was to return to a monastery. He knew what could happen to priests who were not on ceaseless moral guard. He knew an outstanding priest in Milan, and when the man died Borromeo was so stricken with grief that his friends deduced he must have been deeply attached to the man. When they mentioned this he merely observed, "Oh, you do not know the worth of one good priest." His grief, then, was not so much at the loss of his friend but at the world's loss of a good priest who could have salvaged many more souls.

As years went on, Borromeo became a priest, then a bishop, then the cardinal-archbishop of Milan. He sold all his possessions to raise money for the poor whose houses had to be burned to bring an epidemic of the plague under control. He was only forty-six years old when, one night at prayers, he felt a piercing chill pass through him. He arose, left his chapel, went to his bed, laid down and asked that the holy oils be brought to him to be anointed before death.

"At once," he said. The oils were brought; Borromeo prayed with the priest who anointed him, and when the administration of the sacrament was finished he said simply, "Behold, I come." And he died.

During his short life he made an invaluable contribution to the Church when he went one day to his uncle and pleaded with him to reopen the Council of Trent. There were many obstacles. Despite the harmony that apparently existed in the Church, old factions lurked beneath the surface. In Germany, Protestants were gaining strength; embers that were to burst into the flames of the Thirty Years War burned across the continent. In Norway, Denmark, Sweden, parts of Germany, and England, the mere fact of being a Catholic was reason for execution. People hesitated at stirring trouble by reviving of the Trent council. But Borromeo felt further sessions were vital; there were many aspects of the religion still to be spelled out. Pope Pius gave him authority to proceed with his plans. Borromeo chose as his collaborator Cardinal Morone, the accused heretic, and by his choice he freed Morone from all further suspicions.

They were a perfect pair. What Morone could not achieve by frontal attack Borromeo accomplished simply by being himself. One obstacle after another fell away and the council was scheduled for February, 1562. Borromeo assured Pius that the presence of as many bishops as possible was essential. The Pope called in the bishops living in Rome, one hundred of them, and told them bluntly, "I want you to go to Trent. I mean it." When the meetings began, more than two hundred bishops were there, as well as many cardinals from all over Europe and battalions of brilliant theologians.

The council's committees remained in session for almost two years, until December, 1563. Borromeo's influence was felt everywhere. In the end, all crucial points of Catholicism were clearly defined, and from that day on whenever the Church was called upon to explain its position on any prob-

lem it had only to quote the writings at Trent. The sacraments, Mass, the primacy of Rome, the role of the clergy
and the laity—all questions about these were resolved. The
bishops even managed to agree that all bishops—and that included cardinals—could hold only one benefice, and had to
live in it. Multiple holdings were banned; absenteeism was
prohibited. This was a most important step in eradicating
the abuses that had been created by the greed of the bishops.
Another important step pertained to the training of priests,
for only when there were good priests could there be good
bishops, good cardinals, good popes. The council decreed
that every diocese that did not have a university where aspirants for the priesthood could study must erect a seminary.
A definite curriculum was prepared for all seminarians, and
steps were taken to provide for living quarters for them
apart from other students where they could, through prayer
and spiritual exercises, achieve pious maturity. Further laws
were passed to prohibit priests from living apart from their
churches, whether alone or with their families or friends.
By residing with other priests, the hope for personal moral
strength was heightened.

In many ways, the Council of Trent was the turning point
for the Church; in many ways, Charles Borromeo was responsible for it. He was canonized in 1610 and has since
ranked as the hero of the Catholic Reformation.

The road was clear now. The safety of the journey depended on the men at the helm. There could no longer be
any question of what should be done. The need was for men
who could do it.

XIII

𝒞he next pope made reforms a definite duty of the papacy, and there it remained. He was Cardinal Antony Ghislieri, a Dominican friar who had been summoned to Rome by Pope Paul IV to work with the Inquisition. His candidacy was fostered by Charles Borromeo, sufficient indication of the kind of man he was. He took the name of Pius V, and the fact that he was canonized later showed how well he lived up to his name. He was, incidentally, the last pope to be canonized for almost four hundred years. This, however, does not reflect against his successors, some of whom might still be canonized one day; it is merely vivid evidence of his personal faculties for the severe task facing him.

Reforms could not be enforced without hurting somebody,

and so there were many people in Rome who were displeased by the efforts of Pius V to perform his duties. The Pope was bound by the decisions at Trent to do what he did. Besides his own convictions, there were men around him, like Borromeo and Morone, to see to it that the work at Trent was carried out. In the process, Pius incurred the condemnation of numerous Romans. This was inescapable. It was also unimportant.

Laymen were removed from all positions subject to simony, and priests were appointed in their place. The Jesuits got many such offices. Their vow of poverty precluded any individual hopes for personal profits; they lived together in a nearby house owned by their society, so there was no chance for anybody to build his own little dynasty. The change also had a definitely spiritual parallel. The Penitentiaria, for example, had the authority to grant dispensations from matrimonial impediments. In the wrong hands, such authority could be seriously misused and become an occasion of sin. An unscrupulous layman making a marriage investigation could, for a price, easily overlook certain insurmountable obstacles and recommend a dispensation to the clerics who supervised the office. The dispensation would be granted, the marriage performed, and to all appearances the newlyweds lived together with the blessing of the Church, but the dispensation would then have been obtained fraudulently and would not be effective and the marriage would be a sacrilege. This free use of dispensations was a Curial abuse that worried Pius V more than the crimes of simony involved. His house-cleaning, therefore, was concerned with much more than Protestant complaints.

The Dataria also underwent great change. One duty of this office was to impose and collect fines for certain offenses, and the potential abuse in this was that people could buy their way out of trouble. In the first year of his pontificate, Pius did away with the fines. Dataria officials complained that they were now without any income for themselves and that in future they would be unable to make any contributions to the Church treasury. Pius replied that other means of taxation would have to be devised that would not cast shadows upon Vatican justice.

The Trent council had stressed the importance of improving the clergy and gave bishops the responsibility to do so. As the Bishop of Rome, Pius went to work vigorously on this point.

It was customary for a lot of priests to go about the city in ordinary clothes, and the danger in this was that they occasionally got themselves into predicaments where a priest shouldn't be. Pius ordered them always to wear their cassocks. On the other hand, lawyers, doctors and notaries had picked up the habit of wearing the biretta as a sign of their importance. Birettas were part of the ecclesiastical garb; Pius instructed that it should be worn only by the clergy. Adhering to Trent, he also told clergymen to give up their private residences and move into houses adjoining their churches. Furthermore, they were to make themselves available to their people three or four hours every day to give religious instructions.

Some of the priests needed instructions themselves. Pius appointed Cardinal Morone to examine all the priests of Rome, and those obviously lacking proper training were to attend conferences to learn what they needed. Those who proved utterly uneducable were to be removed from their churches and consigned to monasteries. Great attention was given to confession, for it was in the confessional that a priest had the best opportunity to give spiritual guidance to a penitent. Many priests were found sadly ill-trained for this important function; they, too, were ordered to attend special classes. For the training of aspirants to the priesthood, Pius established seminaries in areas comprising the Papal States.

Bishops were a problem. Rome was full of them. Previous popes had ordered them to go home, but they always thought of excuses to remain or they simply ignored the order. Here again Pius made use of Morone. The Cardinal was authorized to interview all bishops in the city to determine which had duties at the Vatican that required them to be in Rome and which had merely set up residence there because they liked the place. All those who had no official reason for being in Rome were given a choice of going home or surrendering their benefices. When this was not thoroughly effective, Pius locked a few bishops up in the Castel Sant' Angelo as a warning to the others.

But the Roman roots went deep and many bishops could not be budged. Pius had to nag at the prelates throughout his six-year pontificate and popes who succeeded him continually harped on the subject until, with time, the rule gradually took effect. The episcopacy, like the priesthood, was considered part of the sacrament of Orders which imprinted a mark upon the soul that could not be taken away, but the holders of it could be deprived of their authorities and privileges, and so it was through making examples of a few bishops and taking great care in creating new bishops that the problem was eventually resolved.

Pius V tried to make an example of himself. Trent councilors had prescribed that a bishop must make regular visitations to the churches and religious institutions under his jurisdiction. Despite the burdens of the papacy, Pius made a point of carrying out his episcopal duties, and if, in doing so, he spied too many bishops in his entourage he declared in his sermons that they could scarcely expect to obey the rules in their own dioceses as long as they spent all their time following him around. Some of them, piqued, went home and gruffly tossed the same sarcasm at their suffragans. But the job was getting done, and that was what mattered.

Pius felt that the cardinals, too, were spending too much time in Rome. The members of the Curia belonged there and, from time to time, other cardinals were called in for specific assignments. But, like the bishops, they always seemed reluctant to go home. Also, many of them brought enormous retinues with them, thereby causing the expenditure of large sums of money that could be better spent in some other way. Furthermore, most cardinals held many benefices, some of which they never set eyes on. Pius ordered that unless a cardinal could show that he took active participation in the administration of the dioceses, monastic estates or other Church properties he held he must surrender them to men living in the area. In addition, cardinals not affiliated with a Curia office were not to be in Rome unless they were summoned or had some definite business with the Vatican. As with bishops, these new rules for cardinals took time to enforce, but at least they had been proclaimed and now it was for future popes to see that they were heeded.

2

Pius was succeeded by Gregory XIII, a former professor of canon law at the University of Bologna who had earned his right to wear the purple coat of a cardinal by his work at Trent. At the time of his election there were seventy-six cardinals in the world, and in four years thirty of them died. The members of the Sacred College fully expected the Pope to appoint replacements, especially since there were several vacant offices in the Curia. But months passed and Gregory did nothing.

One day the subject came up as Gregory was finishing a conference with a cardinal, and the Pope asked, "When have there been the fewest cardinals?"

"During the reigns of Alexander VI and Julius II there were only twenty-four," the cardinal said.

"So many as that?" said the Pope. The impression was soon circulated that he had no intentions of creating new cardinals and that if he lived long enough the College might well cease to exist.

Gregory appointed cardinals sparingly. In 1572, the year of his election, he appointed one—his nephew; in 1574, he appointed a second nephew. The cardinals had no objection to this, for they had come to expect nepotism from popes: a man had to see that his nephews got along in the world. In 1576 and 1577, Gregory appointed two more cardinals, both Austrians.

The cardinals were restless. At consistories they openly broached the subject, naming men they considered worthy. Gregory answered, "We do not appoint a man a cardinal to honor him but to find new laborers in Our Lord's vineyards." Months passed, still with no more appointments. The cardinals took it upon themselves to submit a list to the Pope, and he said, "We will give serious study to this list, but we can nominate only a few. After all, cardinals must be perfect men and"—he glanced at the long list—"we doubt that perfection exists in such abundance."

It was February, 1578, before he made further nominations, and he paid no attention to the list submitted to him. He kept his plans secret. The men to be appointed by him had no idea of it until, a few days before the consistory, he indicated to them that they ought to see their tailors to have new robes made. He named nine cardinals, of whom only two were Italians. This reflected a point which he himself had urged at Trent, that the red hat should be distributed more among foreigners than it had been in the past.

Five years passed without further appointments. Then, on December 12, 1583, Gregory did a most unusual thing. A consistory was held that day, and when the business was finished the cardinals made a move to depart. Gregory asked them to wait a moment. He had something he wanted to discuss with them. The cardinals settled back in their seats, completely unprepared for what followed.

He began slowly, speaking with almost a smile on his face. He said he realized the cardinals were impatient with him for not appointing more cardinals but that he hoped they were as satisfied as he with those he had named, adding that he, however, was not very satisfied with the lot of them. He was, he admitted, eighty-one years old, but he felt he would be around for a while. He said rumors had reached him that some of the cardinals did not think so or perhaps were hoping not. He announced that he was well aware that certain members of the College had already taken steps to control the next conclave, either to secure their own election or that of one of their friends. While the Pope was still alive and in apparent good health, the College had already divided itself into political parties for the coming battle. This, Gregory said, was deplorable. Didn't the cardinals have enough to do without fretting about a conclave whose date was entirely unpredictable? He said he had work to be done in several unpleasant parts of the world and if the cardinals had time to waste at political plots it might be a good idea for him to ship a few of them off on trips. Conclaves, he reminded the cardinals, had been the scenes of most of the evils that had so endangered the Church in past years, and they would continue to be until the cardinals put aside their own ambitions and gave some consideration to God's.

The cardinals squirmed, wondering what the Pope was driving at. He let them squirm.

Then he said he was sorry he was going to disrupt the political cliques that had so recently been formed, but he had an announcement to make that would probably be somewhat disturbing to the cardinals. He then read off a list of appointments to the College—nineteen of them, each a complete surprise. Now the party organizers would have to start all over again.

A roar of protest thundered through the consistory hall. Cardinal Alessandro Farnese, Dean of the College, asked permission to speak. It was granted. The Cardinal said he realized the Pope had the right to appoint anybody he chose to the College, but in the case of so many appointments shouldn't Gregory have consulted the cardinals? Other popes had done so in similar instances. Gregory replied that he had given that aspect some thought but that he couldn't find anything in law or tradition that required him to consult with anybody. If other popes had sounded out the cardinals on new appointments it was because they wished to do so; he did not, and he did not have to.

Perhaps, Farnese said, the cardinals could have been some help to him in making out his list to assure a wisdom of choice. Had it occurred to the Pope that two of his appointees were the sons of heretics?

"I was well aware of that," said Gregory, "but both of them are men of distinction in every sense."

Gregory had actually chosen well. Of the nineteen, thirteen were Italians, and of these only three were Bolognese, so the pope could not be accused of packing the College with friends from his home town. The remainder came from widely separate parts of Italy (giving the entire peninsula representation in the College), none of them with particular affiliations to other cardinals.

Farnese therefore had no further point of argument except that the Pope had disregarded the customary consultation with cardinals on multiple appointments.

"If I had done that," said Gregory, "we would have wasted more time discussing the subject than we are doing now."

With that he left the room, leaving it the strongest and most independent pope in many years. He had established an important precedent: in the future no pope need consider himself obliged to the College of Cardinals in any way.

Gregory's efforts to disrupt the political parties that had formed in the College succeeded far more than he had hoped. He died on April 10, 1585, and by April 24 a new pope was elected. He was Cardinal Felice Peretti, known as Cardinal Montalto, after his native village. He was a Franciscan who had been called to Rome to assist with the Inquisition and rose rapidly because of his theological skill in evaluating heresy. At the conclave, he made no attempts on his own behalf, but rather avoided entanglements in any political talk. During Gregory's reign he had spent most of his time out of Rome at his studies and was not close to any of the other cardinals. They knew him best from his writings.

He might be considered a compromise choice, except that there was no discussion of compromise regarding him. Three ballots were taken and it was soon obvious that, because of all the new faces at the conclave, no established political faction could possibly win without a tremendous fight. None had enough optimism to try. The cardinals settled down to agree on a man, with the sole specification among the majority that he should not have close ties with Spain. Farnese was considered, but he had too many personal enemies who feared he might turn out to be another Carafa pope. When Montalto's name was mentioned, nobody could think of serious objections to him, except possibly that he was relatively unknown. But this did not turn anyone against him. Without his knowledge, his name passed favorably from group to group. On the morning of April 24, the cardinals convened to hear the reading of papal bulls regarding conclaves, but before the reading could start someone called out, "There is no time for bulls. We have a pope: let us go on to the adoration." Someone else cried, "Montalto!" And that was it. A scrutiny was nevertheless required. Montalto voted for the man he felt wanted the papacy most but who, because of his age, would now never get it: Farnese.

Montalto took the name Sixtus V. In his five-year reign the Vatican was completely reorganized.

Sixtus partially restored the traditional manner of appointing cardinals by allowing the Sacred College to participate to a limited degree. He appointed thirty-three cardinals, and in each case he announced, in effect: "These are the men I choose. I will listen to what you have to say about them, but the final decision will be my own." His first appointments met with violent objection from the College. After he read his lists he could not hear his own voice above the shouted protests. But he refused to be swayed by anybody, and after a while the cardinals accepted his nominations quietly.

He had been Pope about eighteen months when he issued a bull that gave the Church a new and effective form. His subject was cardinals; he defined them and the responsibilities he was about to give them.

He limited the number of cardinals to seventy, basing the figure on the appointment of seventy elders made by Moses to relieve him of having to deal with every problem, regardless of how big or small, that arose among the Hebrew tribes. Borrowing from the Council of Trent, Sixtus specified that cardinal-priests must be at least thirty years old at the time of their appointment. Cardinal-deacons could be twenty-two, provided they became priests within one year after their appointment. The seventy were divided into three groups: six would be cardinal-bishops, holding the Rome suburbicarian dioceses, and the Bishop of Ostia would be the dean of the Sacred College; fifty would be cardinal-priests, holding title to the ancient parishes of Rome, but they could also be bishops or archbishops of dioceses outside of Rome; fourteen would be cardinal-deacons —though actually priests—holding title to the dispensaries of ancient Rome.

Sixtus ordered that all cardinals must be men of blameless lives. No one born illegitimately could become a cardinal. Anyone who ever had children, whether now living or dead, whether legitimate or illegitimate, could not become a cardinal. Nor could anyone who had a brother, cousin, uncle or nephew who was already a cardinal. Even if by accident two men related in the first or second degree should find themselves appointed to the college at the same time, the appointment of the second was invalid once the relationship was established. The Church, Sixtus wrote, had no need for the son of any prince, for any statesman or lawyer or canonist but a need for theologians. It would be good for a cardinal to have a doctorate in canon law, but he absolutely must have a doctorate in theology. Also, it was important that the red hat be distributed among foreigners as much as possible, for the Church was not Roman alone, nor Italian alone, but universal. Furthermore it was vital, said Sixtus, that everybody understand that a cardinal was not to represent outside interests in the Church but to represent the Church among the outside. He reminded the cardinals that they were hingemen, but they were supposed to open and close doors for the Church, not for other people who might wish to make use of the Church.

A pope, Sixtus said, needed his cardinals, just as Moses needed his elders, and it was high time that it be established that the popes and the cardinals were all on the same side. One way to do this was to give the cardinals more to do in the Vatican itself. In the past, Vatican offices were directed by laymen, by priests or canons or bishops, and sometimes cardinals were appointed to specific work, most often on a temporary basis. Now Sixtus wanted to create a truly cardinalitial government, with cardinals taking a definite part in everything that was going on.

With this in mind, he said, he was setting up fifteen congregations (committees) and each would have its carefully defined responsibilities. Cardinals appointed to them, on an international basis, would reside in Rome; other cardinals would be in Rome only when they had good reason.

Of the fifteen congregations the Pope established, six were concerned with affairs of the Papal States; the others dealt with spiritual matters. Some of them were, at least in theory, already in existence. Sixtus made them fact.

In view of the times, the most important congregation was that of the Roman Inquisition, which was now empowered to seek out heresy, schism, apostasy, magic, chiromancy, divination, and the abuse of the sacraments wherever the Catholic religion was practiced. The Congregation of the Index was assigned the task of identifying books dangerous to faith and morals, and was instructed to use the facilities of existing universities in its work. The Congregation for the decrees of the Council of Trent was to interpret and enforce the council's decisions in all spheres. The Congregation for the affairs of Bishops was assigned to handle matters pertaining to prelates, their duties, their privileges, their misconduct, their benefices, their jurisdiction. Affairs involving religious orders outside the jurisdiction of bishops were to be handled by the Congregation of Regulars. The Consistorial Congregation was assigned to supervise any changes made in existing dioceses and the creation of new ones. Petitions for favors, graces and indulgences were assigned to the Congregation of the Holy Signature. The Congregation of Rites and Ceremonies was commissioned to evaluate, maintain, restore and safeguard all acts of worship. And the Congregation of the Vatican Press was to publish and promote the use of the Bible, prayer books, devotionals, missals and meditation aides, papal writings and the works of theologians.

Each congregation was given the necessary authority to carry out its duties. The Pope, whoever he might be, was a member of the Congregations of the Council, of the Holy Signature, and of Rites and, since matters of faith and morals were involved, was to have the final voice in decisions. The offices of the various congregations were to operate on a regular business-week basis; the cardinal members were to maintain business hours and must meet at specified intervals, some once a week, to take care of matters before the congregation so that the work did not pile up.

Sixtus' outline for the congregations touched on every detail that might come up in the course of their functions. Authority was particularly defined, so that no man acquired too much and that all men remained subject to the popes. So thorough was his plan that only minor changes had to be made in it over the years, and it was not until 1908 that Pope Pius X overhauled the Vatican administration to meet the exigencies of modern times.

For what he achieved, Pope Sixtus V has rated as one of the great popes of the Church. More than putting the Church on a practical, business basis that sharply curbed abuses and prevented scandal, he gave dignity, stature, and keen purpose to the cardinalate and to the men who filled its ranks. From then on, the rascals among them were to become the exception, not the rule.

XIV

$\mathcal{T}$he short reign of Pope Gregory XV (1621-1623) was marked by three events which affected the cardinals. Other popes had tried to devise means by which the conduct of cardinals at conclaves could be brought under control. For six hundred years, almost all conclaves had been marred by politics of the lowest variety, with the result that several men who were utterly unqualified became popes. The trouble had been that qualifications were not considered as important as personal affiliations. In efforts to protect the papacy, Sixtus V had stressed the careful selection of cardinals as a step in the right direction. However, suitable cardinals could not be assured until men appeared who were free of indebtedness to each other and to the rulers of the world.

Every age had produced its prince of the realm who connived to use cardinals as tools to control the Church. At this particular time, when the Church was struggling to restore its faded glory, Spain was the worst violator of Vatican freedom, but France had its share of guilt, as did the German empire and the states of Italy.

The years had shown that most cardinals, whatever their pasts, experienced a change for the better once they became popes. In many cases, however, good intentions did not make for outstanding pontiffs; if a man lacked the capacity for the high office he could not, even as the vicar of Christ on earth, expect such detailed guidance from God that he would not make mistakes. Usually the mistake had been made at the conclave, where candidacies were more often determined by political debts than by the promise of expert leadership. Something had to be done that would allow the cardinals to leave the debts outside the door that locked them in conclave session.

Gregory XV produced the answer. In a bull dated November 15, 1621, he introduced the secret ballot. From that day on, no cardinal would ever know how another cardinal voted unless some blatant discrepancy forced an investigation. Even the election officials would not be able to violate the secret ballot, again unless something was obviously wrong. Thus, regardless of what a cardinal had promised others, he was a free man once he sat down to write out his vote. Moreover, he had a new responsibility: Gregory prescribed that each cardinal must stand ready to swear that his vote was the result of his prayers, not his pressures. At last the Holy Ghost was to be given a chance to get through to the cardinals before anybody else did.

Gregory's bull instructed, first, that there was to be no campaigning while a pope was alive. Upon his death and burial and after the customary ten days of obsequies, the cardinals were to wait another week, to give foreigners a chance to reach Rome, and during this time they could line up their parties. Then all cardinals present were to be locked in conclave and the rules regarding the gradual decrease in their menu was to be enforced.

There was to be no campaigning after the door was locked. In fact, all conversation should be kept at a minimum. Hours usually spent at talk were now to be devoted to prayer. Also, the Blessed Sacrament was to be exposed in the election hall so that the cardinals would be mindful of the Actual Presence during their important duty.

Gregory ordered two scrutinies a day. At the start of the first session, any party leaders that existed could stand and announce their candidates—but that was all.

The ballot was a piece of paper that could be folded twice. In the top section, the cardinal wrote his own name, then folded it back so that it could not be seen. In the bottom section, he wrote a motto—a Bible verse, perhaps, a slogan, some phrase by which his vote would be recorded. In the center section, he wrote the name of the man he wanted to be pope. In the event that two or more cardinals used the same motto, it was read aloud by the recording officials and the men who used it had to choose a new one and vote again. If the two leading candidates got the same number of votes, then the officials could check the names on the ballots to be sure neither candidate had voted for himself. Since there was slim chance of either incident, the ballots could remain completely secret.

If everything seemed in order, the votes were to be tallied. If nobody won the necessary majority, the names of the five leaders were to be read aloud. Any cardinal could then change his vote if he wished, but he had to use the same motto so that the officials could determine that he was not merely voting twice for the same man. Should there still be no majority, the cardinals were to retire to their prayers until the next scrutiny, at which they would vote for the five leading candidates. On each day, the list of candidates was to be cut by one until two were left, and if no decision could be made between them a committee of three, five or seven cardinals could be appointed to make the choice by compromise.

The system was a good one, in that it served to free the elections of politics and make the conclaves brief, and had it been adhered to all future elections would have come off without trouble. Subsequent popes, however, had the right to make adjustments, and the feature of Gregory's plan that fell away was the elimination of candidates with each scrutiny. In later years there were concalves that lasted anywhere from two or three days to five or six weeks. The election of Benedict XIV in 1740 lasted six months and two days, with 368 scrutinies. The election bull of Pius X in 1908 restored a measure of control that precluded lengthy conclaves in the future. But it was Gregory XV who, in issuing his bull, showed that the control was possible and necessary.

A second event of Gregory's reign was perhaps even more far-reaching. For almost a hundred and fifty years, explorers had been probing the mysteries of the New World Christopher Columbus had discovered. England, France, Spain, and Portugal had made claims in the Western Hemisphere; European communities were beginning to appear up and down the western shores of the Atlantic and in the islands. Missionaries had gone west with Columbus and they accompanied all subsequent expeditions. As years passed, the missionaries were to play as important a part in the development of the New World as did the governments that made huge investments in it. From the start, the Church was concerned. When news arrived that chartered companies were subjecting the American Indians to commercial slavery, the popes wrote European rulers demanding a stop to it. At the same time, the popes urged the religious orders to send their men across the Atlantic to bring the new-found peoples to Christianity. Such efforts were already being made in the Far East. Jesuit missionaries like Francis Xavier were making their way to India, China, and the Pacific countries with sweeping success. And to the south was Africa.

Various Vatican offices had been set up to meet the problems that arose from missionary work, but because the expansion had been so great and so fast there were gaps, duplication and confusion. Gregory recognized that missionary work would become an increasingly vital factor in Church affairs and that it could be effective only if properly directed. With this in mind he added to the congregations established by Sixtus V the Congregation for the Propagation of the Faith and appointed fifteen cardinals to supervise it. In terms of the bulk of work handled and of work accomplished, the new congregation evolved into the busiest department of the Church. Even now, with half the world still considered missionary territory, the activity of this office exceeds all others, with an enormous sum of money appropriated each year to support an army of missionaries devoted to the material as well as the spiritual progress of millions of people in backward countries. Incidentally, the United States, the discovery of whose shores dramatized the need for a well directed Vatican missionary office, is now a leader in the support of missionary work in other lands. Samuel Stritch, the Cardinal-archbishop of Chicago, was appointed pro-prefect of the Congregation shortly before his death in 1958.

A third event of Gregory's reign did not work out so well. On September 5, 1622, he appointed cardinal the young French bishop of Luçon, a man named Armand de Richelieu.

2

Armand Jean du Plessis, duc de Richelieu, came from an old French noble family, several of whose members had married into royalty. His family marked him for the Church, and it was to prove a sad decision for the Church indeed. Because of his connections, he was a bishop at twenty-two, an age considered too young even for ordination according to the Council of Trent. At twenty-nine, he was a delegate of the clergy to the States-General. He spent a great deal of time in Paris, and it was there that he came to know Marie de' Medici, the widow-queen of France and regent for Louis XIII. It was generally believed that she was Richelieu's mistress. In any event, Marie appointed Richelieu her secretary of state in 1616, when he was thirty-one years old.

Pope Gregory XV knew of Richelieu's influence in France while he was still a bishop and he called on the young prelate to help enforce in France the work accomplished at Trent. The anti-papal feelings of France, both in the Church and in the nobility, had never faded, even after the repeal of the Pragmatic Sanction. At Trent, the French delegations had been expected to cause trouble on matters pertaining to papal authorities, and it was mostly due to diplomats like Borromeo and Morone that they did not cause more than they did. According to the council, bishops were responsible for carrying out the decisions reached at Trent. The popes, as bishops, had done so; Richelieu, as a bishop, was expected to do so. Gregory hoped that he would and wrote him along that line.

But Richelieu was more a politician than a priest. And he was a Frenchman. And he was ambitious. The Pope got nowhere with him, but Richelieu was to get far via his Machiavellian tactics for gaining power and holding it.

The kings of France had never been the absolute power in the country; the power was more with the noblemen. When a king wanted to go to war or, as happened in the past, to go on a crusade, he had to turn to his loyal noblemen for the money and the men, rewarding their loyalty with various benefices. Richelieu wanted to change this, to make a French king truly a king. For a Catholic in a country that had become strongly Protestant, the change would be difficult. French Protestantism grew out of the Calvinism of Switzerland and it attracted many anti-clerical noblemen. As such, it was a political as well as heretical threat to the country. There were wars, persecution and massacres. In the end, the Protestant Huguenots were victorious, gaining both political and religious supremacy in over two hundred towns.

Antoine de Bourbon, duke of Vendôme and king of Navarre by his marriage with Jeanne d'Albret, turned Protestant but reverted before his death. His son by Queen Jeanne was considered legal heir to France, thus making the boy, Henry IV, the first Protestant ruler of the country. Catholic nobles refused to accept a Protestant, so with ease Henry became a Catholic. His first marriage was annulled and his second wife was Marie de' Medici. Henry was assassinated by a religious fanatic in 1610, leaving his wife to rule during the youth of her son, Louis XIII.

Henry had, by the Edict of Nantes, permitted Protestantism in the two hundred communities of the Huguenots. Richelieu considered the communities a state within a state and he wanted them returned to the Catholic crown. To do so would require bloodshed, and he was ready for that.

In 1617, Louis considered himself at seventeen old enough to take over his responsibilities, but his mother refused to surrender them to him. The young King then ordered Charles Luynes, the constable of France, to kill Concino Concini, the marshal of France, whom Marie had assigned to keep Louis quiet. Louis then ordered his mother into exile; Richelieu went with her, acting as her emissary to Luynes. Despite his relations with Marie, Richelieu worked himself into the good graces of the King, and it was after frequent requests by Louis that Pope Gregory XV, gravely disconcerted, appointed Richelieu a cardinal. Richelieu managed to reconcile Louis and Marie, bringing her back to Paris, and now with son and mother on his side it took him just a year to get himself appointed the King's chief minister, with complete control of the government.

Richelieu was eligible to attend the 1623 conclave that elected Pope Urban VIII, but he was too involved in the political affairs of France to go. The Pope and the Cardinal never met, but for twenty years messengers and letters passed between them, as Richelieu tried to make the Pope part of his own intrigues. He urged the Pope to make him legate to France, which would have put him at the head of the Church as well as the state, but the Pope refused. It made little difference to Richelieu, however: because of his political position he knew the bishops of France would do what he wanted.

It was ostensibly for religious reasons that Richelieu sent troops against the Huguenots, destroying them in 1628. He duped the Pope into supporting him on the pretext of quelling a heresy, but when he won out he deprived the Protestants only of their political rights, permitting them to continue practicing their religion.

The Thirty Years War was on, a war with the German Protestant princes, England, Sweden and Denmark on one side and the Catholic House of Hapsburg on the other. On the surface, this was supposed to be a war of religions, but actually religion was secondary, if involved even to that extent. The Hapsburgs were strong, eager to revive their old claim as rulers of the Holy Roman Empire, but their battle cry was the Catholic Church, which they said they wanted to restore in the northern areas lost to Protestantism. The northern powers, now all Protestant, proclaimed that they were fighting for their religious freedom, but it was quite plain that Sweden and Denmark wanted only to expand their holdings in Northern Germany and in Poland, while England had her eyes on the European territories facing her across the Channel.

If the Church seriously intended to take any part in the war, she should have sided completely with the Hapsburgs, but Pope Urban was determined to stay out of it. True, he sent some money and a token force to the Hapsburgs, but this was of little help and was done only because, in the circumstances, the Pope could not refuse to do anything at all. Also, the Church might have urged France to aid the Hapsburgs but this would have been a futile gesture because Richelieu hated the Hapsburgs and feared their power. Their mere existence blocked his own plans for France. He was not yet in a position for open warfare against them, but he was in the war in other ways.

Because of the confusion of victories, the chaos of purpose and the frequent switch of allies, it was difficult to tell who was winning the war. The Hapsburgs lost important battles and steps toward surrender were taken, but then fresh troops would arrive from Bavaria or Bohemia or Poland and the fight would be on again. The same was true of the other side. Richelieu placed himself squarely with the Protestants by providing them with money and troops whenever they suffered losses or planned attacks. Then in 1636 he threw his own country into the battle for the kill. Catholic Frenchmen fought side by side with Protestants against a Catholic force that was often enhanced by Protestant supporters who opposed the Swedes and Danes. For his aid, the Protestant alliance promised Alsace to Richelieu if they won, a promise that was eventually kept and proved to be a fresh cause for future wars.

Richelieu died in 1642, six years before the war ended. Thus he did not live to see the final victory for his side in the war he had sponsored. Nor did he see the crushing ruin of the German lands which the many years of fighting had wrought, the severe depopulation of the German people, the distrust that was born between the European countries which would never really die. He was to blame for much of this. He was to blame, too, for the seeds of revolution that were planted when he battled French noblemen in order to grasp absolute power of the country and place in the hands of French kings, who then proceeded to misuse it absolutely.

Pope Urban was still on his throne when Richelieu went to his grave. Death had resolved a problem with which the Pope had wrestled for almost twenty years. Repeatedly he had consulted with the cardinals on the wisdom of excommunicating both Richelieu and Louis XIII. He had, in fact, sent Richelieu many warnings. Had Urban gone ahead with his threats, there was a chance that the Catholic nobles of France, who despised Richelieu, would have used the excommunication as grounds for civil war. There was already enough of war. Time and again, Urban sent Richelieu pleas of "Peace! Peace!"—but to no avail. An excommunication, which at one time would have brought a contumacious emperor to heel, would also have been to no avail.

So Richelieu died a cardinal, a prince of the Church, and it was as much the churchman as the King's chief minister that the people remembered: one man became two enemies. Thus, a century later when the seeds of revolution blossomed into bloody terror, the Church went with the King to the guillotine.

As the bleak hour approached, France found itself with an heir to Richelieu, spiritual and political. He was François Joachim de Pierre de Bernis, a count who could boast that his family's noble blood had been uncontaminated by com-

moners for seven hundred years. At twelve, Bernis jokingly
informed his parents that he planned to enter the Church.
They took him seriously and placed him in the best schools
that would lead him to the priesthood. At nineteen, he was
an *abbé*, one step below sub-deacon, when he was tossed
out of the College of Saint-Sulpice for general devilment
and specifically for getting caught eating a roast chicken in
his bed after lights-out one night. His shocked parents cut
off his allowance, and he found himself on his own in Paris,
a cherubic young man with a good name, good education,
good connections, but no money.

Through relatives, he entered social circles in which he
was able to indulge a pleasure he never outgrew: the company of beautiful women. The women knew he was impoverished, and they devised discreet ways by which they
could occasionally slip him some money. His company was
worth it. He had a delightful wit. In his youth, wit was a
key to any door. It was the era of Voltaire and Casanova,
both of whom Bernis got to know well and, in his own way,
to outshine.

During these days he repeatedly assured himself that by
the time he was forty he would be somebody, and he was
indeed. His first steps toward greatness resulted from his
connections. There lived in Paris a woman named Madame
Lenormand d'Etoiles, who had some wealth, great beauty
and a husband, and whose ambition was to become the most
powerful woman in France, mistress of King Louis XV. It
was the mode of the day for anybody who wanted something
done to go not to the man concerned nor to his wife but to
his mistress, and this was true of the King as well as everybody else. The King's mistress, therefore, was more influential than the King himself.

This was the Age of Scoff, when intellectuals derided all
authority, Church or State. Although Madame d'Etoiles
knew many scoffers, she knew no one who might be able to

bring her to the King's attention. Then she heard of the Abbé de Bernis who, because of his family, was as much at home at Versailles as he was at any Paris table where he could get a free meal. She invited him to her house and told him what she wanted to do.

Arranging friendships proved to Bernis' most profitable asset; people paid for friendships. Thus he arranged for Madame d'Etoiles to attend a masked ball at which Louis would be present. The plan was for Bernis to maneuver her near the King; then, dressed as Cupid, she would shoot an arrow at him. Once she had his attention, she would remove her mask and drop her kerchief at the King's feet. The plan worked perfectly. Next day Louis summoned Madame d'Etoiles and their romance began. In a short time he granted her first step toward power by making her the Marquise de Pompadour.

From the start, Bernis had free access to Madame de Pompadour's chambers, and he was confident enough of her debt to him to freely solicit favors for his friends. With her help, he rose even higher socially, but still he had no money. One day a Bishop said to him, "As long as you are young, you will find your present position in life very pleasant. You are popular, and you are run after. But bear in mind that there is nothing in Paris sadder or more humiliating than an old *abbé* who is poor."

One word to Madame de Pompadour was enough. He received the benefice of an abbey at a time he was more layman than priest. Later on he said another word. He was made French ambassador to Venice.

He was a clever young man. Before leaving for Venice he studied the history of the city-state and the day he arrived there he knew more about the place than people who had lived in Venice for years.

It was a dull town, mostly because of the Venetian distrust of foreigners. Ambassadors lived almost ignobly, ignored, in a cluster of old houses in what amounted to a swanky ghetto. There was practically no social life among them. Bernis changed all that. Fresh from Versailles, he knew how a party should be given, and he was soon giving them every night. He brought the town to life. He was into everything. He would entertain nobility half the night, then bribed their servants the next morning to learn what little more he had to know about Venetian affairs. He was able to report to Versailles on intrigues with Spain or Austria even before French ambassadors there had any idea what was going on.

He was quite sure his future was with the government, but he realized his favored position might last only as long as did Madame de Pompadour, so he took steps to enhance his role in the Church. Venice and the Vatican were at odds; Bernis, whose charm was irresistible, patched up the differences, a deed which years later brought an important reward. Then, before leaving Venice four years later, he arranged to have himself ordained a sub-deacon.

To the bishop who ordained him Bernis punned bitterly, "Now I can sing the Song of Simeon."

He was soon deep in simony. In Paris, Madame de Pompadour explained why he had been so suddenly recalled. Protestant Prussia was acting up and Empress Marie Therese of Austria expected a war. She wanted France to join her side, an unusual request because the House of Hapsburg and the House of Bourbon had been estranged since Richelieu. But Madame de Pompadour thought it was a good idea. It would open French doors for expansion; more important, it would make her friends with Marie Therese—a royal friendship she was denied by the Queen of France who knew she was the King's mistress.

Madame de Pompadour disliked the French foreign minister and, furthermore, felt he would not go along with the plan. Thus she appointed Bernis to negotiate with the Austrians until a pact was ready to present to Louis. Louis approved the agreement, primarily because the mutual-aid pact would keep Austria on his side in the war he was expecting with England. Bernis suddenly found himself the new foreign minister.

As Austria feared, Prussia began to fight. France fulfilled its part of the bargain, and the Seven Years War was on. Bernis suspected that Prussia might hope to ignite another religious war. He therefore moved fast to buy the neutrality of Sweden and Denmark and to hire their mercenaries for the Franco-Austrian alliance. At first the war went well, but then clumsy French generals let important victories slip to the Prussians, and Bernis faced the reality that total defeat was inevitable.

He hinted to Madame de Pompadour that they ought to quit, but she wouldn't hear of it. Even when news arrived that Austria was ready to make a separate peace, she wanted to fight on. Bernis' pessimism irked her so much that she began to urge the King to get rid of him. Then a moment from the past changed everything.

Still grateful for the friendship with Venice that Bernis had salvaged, Pope Benedict XIV informed Louis that he wanted to make the French foreign minister a cardinal. Louis liked Bernis; it was only on his mistress' urging that he was ready to fire him. To do so at this moment would have looked bad. Besides, Louis wanted another French cardinal in the Sacred College. He hoped, with the help of time, to satisfy both himself and his mistress. He sent the royal approval to Rome; the day it arrived the Pope died.

Bernis knew about the appointment; he also knew that he was on thin ice with Madame de Pompadour. No longer welcome in her chambers, he besieged her with affectionate letters, openly admitting that he might not have been the man for the important job she got for him, suggesting that a co-minister be appointed to handle relations with foreign rulers while he confined himself to the ambassadors to the

French court. But she was not about to help him save his neck.

The new Pope, Clement XIII, wrote King Louis that he was aware of the promise of another red hat to France and that he intended to carry it out. Through his private spy-system, Bernis learned of the letter. The King said nothing about it. Aware that he was losing out at Versailles and afraid he might also lose out in Rome, Bernis made a shrewd move: he publically announced his gratitude to the Pope and the King for the great honor of the cardinalate about to be bestowed upon him. Forcing the issue, he won it.

There was great excitement in Paris. Friends who did not realize the situation told Bernis, "Surely the King will now make you his chief minister. You'll be another Richelieu."

That Madame de Pompadour would never permit. It was for years the French prerogative that the kings should place the red biretta on the heads of new cardinals. Within hours after Louis gave Bernis his hat he ordered the new cardinal into exile. Bernis was disgraced.

And yet it was Bernis' luck always to bounce back. His eviction from Versailles convinced the French Queen Marie that she now had in him an ally against her husband's mistress. The two began a correspondence; the Queen saw to it that parcels of food delicacies arrived regularly at his exile home near Vic-sur-Aisne. Also, Bernis was replaced as foreign minister by an old friend, a man who owed many debts to him and who disliked Madame de Pompadour. He vowed to get rid of her, and he achieved this remarkable *coup d'amour* by introducing the King to the younger and more beautiful Madame du Barry.

The change lightened Bernis' exile restrictions and he was permitted to go to the south of France to visit his family. Exile had not mellowed him. During it, he had had himself ordained a priest, and of this he commented, "I have always approved the conduct of those Roman prelates who only bind themselves to the Church late in life, when the age of passion is over." His own passion for lovely women was far from over; at forty-five he enjoyed their company as much as he had at twenty. A battalion of them were awaiting him in his future.

It was a future that began when, on the plea of the Queen and the foreign minister, King Louis appointed him Archbishop of Albi, the third richest archdiocese in France. Now there would be nothing but incredible luxury for him for the next twenty-five years. With it would come a new title for him, a title given in jest but a title he extravagantly earned: the King of Rome.

Pope Clement XIII died in February, 1769. Before leaving Albi for Rome Bernis inquired whether the King had any pet candidate. Louis suggested that Bernis go along with whomever the Spanish wanted; the Spanish wanted anybody who would disband the Jesuits. This was the situation:

The colonization of South America was in Spanish and Portuguese hands. The continent was enormously wealthy, and to get the wealth aboard ship demanded many workers. The only workers available in bulk were the Indians; paying all who were necessary would have been economically prohibitive, so the Spanish and the Portuguese simply enslaved the natives. Jesuits had gone to South America with every expedition. In order to carry on their work among the natives they were given large land grants on which to build their missions. They had more in mind than only the spiritual conversion of the natives: they wanted to introduce the people to the entire way of life they felt Christianity offered, which meant improving the whole man. Their missions, called Reductions, were extremely successful. Thousands of natives were converted and they moved to the Reductions to learn, as well as religion, how to read and write their own language, how to farm, how to use modern tools, how to get along with each other peacefully, and they received the medical aid they needed desperately.

All went well until the slavery business started. The missionaries tried to talk the expedition leaders out of it but failed. They sent complaints to their superiors and rulers, but this accomplished nothing. There was only one course open to them: active resistance. They urged all natives to move to the Reductions for protection, and they went so far as to arm the people to fight off the soldiers who came to enchain them. Thus a string of little wars broke out up and down the coast.

The Spanish and Portuguese governments were furious. At great expense they sent troops to South America to quell the resistance. The defeated missionaries were shipped home. In Lisbon and Madrid they carried on their battle, by words now, against the authorities. As a result, Spain and Portugal outlawed the Jesuits. Hundreds of them were loaded aboard ships, taken to Italy and dumped ashore near Rome; since they had a vow of obedience to the popes, the popes could have them. Now that there was to be a new pope, the Spanish and Portuguese governments ordered their cardinals to choose a man who would promise to disband the Jesuits throughout the world.

Bernis had orders to cooperate.

Among the Roman cardinals was a clique, called the Zalenti, that had pledged itself to keep the conclave free of nationalism and personal ambition, and it was their hope to rush through an election before the foreigners could arrive with their factious pressures. The French ambassador, however, warned that such action would be taken as an insult to King Louis, hinting that a schism might well result. The Zalenti were forced to back down, and it was the middle of March when the French and Spaniards arrived to start the conclave.

Bernis loved it. At Versailles he had been an important man, but still he was not a member of the royal family and there was an impenetrable wall between him and the throne. Now things were far different: in conclave he was surrounded by Church royalty—the papal princes—and he was one of them; it was a fine feeling. He made no attempt to influence the first weeks of the conclave, leaving that to the Orsini cardinal who headed the anti-Jesuit faction. Instead, Bernis carried on as if he were throwing a party and the cardinals were his guests. Few of them knew him, but he made a point of knowing all of them. Every day French pastries were brought to him and he invited the cardinals into his cubicle for a chatty tea. With stand-offs, he paraded through the halls, carrying a dish of delicacies which he insisted they try. And each evening the tense buzz of politicking in the room was punctuated by the popping corks of French champagne bottles. Bernis knew how to win friends.

The least likely candidate present was Fra Lorenzo Ganganelli, a Franciscan who worked with the Congregation of the Holy Office. Devoted to his vow of holy poverty he always refused to wear a cardinal's elegant robes, dressing instead in his tattered brown habit and sandals. He was quiet, withdrawn, almost out of place. Nobody knew where he stood on anything and nobody asked him. His name had been mentioned a couple of times in the month-long conclave, but simply because he was present although unaccounted for.

It was Bernis who first gave him serious thought. On seeing that the conclave was getting nowhere with leading candidates, Bernis sent an aide to Ganganelli one night with a set of questions on existing issues. Ganganelli's answers, though extremely vague, hinted that he was with the Spaniards or at least could easily be persuaded in that direction. Encouraged, Bernis rushed to work. All night he scurried from cubicle to cubicle, couching Ganganelli's answers in careful words that said nothing and yet convinced both parties on the Jesuit question that the Franciscan could well be their man. When Ganganelli awoke in the morning, he was Pope.

The world learned quickly that Bernis had turned the trick and he received more congratulations than did the new Pope. Versailles was most pleased. An official inquiry arrived asking Bernis if he would like to be French ambassador to Rome: a man with such apparent influence on cardinals certainly should protect French interests at the Vatican. Bernis was reluctant at first, unwilling to give up his lucrative benefice at Albi. King Louis assured him he could keep Albi, plus anything else, and earn an excellent salary besides. Bernis settled down in Rome on a millionaire's income. He bought a palace, staffed it with a legion of servants, hired the best cook on the continent, stocked the place with the finest foods and wines in the world and began a reign of nightly parties the likes of which Rome had not seen since Nero. At every party were the beautiful women Bernis so flamboyantly enjoyed. Casanova was a frequent guest; so was every cardinal or bishop who could grant favors whenever they might be needed. In every way except the blood in his veins Bernis was more the King of Rome than Louis was the King of France.

He worked hard, to be sure. To squeeze in all his social functions, he got up at five in the morning and plowed his way through mountains of paper work before the city began to stir, thereby freeing himself for the parade of callers each morning. Because of him, France became a leading factor in Rome and in the world. Nobody left his presence without a gift, and they reciprocated with the gift he wanted most: information. He knew not only all the political news of Europe, but when he sat down each evening with his scores of dinner guests he knew where each person present had spent the previous night.

There were still the Jesuits. Outlawed in Spain and Portugal, they were now banned in France. Due to Bernis' pressure in the right places, Austria closed in on them. The new Pope Clement XIV did nothing, but he must if Bernis was to protect his position. For months Bernis hammered at Clement relentlessly, cajoling, threatening, demanding. Clement tried every way to back out of what amounted to a campaign promise, and at last, with tears streaming down his face, he pronounced: "Under the pressure of the unjust and envious secular forces of the times, in a sea of dark forebodings, a Father's hand sacrifices the Society of Jesus for the tranquility of the bark of Peter."

Now Bernis' triumph was complete. Had it not been for Empress Catherine of Russia, who refused to reject the Jesuits, the society would have disappeared entirely, perhaps permanently, but in Russia they were able to work for twenty-five years, until another pope lifted the ban against them and permitted them to resume their international work. In subsequent years the Jesuits would be denounced, imprisoned and disbanded whenever a political force needed a scapegoat for anti-clericalism, and always they would have Bernis to thank for starting it all.

When Louis XV died in 1774, Rome went into deeper mourning than Paris. It was all a show for Bernis' sake, accompanied by the fear that he might be replaced and Rome would be deprived of its principal benefactor. But young King Louis XVI reappointed Bernis and the party went on.

The conclave held that same year was strictly Bernis' party. On the first day he made up his mind that Cardinal Gianangelo Braschi, the Vatican treasurer, would become pope, but he knew the cardinals well enough to realize that the direct approach, even for him, would be wrong. He changed his cubicle into a buffet, heaped with food and drink sent over by his embassy, and as the conclave awaited the arrival of foreigners he kept up a constant chatter on candidates with an occasional airy, "And then there is Braschi."

The Jesuits were still a conclave issue because of some cardinals who wanted their return, so the alliance was as before. If Braschi had come out flatly against the Jesuits, Bernis' task would have been easier. As things were, Braschi had certain Jesuit sympathies, having been educated by them, and this caused Bernis to proceed slowly. The process took one hundred and forty days, with interruptions caused by deadlocks and an influenza epidemic that put several important cardinals to bed. Slowly, gently, persistently, Bernis continued a soft barrage for Braschi, winning the cardinals over one by one. At last a compromise committee was chosen and Braschi's name was not among those given to the committee for consideration. But Bernis knew that the hottest candidate before the committee was a man absolutely convinced that Braschi should be pope. It was a moment of great drama when the man firmly refused the nomination and cried out for the election of Braschi. In the wave of excitement Braschi was swept into office.

Again Bernis got more congratulations than the new Pope. The crowned heads of Europe praised him for his diplomatic skill that had brought him victory. He had won the race: Braschi was merely the jockey aboard for the ride. Soon afterwards Bernis was made the bishop of Albano, a suburbicarian diocese, a tremendously important benefice especially for a cardinal who was at the same time the ambassador of a foreign power.

It was a power soon to die. In Louis at Versailles and Bernis at Rome the French people had two outrageous examples of unimaginable extravagance. Both men lived blithely in a cream-puff world soon to be smashed by the bloodiest uprising Europe had ever seen. Short-sighted by their own pleasures, neither man could understand why it should happen.

Soon it was all over. In 1789, the States-General forced

Louis to the Oath of the Tennis Court, which ended abso-
lutism in France. The next year, the assembly confiscated all
Church holdings in the country, and the clergy was forced
to take a pledge of allegiance to the assembly that super-
seded obedience to Rome. A great number of the clergy submitted. Prelates of noble blood who refused escaped to England; the lesser clergy who refused went into hiding and for
the next dozen years had to practice their ministry in attics,
in barns, and in the middle of the night.

All Bernis' revenues from France, his salary and his benefices, were cut off. His only income was from Albano, scarcely
enough to keep him in his accustomed luxury. Reluctant to
bring his personal kingdom to a sudden end, he continued
his parties on funds he had invested in Rome, but this lasted
only a few months. In the end he had to break up his palace
into apartments and rent them out. It was his nature to be
affected physically by crises and, as in the past, particularly
during his exile, his health broke. He was in Rome, a sick
man, when in 1793 his King and Queen were guillotined.
With him were two of the royal princesses who had fled to
Rome for safety. He supported them as well as he could, until the time came when he had to advise them to move to the
Spanish embassy for the sake of their own comfort.

Alone in his palace, he wrote his will. In typical cardinal
fashion, he left what little he had to his nephews. And then
he died. With him an era died. Never again, no matter how
much it deluded itself, would the French Church know such
glory and power as it did in the years while Bernis was its
principal spokesman. Because of its role in the crisis of
France, the Church would forever be held suspect by the people.

Pope Pius VI decreed that all French churchmen who
took the oath to the Civil Constitution of the Clergy
were automatically schismatics and were deprived of their
priestly faculties. Yet these men were the only priests per-

mitted to work in France. To the anti-religious, this plight made no difference, but the faithful realized that these men, having lost the lawful exercise of their priestly powers, could not say a lawful Mass nor dispense lawful sacraments. Churches then became like theaters where plays on religious ceremonies were performed, and the churches were empty. There evolved in the country an underground of true priests, traveling in disguise and known only by those they could trust. From time to time, priests were captured and killed, and so were the Catholics who had helped them.

The situation improved somewhat with the rise of Napoleon Bonaparte who, searching for friends on a continent torn by his wars, reached a concordat with the Vatican in 1801 which restored many ecclesiastical rights in France. The harmony was far from complete. Napoleon insisted on the authority to control all Church activity in France, regardless of how trivial. In the midst of his wars he had to take time out to sign an approval for groups of nuns to open orphanages. So great was his power that he summoned Pius VII to Paris in 1804 to coronate him and bless his marriage. He hoped at the same time to force the Pope to endorse his side in the threatening war with England. But the Pope refused to take a stand on the English problem. Furthermore, the Pope bristled when Napoleon would not go to confession before his marriage and coronation ceremonies. It was subsequently opined that Napoleon tried to show his independence from the Church when, during his coronation ceremonies, he snatched the crown from the Pope's hands and put it on his head himself, but the circumstances gave more credence to speculation that the Pope, realizing that he was already a prisoner, refused at the last minute to go through with the sacrilegious ceremonies and Napoleon had to crown himself or not be crowned at all.

Napoleon held Pius a prisoner for months in order to force his submission, releasing him only when world opinion created an international embarrassment which even the ruler of France could not escape. Back in Rome, Pius quickly reinstated the Jesuits, much to Napoleon's displeasure. When the obdurate Pope still refused to give Napoleon at least his moral support against England, the French invaded the Papal States in 1809, captured the Pope and retained him as a prisoner at Fontainebleau for almost five years. Pius was forced to sign a new concordat with France, which practically made Napoleon a pope, but he later repudiated it. The collapse of Napoleon's empire in 1814 freed Pius to return to Rome, and the Congress of Vienna gave back to the Church most of the territories the French had taken away.

For years to come, relations between France and the Church were to swing like a pendulum. For a people who had fought such a bloody revolution to destroy the nobility, the French returned their government to nobility with a frequent ease that was bewildering. Whenever the nobility ruled the Church had greater freedom because the nobility felt that the Church, at least the control of it, was their special domain. It was understandable, therefore, that a great percentage of the people, whether they prayed or not, looked upon the nobility and the hierarchy as partners in the stiff control of the country. Unfortunately, the nobility and the hierarchy felt the same way, a situation that might have lasted forever had not a commoner who became a prince taken steps to correct it.

Charles Martial Allemand Lavigerie was born on October 31, 1825, at Bayonne, in the south of France, the son of a customs officer. Like Bernis, he informed his parents when he was still a boy that he intended to become a priest; unlike Bernis's parents, they did not take him seriously. In fact, throughout his youth he had to insist repeatedly on his vocation, but his family went ahead to make plans for his marriage. The plans were not discarded when the boy entered the minor seminary near his home, nor when he went to

Paris for his major seminary studies. Only on the day of his ordination did his parents realize he had meant it all along.

He often said all he wanted to be was a country priest, but he had done so remarkably well at his seminary studies that his superiors urged him to go on to work for higher degrees. He earned them in record time, obtaining in ten months degrees that normally took two years. Again he asked to be assigned to a country parish, but he found himself instead teaching Church history at the Sorbonne. He drew considerable attention to himself by lecturing on papal infallibility, which he felt was implicit in the Bible and had been established *ipso facto* by tradition. This was a touchy subject in France where, despite everything, the hierarchy was still reluctant to grant additional authority to Rome. Thirteen years later the doctrine was officially proclaimed.

Lavigerie might have remained a professor all his life, but for the unexpected vacancy of the chairmanship of L'Oeuvre d'Orient, a philanthropy created for the purpose of erecting Christian schools in the Middle East. The position was offered to him and on the insistence of friends he accepted it. The work took him to Lebanon and it also required him to work closely with Vatican congregations devoted to missionary endeavors and the Eastern rites. Because of the importance of his program, he was granted an audience with Pope Pius IX and made such a favorable impression that, in 1861, the Pope appointed him French auditor to the Rota, the Vatican court of appeals. Soon after, he was appointed consultant to the Congregation for Oriental Rites and he was made a domestic prelate.

But he was restless in Rome. Endless paperwork chained him to a desk. He wanted to be out among people, and he told the Pope, "I suffer too much here, Holy Father. I wasn't born to be a diplomat nor a political arbitrator. I was born a priest."

He hoped to be sent back to France to a parish; he was

sent back to a diocese. In 1863, he was made Bishop of Nancy. He proved to be another Borromeo, rushing through his diocese like a holy storm, making sweeping changes, demanding more work out of his priests and better training for his nuns. His startling improvements made him the talk of France, and it was only natural that when the archbishopric of Algiers should become vacant in 1867 the post should be offered to him.

He didn't want it. He was happy at Nancy, and there was still so much he wanted to do there, but the Algerian offer had come from two sources he could not ignore: the Pope himself and Emperor Napoleon III. Always a tremendously informed man, Lavigerie knew what he was getting into. Previous bishops of Algiers had encountered nothing but opposition from the colonial government, particularly in relations with the Arabs. The colonial policy was quite plain: leave the natives alone—they'll be less trouble that way. But Lavigerie was not the kind of man who would settle for that. Going to Africa would make him a missionary and he intended to behave like one. His years of study and his experiences in the Middle East had made him an authority on Islam; he knew of Islam's deep hatred for Christianity and he realized that conversions were out of the question, at least for a long time. But he wanted Christianity to make itself felt in the Arab community by the performance of Christian good works. There were many ways Arabs could be helped, lifted to a better way of life, through schools, hospitals, orphanages, technical training, agronomy, and these were the things he wanted to provide. If—as he knew perfectly well—this was contrary to colonial policy, then the policy would have to be changed. The day he arrived in Algiers he gave clear evidence that he would not be a puppet. Leading colonial families had gathered at his house to welcome him with a party and he refused to enter the house until everybody there got out.

He did everything he said he would. In twenty-five years in Africa he never traveled more than twenty-five miles into the interior, but he had an amazingly perceptive knowledge of the continent that led him to remarkable achievements. Realizing the importance of missionaries especially trained for Africa he founded both the White Fathers and White Sisters, who now comprise the largest and most effective missionary factor on the continent, both among the Arabs and below the Sahara. The information which these pioneers supplied for him on African slavery made him the leading figure in the anti-slavery societies being organized in Europe and brought about international agreements for the end of slave trading in Africa.

As for the stiff-arm colonial policy in Algeria, Lavigerie told the Emperor to his face: "Unless you do something to help the Algerians, I warn you they will not rest until they push you into the sea." It was a prophecy that has been emphasized by Algerian uprisings which have persisted to this day.

Lavigerie's role in strictly French affairs shook the royalists of his country. An important step preceded it. He had become very popular in Rome because of his efforts to rally the French hierarchy to accept the doctrine of papal infallibility when it was decreed in 1870. With their traditional sensitivity to the supremacy of Rome, the French bishops winced at the prospect of complete surrender to the papacy, if only in matters of faith and morals. Lavigerie sent scores of lengthy letters to key Church figures in France, presenting historical evidence supporting the logic of the decree and the validity of its claims, and it was largely due to his labors that the French hierarchy received the decree with little more than a murmur. This plus his phenomenal success in Africa led, in 1884, to the expansion of his episcopal area to the ancient archdiocese of Carthage, vacant for more than a thousand years. With it came a cardinal's red hat and the title of Primate of all Africa. He was now a man of first prominence.

Occupying the papal throne was Pope Leo XIII, a man who was to distinguish himself with his encyclical *Rerum novarum,* which deplored the miserable plight of factory workers and the companion evil of slum-living and put forth ideas for labor-management responsibilities that was to become a blueprint for the deveopment of unions. Leo had another interest.

The Third French Republic was struggling for its own life. Its greatest enemies were the royalists who plotted for its downfall and hoped for a return to the kind of monarchy under which they could flourish. Pope Leo knew another governmental collapse in France would mean further bloodshed, and he prayed against that. Also, he knew that most of the royalists were Catholics, and as long as they refused to support the government there would be no end to the anticlericalism again rife in the country. Moreover, he was convinced that the era of monarchy was finished in France and if the royalists, as citizens, expected to have anything to say in the government they had better take part in the government they had.

He could not, as Pope, make any public statement about all this; he would be immediately accused of meddling in the political affairs of France and there could be serious repercussions. But he knew a man who could say something. He waited until Lavigerie was in Rome in the autumn of 1890 and put the matter to him.

Lavigerie was stunned. He readily admitted that the Pope was right, that these same thoughts had occurred to him, but to ask him to say so out loud was inviting catastrophe. Lavigerie depended on French Catholics for donations to support his missions, and his most generous benefactors were royalists. For him to urge the royalists to get behind a government diametrically opposed to their preferred way of life would be suicide. Lavigerie begged the Pope not to give him such a terrible assignment. The Pope replied that the request had been made, the matter was urgent, but he would leave it to Lavigerie to make the decision. Lavigerie went back to Algiers knowing he could not refuse.

Six weeks later the French Mediterranean Fleet pulled into Algiers. The Governor was away; it was therefore up to Lavigerie to give the Fleet officers a luncheon reception. He chose this occasion to make the statement Pope Leo had requested. He could not have had a less receptive audience; the Fleet officers were all royalists, by descent and conviction. And yet in language rich with innuendo he said in his welcome toast:

"Union, in view of the past which still bleeds and the future which is always menacing, is at this moment our supreme need. Union is also—may I say—the first wish of the Church and her pastors at all degrees of the hierarchy. Most certainly, the Church does not ask us to dismiss either the memory of France's past glories or the men whose loyalty and services pay tribute both to them and their country, but when the will of the people has been clearly stated, when the form of government they choose has nothing in it contrary to the principles which alone can give life to Christian and civilized nations and when, in order to save one's country from the pitfalls which threaten it, sincere adhesion to this form of government becomes necessary, then the moment has at last arrived to declare that the period of test and trial is over and all men must unite, despite sacrifices which arise, to work as one for the future and the salvation of the country.

"... Without this patriotic acceptance, nothing is possible indeed, neither for the conservation of order and peace, nor for the salvation of the world from social peril, nor to save the religion itself whose ministers we are.

"It would be folly to hope to provide supports for the columns of a building without entering the building itself, and this must be done to prevent those who would destroy everything from accomplishing their foul deed. Those who obstinately remain outside the building, as some still do despite recent evils, succeed only in showing to the world their own ambitions and hates and in sowing in the heart of France itself the discouragement which will be the precursor of the final catastrophe. . . ."

Lavigerie's words were received in silence. Within moments the Fleet officers walked from the room. For them, insult was added to treason when, outside, Lavigerie's boys' band struck up the *Marseillaise.*

The blast was severe. The French royalist press called Lavigerie everything from a fool to a drunk. The Catholic papers said he had made France weep. The republican papers jokingly invited the royalists to come on in and grab a column. Then came the bitter blow: Lavigerie's royalist benefactors, in and out of the Church, wrote him to forget their addresses the next time he was looking for money.

For two years he did not get a sou from France. For two years his important missionary work gradually slowed, then stopped. This was what hurt him most.

In France, the anticlerical national assembly closed Catholic institutions, dissolved the Jesuit establishments, and confiscated Church properties. Then the light came slowly into many narrow minds; Catholics began to realize that if they had had more representation in the assembly this sort of thing would not have happened. Diehards began to understand that a royalist government was out of the question but there could be a government in which Catholics, armed with votes, could defend their personal interests while aiding in the progress of the country. A bishop here, then a bishop there, finally faced the fact. The trend was strengthened by a papal encyclical in which Leo defined the responsibility of all Christians to their governments as well as their Church in establishing peace and providing justice for all, and in the paper Leo used some of Lavigerie's own words.

Then it came, almost too late: the apology. In Algiers the Cardinal was close to death from strokes brought on by his great worries for funds to support his growing missions. He was already confined to his bed when news arrived that a document had been published in France, signed by five cardinals and seventy-five bishops, acknowledging the wisdom of Lavigerie's toast and urging Catholics to go to the aid of the republic.

Lavigerie did not respond to the praise, just as he had not responded to the earlier attacks. In a letter to his missionaries he said only:

"The thoughts and words I pronounced for years in (Pope Leo's) name he has deigned to recall in this encyclical, which henceforth by the fidelity with which we will follow it will constitute the object of our hopes—not only for our temporal fatherland but also for the Church, which is our Eternal Father."

In a few months he was dead. Obituaries in Paris newspapers read like tributes to a national hero. One editor summed up the thoughts of all: "My God, he was a great man!"

3

In England at this time were three men who would have earned a similar accolade, each in his own way. They were contemporaries, their lives spanning the century, lives that touched each other, sometimes with a bump.

Following the severance with Rome, the Church of England (Anglican) did not change much at first. Henry VIII wanted it that way. His only personal complaint against

Rome was that it interfered with his marital life. His love for Anne Boleyn was short-lived; he had her beheaded for adultery, a strange accusation coming from a man who had practically made a hobby of the same deed. Now that the Anglican Church had served its purpose for him, Henry was no longer interested in it and he put it into other hands.

During the years of Cardinal Bernis, Catholicism was a crime in England. Those who practiced it did so secretly, as was to be the case in France later on. The French Revolution put England in an awkward position. It had been an enemy of France, and yet when the French nobility and hierarchy needed a haven, England, herself a monarchy, could not refuse entrance to the refugees. Into the country rushed Frenchmen, laymen and clergy, and once they settled down they expected to be able to go on with their religion. Again England, despite her laws, could not very well refuse.

In the late nineteenth century the Anglican Church consisted of two parts: High Church, which was almost as ceremonial as Rome, and Low Church, which was strongly influenced by puritanism. In its break with Rome, the Church of England claimed that it had retained Apostolic Succession and that Rome had lost it because of errors in doctrine and practice. Rome, in other words, had gone astray, not London. The Anglican leaders, in view of their claim, maintained that their sacerdotal orders were valid, that their eucharist possessed the Real Presence, and High Churchmen adhered to auricular confession in the Catholic form. Actually, had the Anglican separation been based merely on the matter of Vatican authority over Catholicism the Anglican sacraments quite likely would have retained their validity; this had happened with some of the Eastern rites. But the Council of Trent had so clearly defined the nature of sacraments that any changes were tantamount to heresy. Thus, after long and careful study, the Vatican proclaimed in 1896 that the Anglican ordination rites had been defective since the time of Edward VI and Elizabeth I because of changes in the nature of the priesthood itself. Thus what had started out as a schism developed into a heresy, with all sacraments invalid because the sacrament of Holy Orders—the priesthood—had been invalidated. Viewed in these terms, the Anglican claim to Apostolic Succession was baseless sacramentally as well as historically.

During the eighteenth century Anglicanism developed abuses like those that had plagued Rome: multiple benefices, simony, episcopal control in the hands of the nobility, politics. Moreover, the Church was greatly in the hands of Parliament. A committee of laymen could overrule bishops. The Church as a church lost its spirit. The priesthood weakened. Their theology reflected their own sentiments rather than defensible precepts. Church attendance fell off. Outside of the top circles, the clergy was poor and ineffectual.

The influx of Frenchmen, the required good manners that permitted their religious practices and the ease with which they became part of England led to the Relief Acts of 1778 and 1791 which allowed public Catholic worship, and eventually to the Emancipation Act of 1829 that let Catholics have churches and schools and brought Catholic priests out of hiding.

The English Catholics didn't know how to live in their new freedom and remained reticent for generations. It was an odd experience for a man accidentally to dig his rosary out of his pocket without having to break out in a cold sweat. The reserve of the old Catholics was to prove a problem in the years immediately ahead when the ban against Catholicism was lifted.

The Church considered England to be missionary territory. There was no Catholic seminary in the country. Any young man aspiring to the priesthood had to go to Rome and study at the English College and Gregorian University, founded by Pope Gregory XV and taught by the Jesuits.

The English College had been reopened in 1818, and among the first to enter it was Nicholas Patrick Wiseman, a young Englishman who had been born in Spain, raised and educated in England. He was ordained in 1825 and immediately appointed vice-rector of the College.

At approximately the same time, another young Englishman, named John Henry Newman, was ordained an Anglican priest and assigned to St. Clement's, Oxford. And about to begin his Anglican studies at Oxford was another Englishman, Henry Edward Manning.

The return of Catholicism stirred the minds of England's young men. Unless they traveled abroad they were never exposed to it, and the histories they studied led them to believe that the Anglican Church was, as it claimed, the true church; Rome had gone astray. But now here it was, right in their laps. They began to look at it, examine it, evaluate it; then they looked at the Anglican Church with the same attention. It should be pointed out that these were admirable, sincere, idealistic young men, deep in their studies, hungry for truth, safe in an intellectual atmosphere and still untainted by the weights of life that limit a man's horizons. This was the time of their lives when they would determine whether they would ever be worth anything. Life was urgent; without truth, life was empty. Like the young so briefly are, these young men ached to be right, and they had character enough to realize they had to look outside themselves for it.

With most of Europe in turmoil, it became fashionable at this time for the English who could afford it to vacation in Rome, especially in winter when the British weather was bad. Newman went to Rome in December, 1832, primarily because of his health. Manning went in 1838, hoping to find on the trip some escape from the heartache caused by the death of his wife. Both of them met Wiseman. A sizable English colony had collected in Rome, both Catholic and

Anglican. To provide religious services for them with a sermon in their own language, Wiseman had been assigned to accommodate them. Anglicans as well as Catholics attended, so Wiseman restricted his sermons to general topics, sometimes criticizing the English for their un-English flamboyant behavior with the hot-blooded Italians.

Manning attended Wiseman's services, went about Rome with him, and witnessed various Catholic ceremonies with him. Newman was disinclined to fraternize to that extent with a papist; he did not attend Wiseman's Masses but inspected the English College under his guidance. From what they saw, from what they heard and read, both Manning and Newman returned to England with uncertainties about their own church.

It did not occur to either man that he would end up a Catholic. On the contrary, their initial steps, taken separately, were to justify Anglicanism historically, and without realizing it they were trying to make Anglicanism more Roman. It was Newman who coined the phrase "Via Media," by which he intended to establish that Anglicanism was the middle road between Catholicism and Protestantism, with its roots in early Christianity before the Italians papal-decreed the faith out of recognition. The idea was attractive to many who were seeking a clearer definition of the Anglican Church, but to others, some high in the Church, it was denounced as an unnecessary compromise. Pursuing the idea further, Newman read extensively, and the more he read the less convinced he became of his own idea. Gradually the suggestion penetrated his writings that the Church of England, as defined in the Thirty-Nine Articles on which it was based, was perhaps more Catholic than people suspected and possibly a union between the two churches was possible.

For that matter, the whole experience was shattering. Like others in the coterie that had attached itself to Newman, he had, all his life, believed firmly in his church. To be haunted now by the probability that its history was open to question and its theology might be unsound was torture to a man of principle, for Newman knew that once he was convinced the heart of Christianity was in Rome he would have to make the spiritual journey there regardless of the cost. Manning suffered the same doubts, as he indicated in letters to friends who were similarly concerned. Both men were distressed by the chance that they, not their church, might be wrong, and they knew they could not rest until they knew for certain. They knew, too, that, once convinced, they would be intellectually and morally bound to take steps that would cost them their careers, many friends, even their families, but they had both already put sufficient value upon their souls that they realized if they did otherwise they would be spiritual frauds for all eternity.

As a missionary territory, England was under the supervision of the Congregation for the Propagation of the Faith. Heading the work locally were four vicar apostolics, men with the spiritual faculties of bishops but without the territorial responsibilities. When the years showed that all was going well, the English clergy asked for its own hierarchy. The Vatican agreed. The vicar apostolics were certainly qualified to fit into the new arrangements; to plan for the future successors had to be considered from the start. In Rome, a promising English priest was Nicholas Wiseman. He was assigned to England as vicar-apostolic.

He was a good choice. Having spent most of his manhood in Rome he was attuned to confident Catholicity, an important attitude among the English Catholics who still hadn't learned how to live openly in their new freedom. Wiseman was properly aggressive. Until his return to England, the analytical writings of Newman and Manning went unanswered by any notable Catholics. Wiseman replied to them. His approach was gentle but thorough, diplomatic but uncontestible. He sensed what both men were going

through; he knew that one wrong word, one impatient in-
flection, could send them into retreat. He was willing to
wait.

Wiseman settled in England in 1840. In 1843, Newman
gave up his work as an Anglican priest and, after two more
years of soul-searching, became a Catholic in 1845. Manning's severance with Anglicanism came in 1850. Within
months after both men left the Church of England both took
steps to become Catholic priests. Wiseman was helpful in
both instances in suggesting ways they could use their talents
for the benefit of the Church. Newman joined the Oratory
Fathers and settled at Birmingham, prepared to spend his
life at teaching and writing. Manning, a far more overt person, went to St. Edmund's College with the Oblates of St.
Charles, which he organized. Of the two, Manning was closer
to Wiseman, being like him a man with a frontal-attack personality. After Wiseman became the cardinal-archbishop of
Westminster he assigned Manning to work with him.

In Newman and Manning, the Church acquired in England two greatly different men for others to consider in their
own interests in Catholicism. The old English Catholics favored Newman for he was, like them, quiet and reserved, an
intellectual who preferred the slow approach. Mentally, he
was by far the superior man. Manning, on the other hand,
thought and moved fast. In London he was quickly involved
with the working classes, for whom he crusaded for better
working and living conditions. It was later generally agreed
that his work and writings directly influenced the encyclical
on labor by Pope Leo XIII. In the public view, Manning
far outshone Newman. Inevitably, Newman and Manning
were on opposite sides on various issues, not so much as to
goals but rather as to procedures. Newman often said that
Manning caused anti-Catholic feelings by the way he rushed
at his work without considering repercussions. The paradox
was that on many occasions both men were right, with the

result that it was Newman who won the respect of people but Manning who won the greater following.

Newman's star suffered an unfortunate eclipse when he was invited to become head of a new Catholic University in Dublin. There was talk that he would also be made a bishop, and although he had no desire for the office he felt it would give him greater stature in Ireland to carry on his work. But when the Vatican approved the school there was no mention of a bishop's title. Also, plans for the school had been poorly prepared, and there were so many insurmountable problems that Newman finally returned to Birmingham with a failure chalked against him. When Wiseman died, there was considerable speculation about his successor. Newman's name was mentioned; he was preferred by the old Catholics, but quite likely due to the experience in Ireland he was passed over and the appointment went, to the surprise of many, to Manning.

It was on the subject of universities that Father Newman and Cardinal Manning first came to public grips. The best schools in England were Oxford and Cambridge; both Newman and Manning had gone to Oxford and Newman never lost his deep love for the place. It had been for centuries a Catholic university, but upon the English schism it naturally became Anglican. Newman had served as Anglican chaplain of one of the colleges, and his dream was to return there now as a Catholic chaplain.

Manning forcefully opposed him; so did most of the English hierarchy, on the grounds that Anglicanism permeated the Oxford curricula and it would be impossible for a Catholic to attend the university without endangering his faith. That, Newman maintained, was the very reason Oxford should have a Catholic chapel: there were Catholics at Oxford and their faith was being endangered because they had no priest, no Catholic services and no occasion for Catholic companionship. But, as a priest, Newman could not go against the decisions of his superiors and he was forced to give up the plan.

As the years passed it grew increasingly obvious that the Vatican was about to decree the doctrine of papal infallibility. In Africa, Lavigerie was busy writing fellow-prelates in France to accept the doctrine. Manning at London was eager to go along with it. But Newman was not. From this evolved their most serious difference. Newman, as well as Manning and Lavigerie, knew the doctrine was valid. It had been one of the stumbling blocks to his own conversion, but once he established it historically and theologically to his own satisfaction he had no reservations about it.

Now his reservation was merely a matter of timing. He felt that, for England at least, this was the wrong hour for such a pronouncement. Conversions were proceeding in the country, slowly but steadily, and if they were slow it was because of papal infallibility. At that time, it was not necessary for Catholics to accept it because it had not as yet been defined as Catholic doctrine. To have it so defined at this particular time would be, Newman felt, a threat to the faith of new Catholics and potential Catholics. All he asked was that the acceptance of it, in England anyway, be held off until the Church had deeper roots.

But he was misunderstood. In the public mind, Manning approved of papal infallibility and Newman did not. Even Manning fell into this error; he expected Newman either to leave the Church or start a schism, both probabilities ridiculous.

So once again it seemed Newman had suffered failure. From another view, he triumphed, as evidenced in the noticeable increase in Catholic interest in England, but Newman was not the kind of man to enjoy such a victory. On the contrary, he worked harder at his writing—and it was the finest writing being done in English—to explain papal infallibility and its place in the Church.

He paid the price for his opinions. Because of his position in the Church in England he should have received many more honors. They did not come. When, in the next ten years, Pope Pius IX appointed new cardinals, Newman's name never appeared among them. There was little doubt that the Pope felt Newman might not have been too good a catch for the Church.

But the new pope felt differently. Six months after Leo XIII was elected he sent word to Bishop Ullathorne of Birmingham to sound out Newman on whether he would accept a red hat if it were offered him. Newman's joy was in knowing that the offer meant the cloud of suspicion had been removed from him. He was then seventy-eight and not well; he doubted that he could take on new work in his condition. Had he been a bishop he could have gone to Rome for his red hat, then returned to his regular routine, but as a priest it was certain that he would be appointed to fill a cardinal's role in the Curia. He did not feel up to it. Writing Ullathorne, he explained this, saying that he was pleased and honored to be considered for the appointment but he hoped the Pope would not remove him from his quiet life of studies in the English countryside. He wrote Manning in the same vein. Ullathorne sent Newman's letter on to Manning, with a covering note suggesting that the Pope make Newman a cardinal but permit him to remain at Birmingham, which would have been unusual but not impossible.

For whatever reasons he might have had, Manning forwarded to Rome only Newman's letter to Ullathorne, from the tone of which a refusal of the appointment could easily be inferred. Rumors of Newman's refusal were soon all over London; the *Times* printed a story to that effect. Perturbed, Ullathorne wrote directly to Rome, explaining the situation in detail. A month later the Pope announced Newman's appointment, specifying that he would be allowed to remain in England. Newman received his red hat on May 12, 1878.

He was the last cardinal outside of Rome to be appointed while still a priest, the only cardinal on record without any Vatican assignments. In his case, the appointment was expressly a personal tribute.

Of the three cardinals, Newman has been remembered with the most affection and regard. His appeal was more to the intellectual and he was considered the primary influence in the Oxford Movement which during his time brought so many university students to Catholicism. This, however, should not overshadow the success of Wiseman and Manning in the other social levels of the country. Despite the fact that the three men were often at odds, they were an effective combination, particularly in the circumstances of their time. Without design, each man appealed to a different class of people and thus the Catholic revival in England got off on a broad and healthy basis which, due to the strong personalities of its leaders, it retained.

4

In 1700 a law was passed in the province of New York which decreed that "every popish priest caught within the province should be imprisoned for life, and if he escaped and was recaptured could be hung." In modified degrees, this attitude existed in all of the Thirteen Colonies, with the brief exception of Maryland. The Maryland colony was headed by George Calvert, the first Lord Baltimore, a Catholic Englishman, who named his chartered area after the Catholic Queen Mary. However, the Dutch immigration from northern colonies put an end to Catholic freedom in Maryland for almost fifty years. Even after the American Revolution and the adoption of the Constitution and its guarantee of religious freedom, anti-Catholic restrictions and uprisings persisted during the nineteenth century and never completely disappeared from certain sections of the country, along with other types of prejudice.

The early anti-Catholic sentiments in America had their roots in Europe. During the period of colonization in the eighteenth century, Europe was engaged in a series of wars, and denominational sensitivities were tense between Protestant and Protestant, as well as between Protestant and Catholic.

The Constitutional guarantees of religious freedom were the work of Catholics. Father John Carroll, a native of Maryland and the first American to become a bishop, presented a statement to the delegates at Philadelphia defining the rights of Catholics, and it was directly from this act that the assembly adopted the sixth article of the Constitution which abolished all religious tests for any office or public trust. Catholics, therefore, provided to the United States of America the very pledge of religious freedoms that many non-Catholics have worried about losing if a Catholic should attain high governmental office.

When John Carroll became Bishop of Baltimore—of America, in effect—in 1789, there were 25,000 Catholics in the country. Most of them lived in Maryland; there were about 7,000 in Pennsylvania, 1,500 in New York, and 200 in Virginia. Missionaries in the Midwest and on the West Coast accounted for many of the remainder by conversions among the Indians. Thirty years later, the Catholic population was up to 250,000, and thirty years after that, in 1850, there were almost 2,000,000 Catholics in the country. This tremendous increase resulted primarily from the immigration of Catholics escaping from the Protestant states of Germany, and the pressures of Anglicanism in Ireland. Subsequent mass immigrations from Italy, Poland, Greece, and the Low Countries were due to persecution, war, and famine. The immigrants were poor. Most of them remained in cities in the hope of finding employment, and only later did the movement to the rich fields of the Midwest take place, resulting in the heavily Catholic populations of Wisconsin, Illinois, Michigan, and Ohio.

Before the Revolution, the Church in America had come under the jurisdiction of the Vicar-Apostolic of London, but the break with England necessitated a change. Thereafter the bishops of Baltimore were considered the heads of the Church in the country, until 1893 when Leo XIII appointed the first apostolic delegate to the United States, with headquarters in Washington. Actual control, as everywhere, was in the hands of autonomous bishops who acknowledged the papal representatives and the primacy on honor of Baltimore, all, of course, under Rome. The delegates' responsibilities were to represent the popes and keep the Vatican informed on Catholic affairs in the country.

These affairs were to startle the Vatican on several occasions. One episode was the result of a law requiring all church properties to be held by incorporated boards of trustees composed of laymen. This was sponsored by Catholics in New York, who then proceeded to buy property for a church. Undoubtedly influenced by the Protestant policy of having full control of church affairs in the hands of laymen, the Catholics indicated their intention of going beyond their authority and choosing their own pastors, independent of bishops, and carrying out church business. The idea was utterly contrary to Catholic practice, but it caught on and spread to other cities. In a short time the situation was very serious. Various lay boards used their position as trustees as a weapon against pastors and bishops, threatening to sell the properties they held unless they got their way. There was an unusual underlying factor: most men active in Trusteeism, as it was called, were Irish, and their complaint was that many of the priests serving their parishes were French, in the country either as missionaries or refugees, and there was a difficulty of communication between the priests and the people. This situation couldn't be helped, but Trusteeism couldn't be tolerated.

Pope Pius VII issued a brief condemning Trusteeism, and the bishops had to put up a fight to eradicate it. Finally the matter had to go to court, where it was established that the laymen were acting illegally and the Church was allowed to set up its corporations on a diocesan basis with a board including both the clergy and the laity with the clergy in the majority. Even so, almost fifty years were required to end Trusteeism.

During this same period another idea appeared that seemed heretical, at least to Europeans. It was called Americanism, and blamed for it was Isaac Thomas Hecker, a New York City convert who received papal permission to organize a new society of priests—the Paulists—to work for further conversions in America. Having been a convert, Hecker knew which aspects of Catholicism made potential converts balk, and in a biography of him one of his followers attested that Hecker felt it wasn't necessary for converts to understand or accept all the teachings of the Church, that the Holy Ghost would provide all understanding sooner or later, and that meantime it was enough for converts to practice the active virtues. When this book was translated into French the French clergy exploded, charging Hecker with Modernism—a philosophy that had evolved from an attempt to reconcile nineteenth century science and philosophy with historic Christianity and established religion. Modernism maintained that since God didn't create the world He could be only a spirit for good living in it. The Bible was discredited as history, consequently eliminating the Resurrection, the sacraments, the authority of the Vatican, and the function of churches and prayer other than for psychological support. Pope Leo XIII was quickly assured there was nothing to worry about. If anything, Hecker had merely tried to take the sting out of certain Catholic doctrines which potential converts had difficulty accepting; a bigger thing had been made out of it all than actually existed, and the bishops assured Rome that all care would be taken to clarify the situation.

The foreign clergy, particularly the French, intruded into American Catholicism in yet another sphere. For a long time America depended almost entirely on Europe for priests, but gradually, due greatly to the efforts of Bishop Carroll, Americans entered the Church and became excellent episcopal prospects. However, Europeans felt Church leadership in America should remain in their hands, and whenever a diocesan vacancy occurred there was pressure from Europe upon Rome for the appointment of Europeans to the bishoprics. As a result, the development of an American hierarchy was thwarted, so much so that the American bishops finally sent a delegation to Rome to urge that the system be changed. The Americans proposed that henceforth all United States bishops should send reports to Rome regularly on priests who showed promise of leadership and when a vacancy occurred three names would be submitted to Rome from which the popes could make their choices. The Vatican approved the plan and later adopted it for the entire Church.

It was difficult for Europeans to understand the Americans. After centuries of State and Church unions and thus inevitably State and Church friction, the Europeans couldn't see how the Catholic Church in the United States could expect to thrive in an atmosphere where Church and the State had little to do with each other and Catholics daily rubbed elbows with Protestants. In reply, Cardinal Gibbons of Baltimore said:

"The separation of Church and State in this country seems to (American Catholics) the natural, inevitable and best conceived plan, the one that would work best among us, both for the good of religion and of the State. Any change in their relations they would contemplate with dread. They are well aware, indeed, that the Church here enjoys a larger liberty and a more secure position than in any country today where Church and State are united."

By mid-1960, fourteen American-born prelates had been appointed cardinals. With one exception, they were all active heads of U. S. dioceses at the time of their appointment, the exception being Archbishop Aloysius J. Muench, a native of Milwaukee who, although bishop of Fargo, North Dakota, was serving as papal ambassador to the Federal Republic of West Germany at Bonn. Following custom, Cardinal Muench was withdrawn from the diplomatic service on receiving his red hat and assigned to the Curia, thereby becoming the only American cardinal to hold such a position. Cardinal Stritch of Chicago, appointed to the Curia in 1959, died before he could take over as pro-prefect of the Congregation for the Propagation of the Faith. Muench's appointment, along with that of Archbishop Albert Gregory Meyer of Chicago, gave the United States six cardinals, the others being Richard Cushing of Boston, James McIntyre of Los Angeles, John O'Hara of Philadelphia, and Francis Spellman of New York.

Spellman, who received his hat in 1946, was the ranking American cardinal at this time. Between 1925 and 1932 he had served in the Papal Secretariat of State and was a close friend of Cardinal Eugenio Pacelli, then Secretary of State, who in 1939 became Pope Pius XII. A well-known story about the two men involved a document the Pope had written against prejudice and which was aimed at fascism in Italy. The big question was how to get the document out of Italy, an Axis power, and circulate it to all the bishops of the world. The Vatican had its own printing facilities and post office, but at some point the mailed papers would have to pass through Italian government hands en route to their destinations. With Benito Mussolini in control of the Italian government, it was scarcely likely that such a document would be given unhampered passage through the Italian mails. Spellman was at the Vatican at the time and the Pope reportedly sent for him and asked if he had any ideas. The only suggestion Spellman had was that he personally get the document out of Italy for printing and mailing elsewhere. Because of his position, there was a good chance that his luggage would not be examined by customs inspectors, but to play safe—so the story goes—Spellman offered to conceal it by slipping it under his shirt until he was beyond Italian surveillance. It was in this way that the document reached France, from where it was promulgated, and thus the Church was able to take its stand against prejudices of all kinds.

The first American cardinal was Archbishop John McCloskey of New York, appointed by Pope Pius IX in 1875. His nomination caused considerable surprise in Europe, where the feeling was strong that American Catholicism was still too young for such high-level representation in the Church. There were, however, over five million Catholics in the country, far more than in England where Manning was cardinal and more than in all Africa under Lavigerie. But representation was not the factor; as the popes had said, the red hat was to go to workers. The American hierarchy was working hard. By 1890, the Catholic population was over ten million, and there was a lot to be done.

The appointment of Archbishop James Gibbons to the cardinalate proved important in the task ahead. A native of Baltimore, which subsequently became his see, he did more than anyone to dispel Protestant fears that Catholics intended to take over the country and submit it to the Vatican. Made a cardinal in 1886, he lived until 1921 and was the spokesman for American Catholics throughout the thirty-five years. He was keenly sensitive to the constitutional prin-

ciple of separation of Church and State. He was a close
friend of Presidents Grover Cleveland, Theodore Roosevelt,
and William Howard Taft, close enough to ask for federal
protection against such anti-Catholic uprisings as from the
Ku Klux Klan, but he never broached the subject. Some
bishops considered this weak of him, but it proved to make
the Church stronger. By expecting nothing more than protection under the law Gibbons discouraged other denominations from asking for favors beyond it.

Gibbons was the country's best example of fraternity without surrender between Protestants and Catholics. This was
something European prelates could not understand, something Lavigerie tried to point out to them when he urged
French royalists to take part in their own government. Gibbons was anxious for the Church to become an integral part
of American life, and for this reason he urged the popes not
to issue any bulls or decrees which might further antagonize
non-Catholic Americans or stir further anti-Catholic sentiments. His reply to the French clergy regarding the quasi-
heretical Americanism rejected the charge on theological
bases and defined it in terms of the American Catholic's role
as a citizen of his country. He devoted himself on a broad
scale to the assimilation of the Catholic immigrant into the
American way of life, and in doing so he earned enemies in
certain foreign groups. The Germans, Poles, and Italians
particularly, isolated by language barriers, wanted to retain
various practices they knew in their homelands, but the Cardinal insisted that the American Church had its own personality and that immigrants adjust to it and thereby to the
country. Here, too, Gibbons encountered opposition from
some of his bishops, but he refused to let the matter erupt
into open combat. He once described his personal *modus
operandi* as vigilant, masterly inactivity, and the wisdom in
it was that when he did act he got things done.

In 1896, Great Britain and the United States found themselves at odds on the boundaries of Venezuela. Gibbons, along with Cardinal Herbert Vaughan of Westminster and Cardinal Michael Logue of Armagh, obtained the peaceful settlement. In Canada, an organization called the Knights of Labor had been formed. Gibbons was greatly interested in labor affairs and had worked with Cardinal Manning in establishing the Catholic attitude. Because of certain secret aspects of the Knights of Labor, the Vatican took steps to denounce the organization and forbid Catholics to join it. Gibbons quickly assured Pope Leo that nothing about the Knights was contrary to Church teachings and the Pope withdrew the ban. After the Spanish-American War it was Gibbons who brought about arrangements that preserved the rights of the Church in Cuba and the Philippines, and some historians have felt that he might well have been able to prevent the war itself and negotiated terms acceptable to all had he been given an opportunity at an earlier moment.

Gibbons was among the cardinals who, in 1917, invited the American bishops to cooperate in the foundation of the National Catholic War Council, an organization to help servicemen, veterans, and their families during and after World War I. The work was so successful that the bishops decided to extend the program indefinitely, and in 1919 they issued a statement that declared:

"In view of the results obtained through the merging of our activities for the time and purpose of war, we determine to maintain, for the ends of peace, the spirit of union and the coordination of our forces. We have accordingly grouped together under the National Catholic Welfare Council the various agencies by which the interests of religion are furthered. Each of these, continuing its own special work in its chosen field, will now derive additional support through general cooperation, and all will be brought into closer contact with the hierarchy, which bears the burden of authority and of responsibility for the interests of the Catholic Church."

The council was divided into six departments: executive, education, press, social action, legal, and lay organizations. From the start, it was a success, dealing with Catholic situations at the national level.

But there were men in Rome who were not so sure the council was a good idea. The word "council" was itself frightening, reminding of Basel and Constance where councils had tried to supersede the popes. Immediately certain men fretted that the American council might mean a schism. In four hundred years of Catholicism in America there had been only one schism of any duration—the Polish National Catholic Church which was affected strongly by Protestantism and broke away in 1904 on the basis of rejecting papal infallibility and preferring private interpretation of the Bible; it still exists and has about 100,000 members.

There was, however, no reason to worry about a schism in the council. In fact, as soon as the American prelates learned that Rome still cringed at the word "council" the organization changed its name to the National Catholic Welfare Conference. Further, the conference acknowledged without restraint the authority of Rome and assured that nothing would ever be done to question it. Moreover, the conference explained that episcopal membership would be voluntary and the conference would not operate in dioceses whose bishops were not members. There would never be any American disobedience to the wishes of popes, the conference stated, and doctrinal matters would only be touched on in the process of applying them to the United States.

Even so, Pope Benedict XV was distressed. Give a bishop an inch and he would take a mile; it had happened before and could happen again. Everything depended on the American bishops themselves; Benedict was uncertain. He decided to disband the conference for safety's sake and had prepared a document for that purpose. It was said to be on his desk awaiting his signature when he died. The new Pope, Pius XI, reversed the decision and approved the conference as one of his first acts. In subsequent years the idea of team-work, so American in itself, turned out to be so successful that it was adopted by the bishops of other countries at the express recommendation of the Holy See. In his statement giving the conference his blessing, Pius said:

"It appears with abundant evidence how timely and useful was the organization of the National Catholic Welfare Conference, which you lately established, with its departments, the news service and the bureau of immigration. This organization is not only useful but also necessary for you. Cease not, therefore, to labor in this spirit of unity for the welfare of our holy religion in that great republic where the Church, under God's providence, enjoys such a wide and such a high degree of prosperity."

With that, the Church in America came of age, in the eyes of Rome and in the eyes of Americans. For the American Catholic, the Church and State were blended in a unique and wise way: separate in reality but united in the heart.

XV

*I*t was Pope Urban VIII who, in 1630, gave cardinals the title of "Your Eminence." This was to distinguish them from bishops and archbishops who, holding ranks equivalent to earls and dukes, were addressed as "Your Lordship" and "Your Grace"; bishops later were given the title of "Your Excellency" by Pope Pius XI in 1931. Further dignity was added by having the rank itself become part of a man's name. In other words, he was not Cardinal John Smith, but John Cardinal Smith. With time, additional features were applied to the cardinalate to mark the importance of its members. Cardinals acquired a wardrobe of fifty different ceremonial garments, each with a traditional significance. Of these, two special items were the red hat and the purple coat, and it became the custom to say of a new cardinal that he had been given the red hat or been elevated to the purple.

The colors had their own meaning. Red—actually scarlet —was the heroic color of heroes, of martyrs, and for cardinals it symbolized a willingness to shed blood for the Church. Purple was the mark of nobility; in old Rome, noblemen could be identified on the street by their purple robes. White, the symbol of purity, was reserved for the rulers—emperors, kings, and popes. For cardinals, the dominant color was red—red cassocks, red gloves, red shoes. But it was the broad-rimmed pontifical hat that meant most, for it was presented to them as the first and most distinctive feature of their princely role in the Church. In processions of great pomp the cardinals rode majestically on horseback directly behind the pope, their red hats held in place by golden cords tied under the chins.

When tragedy struck the Church in 1870, it was fitting that the red hats should be permanently put aside. The unification of Italy in that year stripped the Church of her papal states, made the popes prisoners in the Vatican, and put an end to public grandeur. The Church, in a sense, went into mourning, and one sign of it was the change in the use of the red hat. Cardinals were never to wear it again.

When subsequent popes appointed cardinals, the nomination was tantamount to an order to Rome. Arriving, the appointee usually took residence in a religious house—his national college, perhaps, or a monastery or the headquarters of a religious order. He was usually kept busy for a few days having his new wardrobe made. Then a messenger would arrive from the Papal Secretary of State with official announcement of the appointment, informing the new cardinal when he should report to the Vatican for the first of the series of ceremonies that would make him a member of the Sacred College.

The day before that ceremony, the cardinal-elect began to receive official congratulatory visits from diplomats accredited to the Holy See, from high-ranking churchmen, and from friends. The first ceremony evolved into a secret consistory at which the pope could freely discuss problems facing the Church in various countries, canonizations, and any of his personal attitudes on Church affairs.

Then a consistorial official would read a list of the new appointments to the College and the cardinals signified their approval. At this point, the new appointees came forward one by one. Each man in turn knelt before the pope, who placed a scarlet biretta on his head, to be worn in the future only at prescribed religious ceremonies. Otherwise the biretta was to remain on display, on a table between two candles, in the entrance of the cardinal's private residence. (An interesting exception developed to this presentation of the biretta. As a hangover of lay investiture, Portugal, Spain, Austria, and France were allowed to have the biretta presented to a new cardinal by the head of the government. Pope John XXIII was serving as papal nuncio to France at the time of his appointment as cardinal in 1953 and received his red biretta in Paris from President Vincent Auriol. In 1946, Pope Pius XII denied Generalissimo Franco the right to make the presentation to new Spanish cardinals, who subsequently had to go to Rome to get their birettas.)

After the consistorial presentation, the popes could, if they wished, announce further appointments to the College without revealing the names of their choices. This custom, called *in pectore* (reserved in the breast), was started by Pope Martin V (1417-1431) who realized that the public announcement of certain appointments might result in physical harm to the nominees. By declaring, however, that he had these men in mind he reserved the right to reveal their names at a safer hour and thereby allow them to enter the

College with seniority dating to the date of the *in pectore* announcement. The occasion arose when such appointees never received their red hats because the pope who chose them died before revealing their names. The names were usually in the pope's private possession and became known to his successor, but since appointments to the College were the personal choice of each pope a successor was not obliged to honor them if he did not wish to do so. In March, 1960, Pope John XXIII appointed three cardinals *in pectore*, and it was believed that they were residents of Communist countries where the honor of their appointments might stir a religious fervor among the people that would bring on further Communist pressures.

This finished, the secret consistory closed with the presentation of scarlet skullcaps—zucchetta—to the new cardinals.

The second ceremony took place the following day in the Sistine Chapel, attended by invited guests. For this event, the new cardinals wore their formal robes for the first time— the zucchetta, red shoes, red cassock, a magnificent scarlet cape edged with ermine, and the broad-rimmed hat indicative of the office. An aide dressed in purple carried the train of the great cape.

In the chapel, the new cardinals took designated places. Then, in turn, they approached the right side of the altar and knelt before three ranking cardinals to take their oath, pledging to uphold papal bulls even at the risk of death. Next, they moved to the pope, sitting on his throne and surrounded by his court. They kissed his cheek and his hand, then embraced the attending cardinals in order of their precedence. Finally, they prostrated themselves before the pope and the train of their capes was placed over their heads as a sign of their humility in the eyes of God, the Church, and the pope.

At this point, the pontifical hat was brought forward and held over their heads, and the pope prayed:

"To the praise of Almighty God and the honor of His Holy See, receive the red hat, the distinctive sign of the cardinal's dignity, by which is meant that even until death and the shedding of blood you will show yourself courageous for the exaltation of our holy Faith, for the peace and successful living of Christian people and for the growth of the Holy Roman Church. In the Name of the Father and of the Son and of the Holy Ghost."

The hat was then taken away and each cardinal returned to his place, the position of which in the chapel indicated his seniority in the College. The *Te Deum,* the hymn of thanksgiving, was then sung by all, after which the pope left and the cardinals were dismissed. The new cardinals returned to their Rome residences, where they issued statements of gratitude to the pope for the honor bestowed on them. After this began again the round of formal visits from dignitaries paying their respects.

Later the same day Vatican messengers arrived to inform the new cardinal of his appointments to various pontifical congregations. They then presented him with the pontifical red hat that had been held over his head during the earlier ceremonies. But he was not to wear it. Instead, it was to be stored in a safe place in his permanent residence—wherever the pope decided that might be—and used again only when it was put upon his coffin while he lay in state after his death, then hung from the ceiling of his cathedral as evidence that a prince of the Church had reigned there.

The final ceremony was held the next day, again in secret consistory, and the high point of it was called "the opening of the mouth." Until this point, the new cardinal had no authority to speak as a cardinal, in or out of consistories. Now the pope addressed each appointee, saying: "I open your mouth so that in consistory, in congregations and in other ecclesiastical functions your advice can be given." With that the cardinal was given his ring, a sapphire set in gold bearing the pope's coat of arms, and he was told the name of the Roman church to which he had been given title and financial responsibility.

As a cardinal, he received, as well, various spiritual privileges. Unlike a priest or a bishop, who required permission to say Mass or hear confessions outside their own dioceses, a cardinal could carry on his sacerdotal functions wherever he chose, whenever he wished. He could choose any priest he wanted for his confessor and that man was relieved of all other duties in order to travel with the cardinal at all times. Further, he could grant indulgences of three hundred days, as well as other spiritual dispensations otherwise reserved for popes. Although most often a cardinal-priest of the Roman clergy, the church to which he held title could be regarded to have episcopal stature because of him and he could perform there the various religious ceremonies of bishops. As recently as 1905, cardinals were considered beyond civil law, but this was dismissed in deference to law and order administered by the civil authorities of the world. Nevertheless, the Church rule remained that anyone harming or killing a cardinal was excommunicated, as were all his male descendants unless absolved by the pope. In countries of Catholic nobility, a cardinal was given the same rank as a family prince and was accorded the same respect in public. As nobility faded away, the cardinals retained their stature because of their positions in the Church and their leadership of the people. Many of the prerogatives of cardinals became meaningless with time. For example, it was defined that there should always be in a cardinal's carriage a silk umbrella so that if while riding he came upon a priest carrying the Blessed Sacrament on a sick call (which he would recognize by the altar boy ringing a bell as he led the priest along the road) the cardinal would be provided with a covering for his head when he removed his hat in respect. When ordinary progress made it possible for priests to make their sick calls in automobiles the occasion of such an encounter became unlikely.

By adjusting to progress, the Sacred College—indeed the entire Church—sustained its vitality as a living organization in a changing world. If some bit of protocol fell away because a new era dimmed its intent, the cardinalate lost nothing. On the contrary, by keeping step with a changing world while safeguarding unchanging truths, the Sacred College produced men who gave the Church its finest leadership in centuries.

2

The unification of Italy occurred slowly, over a period of some fifteen years and at the cost of wars, revolutions, and counterrevolutions. The unifying forces were of three ideals: anti-cleric radicals who wanted a republic, liberals who preferred a constitutional monarchy under the House of Savoy, and Catholics who hoped to see the popes rule a united Italy. The Catholic idea was unrealistic and unwise; those who held to it were the last ecclesiastical monarchists who remained blind to the travails such ambitions had wrought over six centuries.

In 1870, only Rome was outside the sphere of the united Italy, and that year the city fell. Pope Pius IX became the first of four pontiffs who were to live out their reigns as prisoners on Vatican Hill. Certain aspects of the imprisonment were self-imposed. A pall of mourning fell upon the hill. The popes no longer traveled, they did not entertain, they ate alone, and they had little contact with the outside world other than through their legates and foreign ambassadors. The Church's loss of dignity was serious indeed, but equally serious was the loss of income from the papal states, income that had supported not only the Vatican but important missionary work as well. Henceforth the support of the Church would depend entirely on the generosity of laymen in countries where the Church was free to work and where the people were financially able to help.

Its horizons suddenly limited, the Church turned its attention inward and occupied itself more with internal affairs. By the time of his death in 1878, Pius IX completed a reign of thirty-two years, the longest in Church history. One of the highlights of his pontificate was the Syllabus of Errors, which he issued in 1864. It was a compilation of eighty-four doctrinal errors then prevalent in various parts of the world, and simply by stating them the Pope denounced them. The Syllabus, along with Pius' decrees of papal infallibility and the immaculate conception of the Virgin Mary, gave anti-Catholics effective weapons, and of the three it was the Syllabus that was most misunderstood. Anti-Catholics took it as the official Church stand, backed by papal infallibility, but it was merely an indictment. It touched on theological, spiritual and temporal affairs, specifying such errors as these:

——That human reason, without any regard to God, is the sole arbiter of truth and falsehood, of good and evil; that it is its own law unto itself and suffices by its natural force to secure the welfare of men and nations.

——That the prophesies and miracle set forth and narrated in Sacred Scriptures are the fictions of poets, and the mysteries of the Christian faith are the result of philosophical investigations; and that the books of both Testaments contain mythical inventions and Jesus Christ Himself is a mythical fiction.

——That the Church has not the power to define dogmatically that the religion of the Catholic Church is the only true religion.

Pius' statement against the complete separation of Church and State was used frequently in following years by critics who accused the Church of still hoping to rule the temporal as well as the spiritual world. No Catholic defenders could convince the critics otherwise, despite the statements by the next two popes that cooperation between Church and State did not mean collaboration and that the system that had evolved in the United States showed definite advantages.

In view of the confusion among critics who sought argument but not debate, subsequent popes recognized the need for clearer definitions of the Church's position. The writings on labor by Leo XIII established without question the Church's primary concern for the welfare of people who for economic, social or intellectual reasons could not defend themselves against economic, social and intellectual superiors. Pius X (1903-1914) reaffirmed many portions of the Syllabus, principally by declaring firmly that the truths of religion could not be juggled around recklessly simply to salve the sprouting ego and stumbling intellect of mankind.

The circumstances of Pius' election brought on further changes. He had been the patriarch of Venice, an extremely capable and holy man, and was later to be canonized in 1954. He entered the 1903 conclave with no idea that he would be elected pope. The favorite candidate was Cardinal Rampolla, secretary of state for Leo XIII. Certain countries, like Spain and Austria, had special prerogatives, such as the right to bestow the biretta on new cardinals, the right to declare themselves against the election of certain cardinals at the start of a conclave. This veto was respected in the Vatican. Before the conclave got down to business, it was generally felt that Rampolla would be the next pope. But then the Austrian cardinals arrived with orders from their government to veto Rampolla's candidacy. The conclave turned to the cardinal-patriarch of Venice.

One of the first acts of the new pope was to revoke the right of veto, thereby excluding governments from further intervention in papal elections. This was a daring thing to do, especially at a time when the Church had few friends in governments. But it was necessary in order to let the Church escape from the very kind of interference by governments that critics charged the Church itself was imposing upon the governments.

Pius X also redefined the election proceedings of a conclave, stressing that there was to be no contact between the cardinals and the outside world. In the past, doors leading to the conclave quarters were locked; now all doors were to be sealed off with brick, except the one through which food would be sent in. Even this was made into a revolving door, with the food placed in an outer compartment that could be rotated to the inside without any communication between the men on either side.

Pius ordered four scrutinies a day, two in the morning and two in the afternoon. There could, he said, be elections by acclamation or, if a stalemate seemed unbreakable, by compromise, but there was to be no electioneering, no scurrying around the halls at night, no deals. Any special nominations, any discussions, were to be held openly, but for the ears of the cardinals only. Whatever happened in the conclave was to be held secret by the cardinals. A two-thirds majority would be sufficient for election, but if any cardinal got exactly two-thirds the ballots were to be examined to assure he had not voted for himself. This point was later changed by Pius XII, who decreed that the winner must have two-thirds plus one, so that even if a cardinal had voted for himself it would make no difference.

As a further precaution, Pius X instructed that wooden marbles were to be used as counting devices. As a cardinal put his vote into the chalice that served as a ballot box he was also to place a marble into a companion container. Then both votes and marbles were to be counted to be sure everybody voted only once. Also, if there was no majority, the ballots were to be burned in a fire of moist straw. The black puff of smoke that thus rose above the Sistine Chapel would be a sign to those outside that a scrutiny had been taken and nobody was chosen. After the final vote, the ballots were to be burned by themselves, sending up a white puff of smoke as a signal that the Church had a new pope. Interestingly, the stove used for these fires was misplaced during the nineteen-year reign of Pius XII and at the last minute the 1958 conclave officials had to hurry around Rome to find a new one.

With the safety of future elections thus assured, Pius X turned to another internal problem of the Church: the records of canon law. By now there had been over two hundred and fifty popes, and each one had contributed to the enormous collection of canon laws, writing on every possible subject from the manner in which Mass was to be celebrated to marriage, protocol, and administration. There was bound to be some overlapping, some duplication, some laws that no longer pertained. The Pope decided that all the laws were to be codified, an incredibly big chore, and he assigned to assist in the task a young priest then working in the Secretariat of State, a man named Eugenio Pacelli. It was a huge responsibility for a man whose health was so frail that Leo XIII had allowed him to live at home while doing his seminary studies. But this was the man who was destined to become Pope Pius XII and to reign during the rise of Communism and World War II, a period that required a man of the strength he proved himself to have.

It took almost fifteen years to complete the re-codification of canon law; the importance of the achievement could not be exaggerated. The Church, which claimed to be the defender of law, could now declare that its own legal affairs were in order. With the great maze of Church law now recodified future students and practitioners of the canons could proceed with their tasks with unequivocal precision.

The work was finished in 1917 and Pacelli was appointed nuncio to Munich. His efforts to bring World War I to an end failed when the Kaiser refused to see him. Meanwhile, the city was swept by Communist uprisings. One day Communists drove by Pacelli's house and blasted it with machine-gun fire as a warning, but he ignored it. In 1918, after Germany lost the war, he was appointed nuncio to the new Weimar Republic in Berlin.

But he remained active in Rome, where his skill as a diplomat was highly prized. And he was greatly needed at this particular time. The Church's role in temporal affairs had been virtually non-existent since 1871, when the unified Italian government declared the confiscation of Church properties. The government offered the Church an annual indemnity in return for its lost property but the Church refused it. Thus for almost fifty years the Church was merely a cluster of buildings on the Tiber banks. More serious was the diminution of papal influence in the world. To carry out their mission successfully, the popes could not be subject to any temporal ruler: it would have been legally impossible for a pope as a citizen of any country to enter into negotiations with other countries relative to Church affairs. It was necessary for a pope to be the sovereign of an independent nation, in order that his concern for the spiritual welfare of his followers could be truly international.

After World War I, it began to look as if Italy might be willing to restore the independence of the Church. Progress was slow at first because of the delicacy of the matter. Then came two or three years of more intense discussion. Pacelli was frequently recalled from Berlin to contribute the benefits of his own experience. By 1928, most of the details were worked out and King Victor Emmanuel III authorized Premier Benito Mussolini to proceed with the agreement. The Lateran Treaty was signed at noon on February 11, 1929.

In summary, the treaty recognized the reestablishment of Vatican City as an independent sovereign state, ruled by the popes. Its extra-territorial rights were extended to important churches in Rome, to Church colleges in the city, and to the papal summer residence at Castel Gandolfo. The Church gave up its claim to lands confiscated years before and it agreed to remain outside of all temporal disputes between nations unless it was specifically requested by any of them to advise. Italy permitted the teaching of religion to school children, acknowledged the secrecy of the confessional, restored the Church to its prominence in the country, and banned divorce.

It was well known that Eugenio Pacelli had been largely responsible for the treaty terms, even though he was in Berlin the day the documents were signed. Many important officials felt that it was entirely due to his diplomatic skill that the Church was now free. As soon as the excitement calmed, he was summoned to Rome for a most unusual event: a special consistory at which he was named a cardinal. A few days later he was appointed the Vatican Secretary of State.

There was only one honor left for him, and he received it in 1939 when he was elected pope, ruler of the free state which he had helped bring into being.

He ruled until 1958, and it would be premature to evaluate his reign so soon after it. The Lateran Treaty gave the popes the right to exercise the Church's moral and spiritual power for the preservation of peace in the world, and to this end he worked incessantly. In his first encyclical he condemned totalitarianism. Throughout the Second World War he donated large sums of money for the aid of refugee Jews, and following the war he supervised Catholic forces in the reconstruction of the battle-scarred continent. He was a strong supporter of the United Nations from its inception, and to show where the Church stood on Communism he declared the excommunications of all Catholics who aided Communism or Communists in any way.

At first he favored a strong College of Cardinals. In 1946, he appointed thirty-two at one time, the largest number in the history of the Church. They came from nineteen different countries and ended the Italian majority in the College. The Americans appointed were the Archbishops Stritch of Chicago, Spellman of New York, John Glennon of St. Louis, and Edward Mooney of Detroit. In 1953 he appointed twenty-six more cardinals, including Archbishop James Francis McIntyre of Los Angeles, bringing the College to its full complement of seventy. His appointment of Cardinal Stritch to the Curia was the first such honor bestowed on an American.

It was in 1953 that the Pope's health began to fail, and after that he chose no more cardinals. When his Secretary of State died, the Pope took over the office itself, and some observers assumed this meant he intended to draw in the reins on the authority of cardinals, but there was no reason to expect a turn to conservativism except the Pope's physical inability to carry on all the work that burdened him.

When Pius XII died in 1958, there were fifty-four cardinals, a good number in view of some earlier pontificates but low considering Pius' earlier indications of keeping the College full. His successor was Angelo Cardinal Roncalli, the patriarch of Venice, a man with long experience in the Vatican diplomatic corps in Bulgaria, Greece, Turkey, and France. As Pope John XXIII, he soon proved to be a man of intellect, charm, and wit. He was the first pope in almost a century to travel freely in Rome. Visiting the city jail, he commented to the prisoners, "I have come to see you because you aren't able to come to see me." When President Dwight

D. Eisenhower called on the Pope during a European tour, the two men exchanged formal greetings in the Vatican. John listened politely as Eisenhower read his, then responded with the Italian equivalent of, "Now you're gonna hear a beaut." The burst of laughter from President Eisenhower provided one of the most unusual pictures since the invention of the camera.

However, the Pope early displayed his serious attitude toward his new role. Rather than appoint an episcopal aide to perform his duties as the Bishop of Rome he called a synod of the Roman clergy, the first in four hundred years, and presided over it himself, instructing the clergy to adopt more propriety in their public conduct. In 1959 he announced an ecumenical council on a subject that would make it the most important since Trent: the return of schismatic churches to Rome. He was particularly concerned with certain Eastern rites which differed primarily in regard to Rome's primacy in the Christian world, but the announcement stirred such great anxiety among Western Protestants, who looked upon the council as an attempt to achieve their submission, that the council was subject to Protestant criticism and complaint even before its agenda could be prepared. This led to talk that the council might be postponed indefinitely, but instead the Vatican simply removed it from the spotlight and proceeded with the patience and reserve which had long been one of its principal characteristics.

On the day of his election, Pope John revived the tradition of previous popes by giving the red hat to the Vatican official who had served as chamberlain to the conclave. That gave the College fifty-four members. A month later, John called a consistory at which he announced the elevation of twenty-three more cardinals, putting seventy-seven of them into the College. Thus John broke an almost four-hundred year tradition to restrict the number of cardinals to seventy.

As Pope he had the authority to do this; the decree by Pope Sixtus V to keep the number at seventy had been merely administrative; any pope could have gone above that number; most popes had stayed below it. Americans included in Pope John's list were Archbishop Richard J. Cushing of Boston and Archbishop John F. O'Hara of Philadelphia.

A year later, in December, 1959, the Pope again announced new appointments—eight of them, including Archbishop Meyer of Chicago and Archbishop Muench, an American then serving as nuncio to the West German republic. This gave the United States six cardinals, its largest number in history. Despite the deaths of several of its members, the Sacred College now had eighty-one, again a record. Questioned about these increases in the size of the College, the Pope said: "They are necessary for the good of the Church, which is becoming bigger and more universal every year. Further increases will follow."

The next increase came in March, 1960, and in many ways it constituted the most important nominations to the Sacred College since its inception. Seven men were appointed, now giving the College eighty-eight members, and among them were the first Japanese, the first Filipino, and the first African Negro to become cardinals. Of the three, the appointment of Bishop Laurian Rugambwa, of the Rutoba diocese, Tanganyika, was the most dramatic. Certainly the appointments of Archbishop Peter Tatsuo Doi of Tokyo and Archbishop Rufino U. Santos of Manila were important because of their own achievements and the positions in their own countries, but it was Bishop Rugambwa, the prelate of the jungles, who captured world attention.

Born in 1912, just a few miles from where he would later rule as a bishop and then as a cardinal, Rugambwa was eight years old when his family became Christian. Interestingly, the missionaries who converted the family were White Fathers, members of the society Cardinal Lavigerie had founded in 1868 at Algiers. He belonged to the Nsiba tribe and was related to the chief, which made him something of royalty in a village of mud huts. At the time of his baptism he was already a student at the White Fathers' primary school at Mugana in the mountainous area of northwestern Tanganyika. He later said, "When I saw the good the missionaries were doing for my people and the way young Africans were becoming priests and sharing in the work, I prayed I could join them when I was a man."

While still in his teens, Rugambwa entered the minor seminary conducted by the White Fathers at Rubya, some fifteen miles from his village, and he remained there until finishing high school. His next place of studies was the White Fathers' major seminary at Katigondo, in Uganda, where he continued for five more years. He was ordained a priest in 1943 and was appointed to work with the White Fathers at the Rubya mission. He grew to be a tall, slim man, soft-spoken, gentle, perceptive, a bookish intellectual. The White Fathers recognized his potential for leadership and in 1948 they sent him to Rome to study canon law at the Gregorian University. He received his doctorate in 1951, writing on social and educational development in East Africa. A gifted linguist, he meanwhile managed to add fluent French, German, and Italian to his mastery of Swahili, Luganda, English and Latin.

Soon after returning to Tanganyika, he was named bishop of the newly created diocese of Rutoba, the village some thirty miles inland from the southwestern shores of Lake Victoria. His episcopal palace was a five-room house made out of sun-baked clay; his cathedral, scarcely larger than a chapel, was constructed from home-made bricks. To carry on his work he drove himself over the rough roads of his large diocese in a second-hand American car. Unable to afford a secretary, he handled all his personal and official correspondence on an ancient portable typewriter.

When he received the diocese from the White Fathers it contained the church at Rutoba and seventeen primary schools. In five years, he built two more churches, twenty more primary schools, two high schools, and a trade school. Because most of his people were impoverished farmers he had to seek funds elsewhere, and he subsequently described Rutoba as the diocese that begging built. In 1956, he visited the United States on what he called a begging-tour.

His appointment to the Sacred College came as a complete surprise. Days later he wrote an American friend that he was still stunned and that he doubted he could live up to the responsibility of his new office. But there were no doubts in Rome. So numerous were the requests to witness the presentation of the scarlet birettas that the ceremony was conducted in the enormous Consistorial Hall before an audience of three thousand. When Rugambwa's name was called to approach the Pope, applause broke out that shook the room. Later at the secret consistory at which the red pontifical hat was placed over Rugambwa's head the same enthusiasm exploded among the ordinarily sedate cardinals. Their applause began as Rugambwa left his place to go to the cardinals at the altar to take his oath, increased as he went to the Pope and prostrated himself, and when the hat was held over his head the applause drowned out the Pope's voice.

Regarding Rugambwa's appointment, Pope John said: "All the faithful of his continent will be able to say with joy: 'This is our hour. We wish to do honor in the spirit of Jesus to the furrow which has been opened and which continues to yield new flowerings and abundant harvests for future triumps of the Kingdom of God.' "

In his own statement, made on receiving formal notification of his appointment from Vatican messengers, Rugambwa indicated his awareness that this was also an hour of turmoil in much of Africa, turmoil caused by racialism and revolution from one end of the continent to the other, and

he urged his fellow Africans to "seek the peace of Christ."
He went on: "The Catholic Church uses her influence to establish this peace among men, for always does she see in
them not persons belonging to different races and social conditions, but human beings created by the same God, Father
of us all."

It was perhaps significant that at this glorious moment of
Church history there should be turmoil on the continent being honored with a native cardinal for the first time. There
was, indeed, turmoil on every continent. In all the world
there was only one institution which had survived this same
kind of turmoil over the past two thousand years: the Catholic Church. Its own evolution had been part of it all. While
governments collapsed and other institutions decayed, only
the Church grew stronger and mightier, only the Church
arose from the rubbles of man's repeated crimes against himself. There were, as these pages attest, moments when the
men who ruled the Church were not innocent of entangle-
ment in the chaos, and yet these men were able to attract
others whose character and spirituality were enough to ad-
vance the Church's divine responsibility to preserve truth,
establish justice, and strive for peace. For almost two thousand years, these men have guided the bark of Peter through
every troubled sea, producing from among themselves the
hands that held the helm, and as such they gave the world
the only constant influence for good it has known since the
days the Apostles walked together in Palestine. It follows,
then, that whether they were as individuals either saints or
satans, no other single group of men contributed as much to
the spiritual fulfillment of so many as these: the cardinals.

Bibliography

Burton, Katherine: *The Great Mantle.* New York: Longmans, Green & Co., 1950.

Brieg, Joseph A.: *Vicar of Christ.* St. Paul: Summit Press, 1958.

Brezzi, Paolo: *The Papacy.* Westminster, Md.: Newman Press, 1958.

Brusher, Joseph: *Popes Through The Ages.* Princeton, N. J.: D. Van Nostrand Co., 1959.

Cheke, Marcus: *The Cardinal de Bernis.* New York: W. W. Norton & Co., 1958.

Ehler, Sidney and Morrall, John B.: *Church and State Through The Centuries.* Westminster, Md.: Newman Press, 1954.

Farrow, John: *Pageant Of The Popes.* New York: Sheed & Ward, 1942.

Gilson, Etienne: *History of Christian Philosophy In The Middle Ages.* New York: Random House, 1954.

Graham, Robert A.: *Vatican Diplomacy.* Princeton, N. J.: Princeton University Press, 1959.

Hardy, Adolphe: Four articles on papal elections. Brussels: Le Libre Belgique, 1939.

Hatch, Alden and Walse, Seamus: *Crown of Glory.* New York: Hawthorn Books, Inc., 1958.

Hertling, Ludwig: *A History of The Catholic Church.* Westminster, Md.: Newman Press, 1957.

Hughes, Philip: *A Popular History Of The Catholic Church.* New York: Macmillan Co., 1949.

Kittler, Glenn D.: *The White Fathers.* New York: Harper & Bros., 1957.

Kuhner, Hans: *Encyclopedia Of The Papacy.* New York: Philosophical Library, 1958.

Pastor, Ludwig: *The History Of The Popes.* (40 vols.) St. Louis: B. Herder Book Co., 1938.

Poulet, Dom Charles (Sidney A. Raemers, translator): *A History of The Catholic Church.* (2 vols.) St. Louis: B. Herder Book Co., 1935.

LaFarge, John: Five articles on cardinals. New York *Herald Tribune,* 1946.

Latourette, Kenneth Scott: *A History Of Christianity.* New York: Harper & Bros., 1953.

Mann, Horace K.: *The Lives Of The Popes.* (18 vols.) St. Louis: B. Herder Book Co., 1925.

McSorley, Joseph: *Outline History Of The Church By Centuries.* St. Louis: B. Herder Book Co., 1954.

Meadows, Denis: *A Short History Of The Catholic Church.* New York: Devin-Adair, 1959.

Murphy, John L.: *The General Councils Of The Church*. Milwaukee: Bruce Publishing Co., 1957.

Neuvecelle, Jean: *The Vatican*. New York: Criterion Books, 1955.

Reynolds, E. E.: *Three Cardinals*. New York: P. J. Kenedy & Sons, 1958.

Ryan, Edward A.: *Notes—Cardinal Gibbons After Thirty Years*. Theological Studies, 1953.

Thorton, Francis B.: *Cross Upon Cross*. New York: Benzinger Bros., Inc., 1955.

Thurston, Herbert and Attwater, Donald: *Butler's Lives Of The Saints*. (4 vols.) New York: P. J. Kenedy & Sons, 1956.

The Vatican. New York: Letters & Arts Publishing Co., 1914.

Index